CONTENTS

Your Best Meditation	2
Paul M Harrison.	3
Opening The Curtains Of The Mind	4
Hearing the call and beginning the journey	13
Opening your mind to a deeper existence	38
Beginning at the beginning	42
Open Meditation	45
Closed Meditations	49
The Benefits Of Meditation And Why There Are So Many	51
Yes, You Can Meditate Wrongly	94
Finding Your Best Meditation Position	100
Malas—The One Tool You Need	107
TECHNIQUES	117
Guided Meditations – Doing It The Easy Way	118
Breath Awareness Meditation and Stillness Breathing	123
Mindfulness Meditation	132
Introduction to Buddhist Methods	138
Anapanasati	141
Zen	147
Zen Walking: Enlightenment In Your Feet	153
Samatha	160

Loving Kindness Meditation	171
Karuna Meditation: Nourishing The Soil Of Compassion	185
Vipassana Meditation: How To See The World Within You	193
Hindu & Yogic Meditation	209
Mantra Meditation	214
Bhakti Meditation	228
Chakra Meditation	235
The seven chakras:	237
Third Eye Meditation	240
Yoga Breathing Methods	245
Candle Gazing Meditation (Trataka)	257
Kundalini	262
Self Inquiry	266
Crystals	271
Taoist Meditation	277
Christian Meditation	291
Dynamic Meditation	300
Body Scan Meditation: Tuning in to your internal antenna	308
More Meditations For This Revised Edition	314
Chanting	315
Falun Gong	321
Gong Bath	326
Healing Effects and Benefits of Gong Bath Meditation	329
Contemplative Meditation Techniques	333
Forest Bathing	338
Applications	343

Anxiety	344
Depression	353
Stress	359
Sleep	362
The Path To Enlightenment	367
More journeys of discovery lie ahead in this spiritual must-read	379
The 30 Secrets To Spiritual Love	380

PAUL HARRISON

For mom, whose loving-kindness has always been my guiding light.

YOUR BEST MEDITATION

Book of the World's Best Meditation Techniques

PAUL M HARRISON.

THE DAILY MEDITATION

Special thanks to Deniz. K for her help with the cover design.

OPENING THE CURTAINS OF THE MIND

Isn't it funny how one simple thing can change the course of your life forever?

Having taught meditation to thousands of people all around the world, it never ceases to amaze me how the simple act of being mindful can change lives. But I've seen time and again how meditation can help cure depression, anxiety, and stress, help people get to sleep, and heal numerous health conditions; how it can create happiness and joy; and how it can lead you to live a meaningful life. Meditation has changed the lives of millions, and it can change your life too.

My own experience of meditation began in the spring of 2004. I was training to be an actor at Oxford. It was a fairytale of a time, surrounded by artists, musicians, and my fellow actors, many of whom are unforgettably beautiful people whom I'm blessed to have met. Each day at Oxford was spent reading the classics of Shakespeare, Checkhov, Ibsen and ilk, studying people and characters, putting on performances, and honing the art of acting.

My teachers at Oxford were a truly varied and contrasting bunch, from the ultra-strict to the carefree. But one teacher in particular struck a chord with me: my vocal coach. The moment I met him I knew there was something different about him. He wore a long string of beads, he had black hair tied in a ponytail down to his lower back, and his presence was strong and earthy. It was like he'd walked right out of an old dojo and into our drama class.

I'd already been training in classical singing for Eight years, so I felt a natural kinship to my new vocal coach. I was one of the few students who truly grasped the purpose of the absolutely insane exercises he made us do (which included imitating apes and dancing like zombies).

One day, when we'd stopped for lunch, I was munching on a grilled cashew butter and blueberry sandwich, and chasing it down with a glass of cranberry juice, when my vocal coach spoke to the class. Little did I know that what he was about to say would change me forever.

"Imagine there's a closed curtain around your mind," he said. "Now imagine that curtain opening".

It was not a profoundly complex thing to say. It wasn't particularly philosophical or poetic. But nevertheless, it immediately struck a chord with me. It put my hair on end. He was, in essence, telling me to start being mindful.

Up until the moment I heard that line, my mind had been closed. Stress and fear had led me to shut myself off from the world. It was the unfortunate result of having lived in a rather turbulent home. My father was a very loving man with one terrible problem: alcoholism. When he was drunk, everyone in the house suffered. That pain stopped whenever I went to school, but there it was only replaced by a hailstorm of bullying. Feeling unsafe at both home and at school, I had sequestered myself to the one place where I felt safe. I'd shrunk into my shell and was living in my head, rarely daring to come out.

I'd been closing myself off for as long as I could remember. Since childhood, I'd severed myself from external reality to prevent myself from being hurt. I'd unwittingly decided to close my mind to reality rather than living in a world where my father could be drunk at any moment, a world where I could end up humiliated or beaten-up at school and hiding away in the sickroom.

But somehow I never realised I was doing it. I never realised that I had drawn the curtains of my mind.

Then, when my drama teacher happened to say that line about there being a closed curtain in my mind that needed to open, it was like a lightning bolt struck my temporal lobe and ignited my mind with a profound epiphany. I realised that I was master of my own world and that I had the power to dim the lights of my conscious mind or to turn them up to full. I alone determined how *alive* I was. I chose whether the "curtains of my mind" were open or closed. I could choose to live *mindfully*.

Let me show you what I did in those five minutes that opened my eyes. And I invite you to do it with me.

Exercise: Becoming Mindful

1. Look back on your life. On a level of one ten, rate how *alive you've been to the world*. How mindful have you been? If your mind were a curtain, how open is it? Rate yourself on a level of one to ten.

2. Now sit comfortably somewhere quiet.

3. Close your eyes.

4. Take ten deep breaths. As you breathe, notice the feeling of your breath moving around your body.

5. Tell yourself that you are going to commit to living mindfully. And tell yourself that by the time you finish this book you will have increased your mindfulness

score (your score from point 1 of this exercise) by at least two points.

6. You are going to slowly open your eyes. As you open your eyes, tell yourself that your mind is also opening, and that you are becoming more mindful.

7. With your eyes open, say, "I promise to experience the moments of my life mindfully, and to enjoy each moment as it happens".

My vocal coach made me realise I had been living mindlessly.

I knew there and then that I needed to open myself up to the full richness of life, for good and bad, for better or worse. I swore to myself that I would dedicate myself to living consciously, to being fully awake to the world.

Little did I know back then that this process, this mental attitude of being present and conscious of reality, is called Mindfulness.

Mindfulness: *The art of focusing the mind on the present moment non-judgmentally.*

Before I even knew anything about mindfulness—before I even knew the *term* "mindfulness"— mindfulness became my top priority. My primary goal in life became to live every moment consciously and with clarity.

Within a few days of practising mindfulness, it felt as though someone had turned the brightness and contrast levels up on my life, as though they'd taken my old CRT TV and replaced it with a 4K 3D monitor.

It was such a joy just to be *truly alive* to the world, to notice what I hadn't noticed before, like how a clap of distant thunder sends a tingle through my skin, or how the whistle of the wind in the trees makes the leaves dance. The world was coming to life in a million colours and in an orchestra of sound. I felt a level of joy I'd never felt before. I spent the next few weeks in a state of pure joy, feeling intimately connected to the world.

But then it suddenly dawned on me: What if other people weren't experiencing the same state of consciousness and mindfulness that I was?

In my teenage years I'd always considered myself to be a freak, to be the odd one out. It always seemed to me that it was I and I alone who was living closed-off from the world, as though everyone else in the world was living in the same grand hall while I was hidden alone in some dark cupboard. It hadn't occurred to me that everyone else was in the exact same place as me.

One day, when I was walking with an old friend through the local park, we happened to pass by the most beautiful swan, which was gliding so gracefully on the lake. Bathed under a red sun, the whole scene seemed more like a romantic oil painting than real life. Completely captivated, I stopped to take in the breathtaking sight. But my friend just kept right on walking. Noticing that I'd stopped, she said, "Come on, we're in a rush."

"A rush for what?"

"X Factor's starting in half an hour."

X Factor? A "reality" TV show? That's what was so important? She tapped her foot on the ground impatiently. Somewhere between that impatient foot-tapping and that serene swan on the lake, I realised the horrifying truth.

I realised that it wasn't just me who had been living mindlessly and with "the curtains closed"; it was my family, my friends, the people passing me by on the street typing away on their cellphones, the people staring at the TV. I felt like Cillian Murphy's character in *28 Days Later*, when he wakes up as the only person on Earth, surrounded by zombies. Because the reality was that the vast majority of people were barely conscious of the brilliance and beauty of the world around them. They were stuck in their thoughts, worrying about their work, thinking about tomorrow— always, always tomorrow, never now.

The majestic swan flapped its wings, beads of silver water dripping, and flew off into the distance, a white fleck fading into the crimson sun. Stunning. But no one witnessed it but me. Beyond the swan, the crowns of oak trees reached towards the heavens. Beyond them, the sounds of the city, where people were too busy with stresses and pressures to stop and enjoy the beauty of it all.

I knew then that the best thing I couple possibly achieve in life would be to spread mindfulness and meditation. And so I dedicated my life to it.

Perhaps you yourself feel like you are sometimes not alive to the world. Perhaps you have so much stress and pressure that it feels impossible to enjoy life and to live in the moment. But I promise you that by the time you finish reading this book you will know how to live life fully. I will show you how, a little later, when I share with you the most powerful mindfulness and meditation techniques in the world.

Mindfulness and meditation empower us to let go of the stresses, the thoughts, the anxiety, the depression, the worry, and all those other problems; so that we can enjoy bathing in the brilliance of the moments of our lives.

And so, before I knew it, I'd taken my first step on a new journey: The journey to spread consciousness, or *mindfulness*, to as many people as I could.

Of course, at that time, I didn't actually *know* a great deal about mindfulness and meditation. It was a new field of study for me. I knew it made sense. I knew it made a powerful difference in my own life. I felt it could help others too. And though I didn't know much about it, I already knew what mattered. I knew I had a goal—to help people to live in the moment without the stress and worry that holds them back. And I knew I had a means of achieving it—through mindfulness and meditation. My quest began.

I started learning everything I could about mindfulness and meditation, learning from the very best in the field, some of the most brilliant and inspirational minds in the world, among them being spiritual gurus, lecturers, and scientists, as well as everyday friends and acquaintances who happened to have some truly insightful wisdom to share. In between taking my acting lessons and performing in stage shows I tirelessly studied meditation, eagerly digging into the culture, the science, the *when*, the where, the *how* of it. I was a tiny sponge in a whole ocean, soaking up all I could.

I was lost in a journey of discovery. And in this book, I am going to take you on that same journey so you can discover meditation, discover the power of your own mind, and discover yourself.

You, however, will have one advantage that I did not have: This book. I've conveniently organised the most powerful meditations in the world into this one book, so you have a clear and comprehensive guide to meditation. But as you read it, I want you to promise me one thing: You will enjoy the journey you're about to go on.

Looking back now, I realise that the journey itself is what means the most. As much as I love meditation and teaching meditation, that journey of discovery is the most beautiful thing in the world. After all, life is in the journey, isn't it? It's not where we end up; it's the paths we take, the scenery we take in. My own spiritual journey has been one of the most adventurous and enjoyable paths through which I've wandered. It's that same sense of journey and discovery that I want to share with you in this book.

With that in mind, let me ask you to perform this second little exercise, which will help you to let go of your ideas of *what should be,* and *what I need,* and all those other pesky thoughts that stop you from being alive *now.*

Exercise: let go and live in the now

1. Sit comfortably with your eyes closed.
2. Bring to mind all your *shoulds,* your *expectations,* your ideas of what is right and wrong about your life. Bring all of that to mind.
3. Now imagine that in front of you there is a huge ocean. See the waves. Now throw all your thoughts and ideas into the ocean and watch them drift away.
4. Now say to yourself, "I vow to accept the moments of my life as they come to me, starting with this moment right now."

Have you let go? Good. Because I want to embrace the moments of this book.

In this book, you will learn every major meditation technique, and you'll discover how to use those techniques to create happiness, joy, love, and peace, and to end problems like anxiety and depression. Together we will journey through numerous religions, spiritualities, and cultures. As we journey through meditation, I would like to ask just one thing: Regardless of who you are, regardless of what you believe, *have an open mind.* There will be times when you question or outright disagree with some of the beliefs and practices in this book. But being right or wrong, believing or not believing, agreeing or disagreeing... these are not as important as the journey itself. We're moving across a vast landscape. Wherever we stop on the map, have an open heart and mind. Take the full journey. Appreciate every step.

As you progress through this book, you will experience many powerful and beautiful moments. Enjoy those moments. Live them. Embrace the journey we're about to take together. Life is a journey, and this book represents just a few oh so precious steps.

> **"Walk as though you are kissing the earth with your feet." – Thich Nhat Hanh**

HEARING THE CALL AND BEGINNING THE JOURNEY

"Just to let be and to live this moment, this step, now. That is all we truly need."

Looking back on that moment when my drama teacher told me to open the curtains of my mind, I realise that those words resonated with me because they were undeniably true.

For years I'd been living life inside my head, not truly living in the moment or experiencing the full richness of life. I'd barely been conscious. And I hadn't noticed it until my drama teacher pointed it out.

"I want to thank you, truly," I said to my teacher, my mind still abuzz with the poignancy of his words.

"For what?" he asked, his deep brown eyes searching me curiously, completely unaware of the importance of what he'd said only minutes before.

"I've always known something wasn't quite right with my mind. When you said about opening the curtains of the mind, I immediately realised what was wrong. And now I think I can change it."

"That's fantastic, Paul," he said with a big, broad smile.

I nodded to myself, because for the first time I knew what the problem was. The problem was that I was closing the curtains of my mind. I was preventing the true light of day from coming in, and I was preventing my consciousness from reaching *out*.

Happiness is accepting things precisely as they are. Unhappiness is rejecting reality and twisting the real world into your falsified view of things. Stripped of all worldly possessions, you could still be happy if you accept reality as it is, if you didn't think "If only I'd…" or "Why can't I be like *them*…" or "How did my life get so bad…"

How often do you think negative thoughts like that? Imagine if you could get rid of those thoughts and start to simply enjoy the experience of being alive.

You do not need anything to be happy.

Some of the happiest people in the world are poor. And conversely, some of the unhappiest people are rich because they're constantly comparing themselves to others and wanting more and more. They're always focusing on what they don't have; counting their sins rather than their blessings. Statistics show that more people are depressed in affluent countries than developing countries and that highly successful individuals are much more likely to develop depression. Though we tend to believe that "real world problems" are the main cause of stress, anxiety, and depression, the real culprit is much more fundamental to the human mind: it's the inability or unwillingness to accept your life as it is. It is ignorance.

Ignorance, the "inability to accept the truth" is what causes suffering. Seeing the true light of day and living in the moment cures pain and creates happiness. That's ultimately the power of mindfulness: it lets us live in the true present moment.

Research shows that people who live in the present moment with a nonjudgmental attitude (i.e. they live mindfully) are happier, less stressed, and less prone to anxiety and depression. But most people are lost in ideas of the past or future and so lose touch with the present moment.

Lost in the stress of day to day life we forget to actually *live life*. We spend so much time and effort trying to create a good life that we forget to actually *live*. We put so much time into getting a good job, securing a mortgage, having a family; but then we forget to enjoy that good job, to make the most of time with the family, to appreciate our homes and our possessions. Sometimes we need a wake-up call to realise that our lives are happening right *now*.

You're alive now. Live this moment.

Simply "being alive", living in the moment, is so obvious that most of us forget to do it. It's *profoundly obvious*, like when someone says "The sky is blue".

"Well, of course, the sky is blue," you say. But then you stop, and for the first time in days, you look up at that grand majestic overhanging canopy, and you realise just how blue it is, and how beautiful. It's always been there. It's always been beautiful. But you've taken it for granted. And then one moment you actually stop and just look up, and you're utterly awestruck by the beauty of it. That's what meditation gives us: the ability to stop and appreciate the beauty of it all.

Thankfully none of us is completely mindless. There are many times when we do live in the moment, and there are many times when we meditate too, even though we may not actually be aware that we're doing it. Even if you consider yourself to be an absolute beginner at meditation, you will already have meditated many times in your life.

Think about the last time you were stressed. Let's say you had a bad day at work. Your team didn't make your projected quarterly figures. You were angry. Your mind was consumed by thoughts: thoughts about how it was everyone else's fault, thoughts about how maybe it was your fault, worry about getting fired, guilt that maybe you'd let your team down.... There was so much going on in your mind that you could hardly see straight. You needed to get away, to chill out, so you took off, perhaps to the park near your office. Your mind shut down because it needed to. The stress dissipated. You sat there in the park not doing anything, just relaxing, just focusing on the moment. You let all those thoughts slip away like water down the drain. Your mind emptied. Into your empty mind poured the pure light of day. Suddenly all that was there was the present moment, the blue sky, the scent of the freshly mowed green grass, the happy people walking by with that golden lab' chasing a ball....

Those moments when you were living in the moment? That was meditation. That was precisely the same thing that happens when a Zen monk sits to focus on their breathing for twenty minutes. They simply sit and allow life to come to them as it is, not polluted with thoughts and feelings, just pure like spring water.

The same thing happens when you experience a moment of pure joy. Think about the last time you saw a beautiful night sky. A few days before writing this chapter, it was the total lunar eclipse, when the Earth's shadow blocked the sunlight from reflecting off the moon, turning the moon red. A stunning moment. Maybe you witnessed it too. And if you did witness it, you probably noticed how the world stopped and everything felt still, and how there was nothing in life but yourself, the stars, and that red moon.

That was meditation.

Or the last time you made love, and you felt a deep and profound connection, and it was like the world stopped and there was just the two of you.

That was meditation.

You see, you already meditate often. You meditate when you need to relax and when you experience moments of pure joy. You may never have thought of those moments as "meditation" before. But that's precisely what they are. They're moments when you let the stress and the thoughts and the feelings stop; when you simply live in the moment. That's what meditation is, and that's what you and I and every other person on Earth has naturally been doing our entire lives.

 **Meditation:** *The intention and practice of focusing the mind on the present moment.*

Those moments of meditation that we all enjoy are immensely important to our wellbeing.

It isn't by accident that we naturally meditate, that when we get stressed, we come to a stop, sit somewhere quiet, and focus on nothing but the present moment. That's nature's design. Our bodies and minds need those meditative moments to rebalance, to calm, and to heal.

For millennia men and women have sat and listened to the waves or gazed out over the stars, letting their minds unwind. It's the oldest form of therapy in the world. And it's something we would all do naturally if it weren't for the fact that society makes it difficult. Work, health, family problems; when all the stresses of the day are done there's often not enough time to just sit and *be*.

Think about the countless times you've said to yourself "I'll relax when I just get this next thing done". But many of us never actually relax. We just keep going until we're exhausted, and then we hit the sack. We never allow ourselves to enjoy that most basic form of therapy: simply *being.* And because we don't allow ourselves to simply *be,* we don't allow ourselves to heal. The result is the plague of physical and mental health problems that afflict us all.

Inevitably, the less you allow yourself to relax, the more stressed you will be. Stress is perhaps the biggest enemy of all, causing more suffering and harm than war, plague, or famine. Stress is the number one leading cause of death, and the cause of innumerable health complications, ranging from high blood pressure to diabetes and Alzheimer's.

But there's good news.

The more you allow yourself to enjoy those "natural meditations" as well as the traditional meditation *techniques* that we'll cover later on, the more you'll relax. The more you relax, the less stressed you'll be, and the better health you'll enjoy.

Meditation is truly powerful. But it's powerful *because it's natural.* It is the absolute most natural thing in the world. The mind needs to slow down and to calm. It does that by living in the moment. That's nature's way of allowing you to heal. But society makes it all but impossible for you to live in the moment. You have responsibilities and pressures, things you need to take care of, and it can be a real challenge to be mindful.

Enter meditation. Meditation redresses the balance. Meditation gives you those precious minutes in which you do nothing *but* live in the moment, nothing *but* be mindful.

That's why the next time you tell yourself you need to take

ten minutes to relax, you should do it. Give yourself those natural meditative moments. That is the best way to begin to learn to meditate: to embrace those times when your mind and body *naturally* meditate, times like when you look up at the sky, and you feel like doing nothing but just gazing; times like when you lie in the bath and you want to just stay there meditating on the feeling of the warm water on your body. Those moments are nature saying to you "This is your time to meditate. You need it. Take twenty minutes and relax".

The very best thing you can do for your health is to *let yourself enjoy those natural meditations.*

See a sunset? Appreciate it. Love the feeling of cold water on your body? Enjoy it. Feel like closing your eyes and focusing on your breath for a few minutes? Do it. Those are all meditations; they will all improve your quality of life and your health, and they are also the very best way to begin to learn meditation.

With that in mind, let's take a look at some very easy ways to start to be mindful.

Easy Mindfulness Exercises To Get You Started

One of the best things about mindfulness exercises is that there are a million ways to do them.

As Richard J. Davidson, PhD [a neuroscientist at the University of Wisconsin] told The New York Times, "In the Buddhist tradition, the word 'mindfulness is equivalent to a word like 'sports' in the U.S. It's a family of activity, not a single thing."

There is no one mindfulness exercise. There are many. You can be mindful just by focusing on your breath. You can go for a Zen walk or do some mindful writing. There are thousands of ways to get started.

Perhaps the best place to start, however, is with some of the traditional mindfulness activities.

e To

Traditional Exercises

Mindful breathing: Mindful breathing simply means focusing on the movement of the breath around the body. (More on this later on).

Tai chi and QiGong: Tai Chi and Qigong are Eastern physical exercises that use slow and conscious movements. These are great for slowing the mind.

Body Scan: Body scan is a traditional type of meditation. In this exercise we slowly move our consciousness around the body while relaxing our muscles. This is very similar to *progressive muscle relaxation* and is one of the best mindfulness exercises for anxiety and stress. (More on this later on.).

Mindfulness-Based Stress Reduction: Jon Kabat Zinn founded the practice known as Mindfulness-Based *Stress Reduction* in the 1970s. It's a complete system of mindfulness exercises for stress relief.

Mindful eating: Mindful eating is all about eating slowly and consciously. This exercise is excellent for anyone who comfort eats or eats mindlessly.

31 Beginners Mindfulness Activities For Adults

1: Mindful Thinking

One of the best places to start is with some mindful thinking.

Mindful thinking revolves around the idea of being conscious of our thoughts and correcting them, so they are more rational, more compassionate, and less harmful.

Mindful thoughts should be compassionate, non-judgmental, rational, unbiased, balanced (balancing positive and negative, so we are not biased in either direction) and accepting.

Now and again, take five minutes to listen to your thoughts. Challenge any negative or biased thought. This will boost your mental health and improve your happiness.

2: Daily Mindfulness Activities That Adults Do Anyway

One of the best mindfulness activities for adults is simply to do whatever you are doing and focus 100% on the task. In other words: Just do what you're doing.

Walking? Walk.

Breathing? Breathe.

Speaking? Speak

Whatever you do, do it mindfully. A moment lived mindlessly is a moment lost forever.

The universe created this moment for you. Embrace it. Be grateful for it. Live and love the moments.

3: For Gratitude

The best mindfulness activity for gratitude is to focus on the moment, be aware of the blessings of the present moment, and express gratitude for now.

Recognise that this moment right now is infinite. This moment stretches across space and time. This moment connects us all. We might be in different countries. We might be different people. But we're all *now*.

This moment is what holds you and me and the whole world together. And that's pretty awesome when you think about it.

Show appreciation for the individual moments of your life.

Mindful gratitude script

1. Close your eyes
2. Listen to the world around you
3. Say (or think): "Thank you for this moment."

This can also be a great mindfulness exercise for families. Simply sit in a circle and take it in turns to state one thing you are grateful for about each person in the group.

4: Perceive Beauty In Everything

There is beauty in everything. Every person. Every flower. Every teardrop. Every smile. Beauty permeates the very fabric of existence. But you have to be mindful to recognise that beauty.

The science of Positive Psychology has proven that people who can see and appreciate beauty are happier and healthier than others. What natural beauty is there around you right now?

5: Smile!

There are so many benefits of smiling. Smiling is contagious, makes the world a more positive place, strengthens the immune system, improves your social life, and releases endorphins.

You can turn smiling into a simple mindfulness meditation exercise. Simply smile and focus on the positive energy you feel around your mouth and face. This will make you happier.

6: Reminders

It is important to set reminders to be mindful. The very word itself comes from Pali and means "To remember".

Set an alarm to go off every hour. If you have an Alexa / Google Home or similar device you can set the voice to give your reminders to be mindful

Or you could use a more traditional alarm, like a Tibetan Singing Bowl or bird call. When the alarm goes off, take sixty seconds—just sixty seconds—to be mindful. That's all it takes, sixty seconds.

When you have a few reminders, it is a lot easier to remember, and it will help you develop the habit of mindfulness.

7: 5 Senses Mindfulness Exercise For Anxiety

We come to life when we live through the senses.

Your senses are always working. You're always seeing things, hearing things, smelling things... be aware of those senses. My favourite way of doing this is with the "5 Senses Mindfulness Exercise".

Simply read the following five senses script in your head, filling in the blanks:

"I am feeling..."

"I am seeing..."

"I am hearing..."

"I am smelling..."

"I am hearing..."

"I am mindful."

8: Mindful Breathing

One of the critical tools we have is our breath. But it's not just a tool for the body. It's a tool for the mind too. Zen Master Thich Nhat Hanh said, "Feelings come and go like clouds in a stormy sky. Mindful breathing is my anchor."

In other words, when we are in the chaos of life, we can return to our breath to restore mindfulness.

When you feel stressed or anxious, take a few deep breaths in through your nose and out through your mouth. Meditate on the movement of your breath.

9: "Right Speech" [For Groups]

One of the best mindfulness activities for groups is *right speech*—the idea that all speech should be kind, compassionate, and loving.

Enlightened people have mastered the art of right speech. We always speak consciously and with love and kindness.

For newcomers, it can be a challenge.

Try using speech as a mindfulness activity for groups of adults. Find a group of friends and tell each person that they are going to speak mindfully. One person starts talking. The others listen mindfully. When someone says something mindless or "ignorant" the other people in the group ask them to rephrase it in a mindful way (a compassionate, enlightened, rational and non-judgmental way).

10: Practice The "Middle Way."

Did you know Buddhists are more satisfied in life than the average person?

One reason is because of the Buddhist habit of *majjhima patipada*, which is the "middle way".

The middle way is about moderation. It is about *not indulging* and *not starving yourself*. In other words, living in moderation.

Whenever you are making a decision such as what to eat or what to do in the evening, ask yourself how you can do something that is satisfying but also healthy, fun but also practical. Look for the middle path.

11: Mindful Eating

The next time you eat something, choose the food mindfully. Eat mindfully and slowly. Pay attention to what you're eating. Be aware of what it is, where it comes from, what it tastes like... everything.

This is one of the best mindful activities for beginners because not only does it help you to be conscious, it also changes the way you feel about that most important thing: food.

12: Mindfulness Activities At Work

One of the best mindfulness meditation exercises at work is

to do a little bit of yoga in your office chair.

The majority of people live too sedentary lifestyles. Scientific research shows that a sedentary lifestyle contributes to premature death.

To counteract this, do some simple yoga poses and stretches in your office chair, while mindfully meditating on the movement of your body.

13: Practice The Yoga Habit Of Pratyahara

Pratyahara is a yoga practice for the mind. In pratyahara yoga, we *reduce negative influences* (such as negative people) and increase positive influences.

We can turn this into a mindfulness activity. To do so, be mindful of the effect different people, objects, and sources of information (like TV, Facebook etc.) are having on you.

When you come across negative influences, find ways to reduce them—such as turning off the TV or ending an abusive relationship.

14: Do One Thing Absolutely

One of the most straightforward mindfulness meditation exercises is just to do whatever you are doing, but slowly and more consciously.

Take the time to slow down each day. One way to make this a habit is to choose specific times when you will slow down (such as at lunch break).

15: Connect With Your Body

This is another simple mindfulness activity for anxiety. It comes from yoga. Take moments to be consciously aware of your body language and your posture. Hold your body with intent, like you would when practising yoga poses.

Anxiety can be caused by negative body language, and by correcting your body language, you can reduce anxiety. When we are anxious, we hunch over and slouch. Conversely, when we are confident, we stand tall. Take moments to correct your body language and mindfully observe how you feel when you stand properly.

16: Laughter

There is a kind of alternative yoga called *Laughter Yoga* that can make a fun mindfulness activity for groups.

Get into a group and deliberately start laughing. Now consciously observe the energy of laughing. It is a fun, playful energy. Also listen to other people in the group laughing. This will make you feel happy and playful.

17: Showering

Close your eyes while showering and focus on the sensation of water falling on your body.

18: Meditation

Obviously, the very best mindfulness meditation exercise is meditation itself. The key to using meditation as a mindfulness exercise is to make it a habit.

I recommend setting an alarm that reminds you to meditate every day.

Start with just consciously breathing. Close your eyes focus on the movement of your breath around your body. Take 108 breaths. Then express gratitude for your meditation.

19: Water Mindfulness Meditation Exercise

Water is one of the most divine things in the world. It's pure, and it's perhaps the number one representation of the power of nature. The next time you're around water, just take a moment to meditate on it. Focus on the flow of the water. Feel the energy and notice how free water is. Ask that sense of freedom to enter your own life.

Rain too. Rain is the healing of the land, the purifying of the world. Rain connects the sky to the earth. It's symbolic of the perpetual cycle of life. Whenever there's rain, be conscious of it. Stand out in the rain and feel the cold droplets cleansing your spirit.

20: Zen Walking

One of the best mindfulness meditation exercises from Buddhism is "Zen Walking". We will look at this method a little later.

21: Read Inspiring Books / Quotes

Books are beautiful. When you read a book, you experience many of the same states as you do when you meditate. Your mind slows down. You relax. The noise dissipates. Your heart rate lowers.

22: Intention

One of the best mindfulness exercises for adults is *conscious* intent.

It can be easy to turn your day into a blur. You start with ideas of what you want or need to do, and you set about doing them. But the plan doesn't quite work out, so you end up doing two things at once, then three things… and you're not really focusing on any of them. Tell yourself the one thing you're going to do. Do that one thing. Complete it. Then move on.

This is a habit of mindful *intent*. We are choosing to do one thing, and then focusing on that one thing absolutely

24: Scents

The sense of smell is immensely powerful. When we smell things, we bring memories to mind. Therefore, we can use the sense of smell to get in touch with our memories.

25: Get In Touch With Your Intuition

Intuition is very powerful. Science suggests that people are at their wisest when they listen to that little voice inside. Let your inner voice speak to you and listen.

27: One Minute Breathing

Mindful breathing is the best mindfulness exercise for anxiety because when we breathe properly, we relax.

This exercise is highly versatile. You can do it just about anywhere, whether you're lying in bed or out for a walk. And it only takes sixty seconds.

Simply breathe in through your nose, hold for a count of five, and then breathe out slowly. As you breathe, focus on letting your breath flow naturally and easily.

At times your mind will lose its anchor, and you'll find yourself flooded with thoughts. Simply observe those thoughts. Let them be. Let them go. Watch your breath with your senses. Observe as your breath becomes one with the wider universe.

If you thought you would never be able to meditate, guess what? You're now meditating, and it only took one minute.

28: Nature

Simply spending 20 minutes mindfully observing nature will make you happier and healthier.

This is a very easy mindfulness meditation exercise, but it's also highly potent and it's is one of my personal favourites, too, because it connects us to the beauty of nature.

29: A Mindful Day

Use this exercise to be mindful all day. This technique uses what I call "Anchors". These are basically reminders to be mindful.

It's easier than it sounds. If you'd like to do this exercise, simply pick a few things that you do every day—for instance, turning the door handle, having a shower, opening the curtains...

When you open the curtains (for example) allow yourself to be completely conscious. Take that moment, those few seconds, to be completely mindful—the same with turning the door handle or having a shower.

You perform these simple tasks every day, so use them as reminders. Through a process of repetition, you will train your brain to be conscious at those moments naturally. The process will soon become automatic. Then, you'll have mindful moments without even having to try.

I love this one because it allows you to take mundane everyday activities—like turning a door handle—and turn them into your own little moments of consciousness.

29: Mindful Listening

Practising this mindful listening exercise will make you more aware and more focused on the present moment.

Everyone loves a good listener, right? But even better than a good listener is a mindful listener.

This mindful listening exercise is all about listening to people in a non-judgmental fashion. Not only is this excellent for the person you're listening to, but it's fantastic for you too. It's great to do this one in groups because it improves communication in relationships.

Most of us are highly influenced by the things we hear. It can be quite easy to become irritated when someone says something thoughtless, for instance. But when you practice this method, you stop being affected by words.

When you're listening to someone speaking, just focus on the sound. Don't judge, just listen. Tune in to the sound of their voice and observe it consciously. If what they say causes you to think or feel things, consciously observe those thoughts and feelings and remind yourself that they are *only* thoughts and feelings.

You can also do this listening exercise with music. If you play an instrument, you likely do this already. I've played the piano for thirty years. When I play, I sink into the music. I let it take me. I flow with the sound of the piano.

And if you're not a musician, hey, no sweat, just put a piece of relaxing music on and listen to it mindfully. You'll find this supremely tranquil.

30: Doing Anything At All

Many of us are starved for time. I know there are often days when I'd do anything for five minutes just to chill in. It can be hard to practice even the most simple mindfulness meditation exercises on days like those. What do you do?

The trick is to take an activity that you'd do anyway. For instance, you have to do the dishes. Why not do the dishes mindfully? Or how about eating. You have to have dinner, why not eat mindfully?

Three awesome things happen when you do chores mindfully: 1) You get a good spot of mindfulness, 2) You complete the task you have to do anyway, and 3) You do that task quicker and better than normal because you're focusing on it.

So, do the thing you need to do, just turn it into a mindfulness activity.

You remember the scene from The Karate Kid when Mr Miyagi is teaching Daniel to clean his car, and he says "Wax on, wax off". He's teaching Daniel to clean his car in a mindful way. The trick is to be one with the movements, one with the "wax on" and one with the "wax off". Be mindful.

By performing your regular activities more consciously, you'll get the task done better and quicker, and you'll get some free mindfulness. It's a win/win situation.

31: Describe Things To Yourself

One of the simplest mindfulness activities is just to describe things to yourself.

Try mindfully describing the beauty you see. The beautiful sky, for instance. What do you see when you mindfully observe a beautiful sky? Describe it to yourself.

The trick here is to observe the things you're experiencing through your senses.

If you're out for a walk, describe the sky—the colours, the shapes, the feelings it creates in you—describe the scenery, describe the motion of walking, and so on.

This simple technique trains your mind to be aware of your senses. It improves the communication between your conscious mind and your unconscious mind. And all you need do is describe a few things around you.

32: Exercises With Pets (Horses Dogs, Cats...)

Grab a cat/dog/horse/octopus (hey, whatever works) and snuggle it. Close your eyes. Feel that sense of love and warmth. Be consciously aware of that. This will put some love in your soul.

Every morning when I wake up, my cat, Willow, want snuggles for at least twenty minutes. So, I snuggle her, close my eyes, and listen to her purr. It's my little mindful-snuggle.

Mindfulness Exercises For Kids

There are so many reasons to start teaching kids to meditate. By practising some mindfulness exercises, kids can focus their minds, improve their health, and feel good about themselves.

There are so many benefits of mindfulness for children. Let's take a look at how kids can start to be mindful.

1: 10-Minute Exercise For Kids 10+

This is an easy mindfulness exercise for kids over the age of ten.

Ask your child to close their eyes and focus on their breathing. Keep an eye on the wall. When two minutes have passed, proceed to the next step. Ask them to focus on what they are hearing. It may help if you ask them to describe, in detail, the sounds they are hearing. This makes them tune in to the sounds around them, which will cause them to focus on the present moment, which decreases rumination and helps to reduce negative thoughts.

Ask them to pay attention to the sensation of touch. Have them describe what they can feel (for instance, wind on the face, soft grass at their feet etc.).

Ask them to focus on scents. How does the air smell? Are there any other scents they are aware of? Now move to the sense of taste and repeat. Finally, ask them to open their eyes and simply *look* around. You may ask them to focus on light, on shades and on other visuals to make them more aware of sight.

This exercise makes kids more aware of the present moment and helps them to focus on one thing at a time (in the exercise, they focus on the senses one at a time).

In this age of constant stimulation, many children (and

adults) struggle to focus. This technique boosts focus and concentration by asking your kids to zone in on one thing at a time.

2: Mindful Breathing For Kids 5 +

Ask your child to sit comfortably with good posture and to close their eyes. Bring their attention to the sensation of their breath coming and going through the space between their mouth and nose.

Ask them to place both their hands on their stomach and to feel their breath rising and falling from there. You may also ask them to repeat a simple word as they breathe in and out, saying "In" on in-breaths and "Out" when exhaling. Work in cycles of five breaths. Have them count five breaths and then ask them to be aware of any thoughts or feelings in their mind. If they are experiencing thoughts or feelings, ask them to let go and to return their attention to their breath. This is great for relaxation and also improves focus and concentration.

3: Listening Activity For Kids 8+

If your kids struggle to listen, try the following. Ask them to focus on their breathing for a few minutes. Explain to them that they are going to hear a sound and that they should focus on the sound as it gets quieter and quieter. Ask them to nod their head when they can no longer hear that sound. Now, start playing some relaxing sounds. For instance, you might like to use a Tibetan singing bowl or an alternative source of what I call "Zen Sounds"—sounds that produce an inner calm.

Gradually quieten the sound. When they nod their head (saying they can no longer hear it) have them count five breaths again. Repeat this exercise once for each year of their age.

The purpose of this activity is to increase kids' auditory awareness while also quieting their minds. Because they are focusing on listening to a quiet sound, they will naturally quieten their mind (because they need to be inwardly silent in order to listen). This produces mental peace and inner silence. As a nice little bonus, it also improves listening skills.

4: Eating Exercise (8+)

This food-based exercise will help kids to be more consciously aware of their diet, which is excellent for their wellbeing.

Gather some food into a plate or bowl. Remove any wrappers. Have your child count to five breaths. Now ask your child to be mindful of the food on the plate, being aware of the feeling, the image, and the scent of the food. If they are holding cutlery, you may ask them to be mindful of that too.

Ask your child to take a small portion of the food and to eat it slowly while focusing on the taste. Ideally, they will chew slowly and will focus on the activity of eating. Once they have finished eating, ask them to describe the taste and feel of the food.

As well as heightening mindful, this exercise makes kids more aware and more appreciative of food.

5: Mindful Walking For Kids 8+

Mindful Walking is one of the traditional meditation exercises in Zen Buddhism.

Take a short walk with your kid(s) somewhere relaxing and safe. Ask them to focus on the sensation of movement in their feet and legs. Continue walking slowly, while focusing on the movement. If your child shows a lack of concentration at any time, stop walking and have them count five breaths. After the five breaths, continue to walk mindfully. After 20 minutes of walking, stop. Ask them to describe how they feel.

This is one of the easiest and most relaxing meditations there is. Try it at the beach or in the park for a truly relaxing experience.

6: Play Activities [Ages: Five-Ten Years Old]

In this exercise, kids play a fun game—such as finger-painting, using a sand table, or a similar activity. Start by asking them to take ten conscious breaths to relax and focus. Now tell your child that they can play in whatever way they like but with one condition: they must be mindful of everything they do. Whatever they choose to do during play, they must focus on it absolutely, as we do when meditating. Ask your child to be aware of all five senses, being mindful of taste, touch, sight, sound and hearing. If they lose focus, use five mindful breaths to regain their attention.

7: Art-Based Mindfulness Activities For Kids 7+

Many children love painting and drawing, both of which can easily be turned into a meditation practice. Try this simple mindful art exercise.

Find an object that your child wants to draw or paint. Now ask them to observe every aspect of the object for 5 minutes. Ask them to describe the shape of the object, the feeling, and so on. This encourages them to practice mindfulness.

They can then draw or paint the object, but they must focus absolutely on the object while they create their art.

8: Cooking (5+)

Here is a great exercise for kids who enjoy cooking.

Get hold of a fun and simple recipe that your child might like to cook (some healthy cookies, for instance). Gather the ingredients, along with any utensils you need. Go through the recipe. Each time you get to a new item, ask your kids to consciously observe that item. Ask them to watch the effect that each new ingredient has on the colour, taste, touch, and smell of the food. Once the food is ready, have them eat it mindfully

(see number 4 in this list)

This mindful cooking exercise boosts present-moment mindfulness, encourages kids to be more mindful of what they are eating, and teaches them to cook, all at the same time.

Now that we've looked at some very simple mindfulness exercises, it's time for us to go deeper. Let's start to dip our toes into some more serious forms of meditation.

OPENING YOUR MIND TO A DEEPER EXISTENCE

In the spring of 2004, having finished drama school and about to move home to Birmingham UK—a cultural hotspot that's home to many of the best musicians, artists, and authors of all time, including Electric Light Orchestra, Judas Priest, Duran Duran, J.R.R. Tolkien, John Wyngham and more—my fascination with meditation and spirituality started to gather momentum.

I was moving with my girlfriend (now *ex*-girlfriend) into a large house in the city centre. We were excitedly unpacking large boxes full of assorted books and games when I happened to find a cute little pink pocketbook titled "1000 Meditations". Flicking through the pages, I found a large quote in the centre of a page. The quote read: "The voyage of discovery is not in finding new landscapes but in having new eyes." The quote was written by Marcel Proust, the French twentieth-century novelist. On the next page was written, "There are things known, and there are things unknown, and between both are the doors of perception—Aldous Huxley". Then, "Dwell on the beauty of life. Watch the stars, and see yourself running with them—Marcus Aerilius."

Like an excited kid at Christmas, I spent the next few hours showing my girlfriend the book and reading every single quote from it—this was before Google made it unsatisfyingly easy to find out what absolutely any famous person has ever said about anything. The combination of moving home and creating a new life while reading these deep and philosophical quotes stirred my imagination. I felt invigorated. I ventured out into my new city, Birmingham, on a voyage of discovery, with what Proust called "new eyes".

> **"The voyage of discovery is not in finding new landscapes but in having new eyes."**
>
> *– Marcel Proust*

Birmingham has many wonderful bookstores and some fantastic festivals and carnivals where you can meet truly fascinating people. I spent hours in the bookstores reading up about spirituality and meditation. I visited all the festivals and carnivals and met absolutely anyone I could who happened to know anything about my newfound fascinations. Wherever I could glean insight, that was where I'd go.

The whole time I was embarked on my voyage, I felt an electric pulse of excitement about me. I felt like Frodo when he first ventured out of the Shire, or Luke Skywalker when he strapped himself into the Millenium Falcon and blasted out of Mos Eisley, leaving his humble home to take in the fullness of the universe. I was utterly enthralled and captivated.

Like Luke, when he's learning The Force, I was eager to push on, to get to know everything I could about spirituality and meditation. I learnt about the body-mind, about enlightenment, about the story of the Buddha, the philosophies of spiritual leaders throughout history. But it was meditation that fascinated me the most, and I think because it is so spiritual and yet also so practical.

One of the best things about my journey was the fact that I wasn't alone. My girlfriend was experiencing her own journey of self-discovery, and many friends were similarly interested in philosophy, metaphysics and many other wonderful subjects. We'd discuss our readings with each other at coffee shops, excited to share this magical thing known as spirituality.

But at the same time that I was eagerly discussing meditation with friends, there were many people who would raise a dubious eyebrow or scoff derisively whenever I mentioned anything remotely spiritual.

It was as though the world were torn in two between those who accepted the Eastern philosophies I was digging into and those who thought they were stupid, offensive, or even satanic.

What I was experiencing was a rift in our society, a rift that began back in the 1960s—when meditation first began to become popular in the West—and has lasted to today.

Even now, meditation techniques from the East are gaining tremendous popularity in the West, where those techniques are being influenced by modern society and led in new directions. It's like two great ocean currents, East and West, hurtling into one another and changing the direction of the ocean.

For the experienced meditator, it's an exciting time. But for the newcomer, it can seem a little intimidating. There are simply so many different techniques being discussed in the media and in spiritual groups right now. It's hard to know where to begin.

If you're new to meditation and just beginning to learn about different meditation techniques, it's best to start with a holistic point of view, taking an overarching peek at the different types of meditation available. That's what I did back in 2004, and I think that's the best way for you and me to begin our journey into meditation.

So, let's start our voyage. Let's open the door to the temple of the mind and dig into the rich culture, history, science, and art of meditation.

BEGINNING AT THE BEGINNING

Where do you begin to learn about meditation?

For myself, back in 2004 when I was starting out, I simply read absolutely everything I could on the subject of meditation, along with attending lectures, meeting many amazing people, and soaking up wisdom like a sunbather soaks up rays.

It wasn't long before I'd dabbled with breathing meditation, mantra recitation, binaural beats, visualisations, and much, much more. The world felt like one big candy store in which every day contained its own philosophical lessons and meditations to be discovered. Every day the morning light breaking over my skin brought with it a desire for discovery.

It was an exhilarating time, but it was also more than a little confusing. Meeting and reading different spiritualists and gurus, it was clear that there was no one *right way* to learn meditation. Back at Oxford, we'd had spirited debates about what the right way to learn acting was, the right way to control your mind so you can step into the shoes of a character on stage. Meditation was similar but even more complex. Every guru was advocating his or her own belief system and techniques. Knowing which to do and which to avoid was no mean feat.

What else could I do? I thought I would try them all.

So I *thought*. But it soon dawned on me that there are far more meditation techniques than I had ever expected.

Believe it or not, there are several thousand specific meditation techniques catalogued in archives and texts throughout the world. Indeed, Tibetan Buddhism alone has over a thousand types of visualisations, which is just one *category* of meditation.

It is quite simply impossible to *try it all* when it comes to meditation. If you tried one new meditation technique each day, it would take approximately ten years to get to the end of them all. And obviously, we don't want to wait ten years for results. We want answers and solutions now, the ever quick and easy twenty-first-century way.

So, to make it quick and easy to find the right meditation techniques for your, I've gone ahead and assorted the most popular meditations into their respective categories.

If you already have a lot of knowledge about meditation, you might be wondering just precisely how I went about organising those thousands of techniques into different categories.

There are many different ways in which you can assort and organise meditation techniques. You can arrange them by the religion that they come from, by the health benefits they offer, by the specific type of activity that they entail, or in many other ways. But the absolute most basic way to categorise meditations is into two sorts: Open and Closed.

"Open" and "Closed" Meditations

Like the pupils of your eyes, the mind can be *open* to receive the fullness of your environment, or it can be *closed* to focus on one thing. That's why meditation is divided into two distinct categories: Open and Closed.

Think of the mind as the pupil of your eye. It can be open, letting in the entire world, or closed to focus on just one object.

OPEN MEDITATION

OVERVIEW: Open meditation techniques are those techniques in which we do not focus on one specific object but instead open the mind to the entirety of our surroundings. Here, you're not focusing on the breath or on a sound, you're focusing on absolutely everything.

In Open meditations, we are aware of the totality of existence. We are aware of our thoughts and feelings, physical sensations, and all the information that comes to us by way of our senses (sound, smell, taste etc.). We non-judgmentally observe the world, allowing our focus to extend to everything in our environment.

Like a butterfly arising from out of a chrysalis to take flight into the world, the mind is freed from its usual shackles of thoughts and stresses, freed to take in the fullness of existence.

If you've ever taken a flight, you'll probably remember what it's like when you're taking off. Your troubles melt away; you feel that liberation as the plane lifts into the sky, you gaze out the window at those streets that seemed so big just a short while before. Suddenly you can see everything clearly, all at once. You see the rows and rows of tiny houses, the little coloured dots of cars, like Skittles, heading down silver-worm roads, and those almost indiscernible specks of humanity going about their daily lives. It's a completely different perspective on reality. It's relaxing, humbling, and liberating. Open meditation is similar. When you practice open meditation, you let your mind zoom out, your focus opening up to take in the fullness of reality. Everything comes to you, the sights, sounds, feelings... you're aware of it all at the same time. It's as though you've completely stopped and life is occurring around you, but your mind is still.

Open meditations are wonderfully relaxing, but they represent a lot more than just a few moments of peace. Practising open meditations is fantastic for your brain. The change in perspective—zooming *out* of yourself and *into* the totality of existence—is remarkably good for your creativity and your sense of freedom.

When you spend your every moment focusing on just one or two things, you tend to get a very limited world view. You forget the million opportunities and events happening all around you. You constrict yourself to just the things you're thinking about: your job, your family, etc. Open meditations give you the opportunity to loosen that grip and to take a more holistic view of reality.

That's why open meditations can be immensely helpful when you get in a rut. Imagine, for instance, that you're a stay at home parent and your every focus is put into raising your kids. That's fantastic and a truly noble cause, but for your own sake there should be times when you're able to let it all go for just a few moments and take in the whole world. That's where meditation can help. Let someone else look after the kids for twenty minutes and practice an open meditation. You'll find that you're suddenly much more aware of the richness of life.

Open meditations are also excellent for your creative brain. Creativity is all about *openness*, about the ability to see things from alternative perspectives. Picasso, for instance, would never have become one of the most famous artists of all time if he'd limited himself to only ever seeing the world in the traditional way. His open mind and his ability to look outside the box led him to create some of the most famous artworks in history. You can create a similarly open mind by practising open meditations.

Open meditations are like the stretches you do in yoga. They loosen up your mental muscles and allow for more freedom of movement, more freedom of thought. But also just like yoga, not only do you need to stretch your muscles, you also need to *strengthen* them by staying in one pose (or "asana") for long periods. That's precisely the purpose of the next group of meditations, "Closed" meditations, which strengthen the mind through focus.

Here's how to do it.

EXERCISE: Open Meditation

1. Close your eyes and take ten mindful breaths
2. Now gradually observe the sensations in your body. Simply watch them as though you are watching a movie.
3. Feel the surface you're lying or sitting on and mindfully observe that.
4. Listen to the sounds around you.
5. Imagine gradually stepping back away from yourself (I like to imagine I am moving upwards, away from my body) and look down at yourself and the world around you.
6. Imagine you are hundreds of metres above your body. Look down and simply observe yourself and your surroundings. Hear, see, smell, taste, and touch, but from a distance. It is almost as though you are holding the present moment like a picture in your hands, which your holding at arms'-length.

7. Feel the space all around you and notice the distance between yourself and your sensory awareness. The more you focus on the empty space, the less reactive you will be to mental thoughts and feelings, bodily sensations, and external stimuli.

8. Spend twenty minutes observing the world from this new perspective.

CLOSED MEDITATIONS

The old Zen proverb "When sitting sit" best explains closed meditations. These techniques are about doing and being one thing absolutely. For instance, if you're focusing (meditating) on your breathing, your breathing becomes everything. If you're listening (meditating) to a sound—the honeyed reverberations of a Tibetan bowl, for instance—that sound becomes the only thing in the world. That's closed meditation: meditation in which the mind is absolutely focused on one thing.

"When sitting, sit."— Zen proverb

Think about the last time you felt a profound connection with someone—for instance, the last time you made love. It was as though you and your lover became one. You merged. You felt their breath on your face, their skin on your skin; you looked into their eyes, and it was as though you were stepping right into those eyes. All that existed at that moment was you and your lover. That was a moment of closed meditation, a moment in which the whole world vanished, and there was nothing but your consciousness and the object of your meditation (in this instance, your lover). That's the state of mind we refer to when we talk about closed meditations.

Closed meditations are significantly more popular than open meditations and come in many more variations (as you'll see later on). There are thousands of different closed meditation techniques, which are used for a whole host of reasons. For instance, chakra meditation (a meditation in which you focus on energy centres in your body) can help to harmonise your body and thereby to improve the functioning of your vital organs, restoring health and helping to eliminate illnesses and diseases. Breathing meditation can help to still and relax the mind. Other closed meditation techniques may boost your levels of joy or compassion, increase your ability to focus at work, and so on. There are so many different closed meditation techniques that I have yet to find one single real-world problem that cannot be helped by a closed meditation.

We'll look in-depth at specific closed meditation techniques a little later on. But for now, suffice to say that we can open the mind to everything or close the mind so that it is focused on one specific thing. There are some meditations that come halfway between the two, meditations where the mind is focused on *a few* things, meditation in which the mind (as the door) is ajar, so to speak. But loosely speaking, every meditation technique belongs either in the Open Meditations pile or the Closed Meditations pile.

Soon, we will look at the most powerful meditation techniques in the world. But you might wonder why there are so many different methods and why you need to know about them. After all, many people think that meditation is just one thing. However, there are in fact many different forms of meditation and they each have their own unique benefits. To get what you personally want from meditation, you have to understand the benefits of the different methods. So, let's take a look at the different benefits of meditation and how different *forms of meditation* have different benefits.

THE BENEFITS OF MEDITATION AND WHY THERE ARE SO MANY

There's one thing many beginner meditators fail to understand about the practise. That is, that there are many different forms of meditation and *each form has its own unique benefits*. Some benefits are universal. For instance, most meditations are relaxing and help the mind to focus. But the majority of benefits are unique to one form of meditation For instance, Loving Kindness Meditation is one of very few meditations that will make you feel more positively connected to other people.

Because different techniques have different benefits, the only way to take full advantage of meditation is to know the benefits of different techniques. That way you can choose which meditation you need to do at any given time.

What follows is a comprehensive list of the different benefits of meditation, with notes on the types of meditation that offer that benefit.

Physical Benefits of Meditation

1. Reduced Oxygen consumption

Meditation lowers the rate at which we consume oxygen (according to the Mayo Clinic), and this, in turn, offers many health benefits. Researchers state that while you are meditating, your oxygen consumption drops to 20%, which is a 10% reduction. This helps you to relax and is also very helpful for getting to sleep.

While you are meditating you relax, your heart rate lowers (according to research from Harvard) and you breathe slower. Because of this, your body requires less oxygen. In fact, while you are meditating your body's oxygen consumption is at the same level it is when you are six hours into sleep. Even better, during this time, your body is given the opportunity to heal itself, as we'll see in a moment.

I personally feel my entire body relaxing every time I meditate, and you can tell the difference it makes to your breathing.

2. Healing

Above, I mentioned that when you meditate, you lower your heart rate, breathe slower, and lower your oxygen consumption rate. This means that your body is having to do less work.

Because your body is having to do less work, it is given an opportunity to heal itself. That downtime, when your body is not working so hard to provide enough oxygen to keep your heart rate up, is basically the equivalent of a break. It's a time when your body can slow down, relax, and heal itself.

3. Eliminating free radicals

Free radicals are agents that attack your cells from the inside-out. Your cells consist of atoms with a nucleus at the centre. The nucleus is surrounded by a cloud of electrons, which are negatively charged particles. However, sometimes atoms lose their electrons. This causes the atom to become a free radical, which can attack your cells, which is one of the primary causes of illness and ageing. The solution? Antioxidants. Antioxidants are nutrients in the body that can give their electrons to free radicals, which stops the problem.

Our bodies naturally produce antioxidants, but stress, toxins, and other factors can make us damage more cells than we produce. Some of the worst causes of this are depression, anxiety, and stress.

Because meditation promotes relaxation and prevents and treats problems like stress and depression, it slows the rate at which cells are damaged, decreasing free-radicals and slowing the ageing process.

4. Reduces Risk Of Chronic Disease

One of the most valuable health benefits of daily meditation is that it helps with chronic diseases.

Stress is the most significant cause of illness and death. Stress causes the body to activate the fight-or-flight response, which affects the entire system in seconds. Blood flow increases, and heart rate and breathing rate escalate. Your entire body is revved up, ready for fight-or-flight. When this happens frequently, you significantly increase your chances of illness, including stroke, heart disease, digestion problems, diabetes, and more. And all because of frequent stress.

When you meditate, you reduce stress and reduce the numerous health quandaries that stress causes. Just twenty minutes of meditation daily will substantially decrease the negative impacts of stress.

6. Heart health

When you meditate, you enter a very relaxed state. Your mind slows down. Stress reduces. Breathing slows down so you need less oxygen. And because of all this, your heart rate normalises. Your entire system is then relaxed, which helps the inner organs to function properly. This, in turn, allows blood to flow through your body unimpeded.

Research conducted by the Division of Cardiology at the Cedars-Sinai Medical Center shows that meditation regulates heart rate and improves blood flow. Another study by the National Institute of Health in 2009 shows that meditation improves blood pressure.

A Harvard study by Dr Herbert Benson proved that meditation dilates the arteries, which enables blood to flow more freely.

Put all this together and it's clear to see how meditation massively improves heart health.

7. Healthier skin

What can meditation do for your skin? Well, in my experience it helped my skin to be clearer and healthier and I always look better after meditating because I'm more relaxed.

Your skin is the largest organ in your body and an essential one. It protects you from diseases. It protects your organs from temperatures that might damage them. It prevents unhealthy chemicals and substances from entering your inner body. It is one of the most crucial ways in which your body protects itself.

Scientific research has proven that meditation improves skin resistance and increases the rate of new cell production.

When your skin cells age, they are gradually pushed out and replaced by newer skin cells beneath. But it takes time for the body to remove dead skin cells and to build new ones. The more stress, anxiety, and depression you suffer, the harder it is for your body to create these new skin cells. When you meditate, you give your body a break. You essentially allow your body to relax and focus on what it needs to do, part of which is building new skin.

8. Lower risk of cardiovascular disease

Heart.org tells us that "taking a few minutes to relax each day could lower risk of cardiovascular disease". They recommend using 20-30 minutes of breathing meditation or other meditations in which you focus on an object or sound.

When you feel stressed, your body releases adrenaline that makes your breathing speed up and increases blood pressure and heart rate. Over an extended period, this stress response has a significant effect on your body. That's why reducing stress is so important for your health.

9. Better breathing

Your lungs are one of the most important parts of your body and definitely the most important organ for respiration. But many people do not breathe correctly.

The best form of breathing is "diaphragmatic breathing", a technique in which air is drawn deep down into the diaphragm. You will know if you are breathing diaphragmatically because your rib cage will rise and fall.

Stress leads to shallow breathing, which makes it harder for air to enter the lungs. The best way to correct this problem is by relaxing. Of course, there are lots of different ways in which you can relax, but meditation is one of the best.

When you meditate you relax, and when you relax, you improve your breathing, helping air to enter your lungs.

10. Relieves asthma

Asthma occurs when a trigger (for instance, dust) makes your bronchi (airways) narrow and your lungs become inflamed. Mucus then develops that makes it even harder to breathe.

Several scientific studies have discovered significant

benefits of daily meditation for the prevention and treatment of asthma. In 2000, the Natural Therapies Unity of the Royal Hospital for Women in Sydney Australia studied the effect of daily meditation on asthma. 47 asthma patients were studied. Half the group meditated while the rest practised general relaxation techniques. The group that meditated observed a significant reduction in the symptoms of asthma compared to the control group.

11. Strengthens endocrine system

The "endocrine system" refers to the glands that regulate tissue function, sexual function, sleep, mood, and metabolism, and produce hormones. Those hormones instruct other cells about how to function, and they also instruct your glands about when to produce saliva and sweat.

Your endocrine system is given orders by your brain, which tells you when to blink, breathe, and other vital functions. But when you are stressed, your endocrine system is forced to release hormones, which can lead to unnecessary and unhelpful bodily functions, like sweating when you don't need to just because you're under pressure.

Research via MRI scans shows that people who meditate have more activity in the parts of the brain that regulate the endocrine system. This leads to improved mood, slower ageing rate, and better immune system functioning. Meditation also reduces the rate at which your endocrine system deteriorates as you age, which is yet another way in which meditation slows the ageing process.

12. Boosts immune system

Your immune system is one of the most important aspects of your overall health and wellbeing. It provides an indispensable role in helping you avoid illness. And it is directly related to both body and mind.

In the 1980s scientists discovered that the immune system is intelligent. It understands the chemical messages transmitted around your body. Your mood, thoughts, sensations, and beliefs all affect your immune system. And when you meditate, you influence those messages.

Meditation creates a positive environment in which your immune system can thrive. And this is so advantageous that it can even help people with HIV.

UCLA researchers discovered that people with HIV who practised mindfulness meditation slow down the reduction of D-4 cell count. These are cells that your immune system uses to reduce illness. At the same time, when you meditate, you boost the production of antibodies.

Researchers investigated a group of biotech workers who meditated for eight weeks. The results showed that after meditation, the workers had substantially enhanced levels of antibodies.

As though this wasn't enough, meditation also improves the functioning of brain areas related to the immune system, namely: the prefrontal cortex, the right anterior insula, and the right hippocampus.

This research proves that meditation has a significant effect on your immune system

13. Loving Kindness And Mindfulness Improve Hygiene

Personal hygiene and mental hygiene are essential to our health. Good personal hygiene helps to prevent the transference of impurities to the body. And good mental hygiene helps to preserve mental strength.

Scientific analysis reveals that bad hygiene is caused by a few fundamental conditions; most notably, depression, lack of self-love, and anxiety—all of which are relieved through meditation. A lack of mindfulness can also lead to bad personal hygiene because when we are mindless, we are more likely to perform tasks that spread contagions (like putting a finger in the mouth).

14. Allergy sufferers

The more stress you have in life the harder it is for your immune system to deal with allergies.

Stress and anxiety increase the duration and severity of allergy symptoms. Conversely, the more relaxed you are, the shorter and weaker your allergy symptoms will be. This is because when you're stressed, your immune system is rendered ineffective. But there are steps you can take to counter this. When you relax, you make it easier for your immune system to operate. For this reason, meditation helps with allergies.

15. Arthritis

In 2010 Dr Rosenzweig at Drexel University (a research centre that is highly regarded for its studies on arthritis) studied the effect of Mindfulness-Based Stress Reduction

(MBSR) on arthritis and other chronic pain conditions such as posterior pain.

The researchers studied the effects of MBSR on more than 1000 people with arthritis and similar conditions, and observed a significant improvement in quality of life. Pain symptoms were also substantially decreased.

Dr Rosenweig associates the pain reduction with improved mood. Naturally, people suffering from chronic arthritis and other conditions frequently suffer from poor moods and may even suffer depression as a direct result of their condition. This negative mental state can increase pain symptoms and make it harder for the body to heal. Meditation improves mood and helps the body to relax, which helps to treat arthritis psychosomatically.

One thing that is important to note is that the effects of meditation were different for different people. Some of the patients had significant improvements, some less. However, Dr Rosenweig informs us that Mindfulness-Based Stress Reduction does offer efficient treatment for arthritis, mostly because of reduced pain.

16. Weight loss

Meditation can have a tremendous impact on weight loss for numerous reasons. For starters, certain forms of meditation can increase metabolism so that we burn calories faster. Meditation in general helps us to relax so we are less likely to stress eat. Mindful Eating makes us more aware of what we are eating and how our food contributes to our body. And methods like Vipassana (which you will learn later in this book) can improve our self-awareness and reduce cravings.

For these reasons, meditation can be a game-changer for anyone wanting to lose weight.

17. Premenstrual syndrome

Premenstrual Syndrome (PMS) is a variety of mental and physical symptoms that exhibit during menstruation. These symptoms may include depression, anxiety, bloating, insomnia, mood swings, and headaches.

For many years, doctors have treated PMS with mood medications. However, there is a healthier way to improve your mood: meditation.

Recent research into the effect of daily meditation on PMS confirms that meditation helps women to overcome the emotional symptoms of premenstrual syndrome and that this, in turn, helps with the physical symptoms. Meditation promotes relaxation and heightens feelings of love and happiness. These emotions help your muscles to relax, which in turn can help to reduce the symptoms of PMS.

17. Decreases muscle tension

Muscle tension is one of the most common health problems in the world. When your muscles are tense, they remain contracted. This is often caused by stress. Recall the last time you were extremely stressed, and you might remember being hunched over, having stomach cramp, and feeling tight.

Whether it's stress from family problems, work, or anything else, your physical tension can lead to health problems and can damage your nervous system. Muscle tension can even cause reduced blood flow, preventing your muscles from getting the oxygen they need. This can lead to short or long term damage to your muscles.

Meditation helps blood to flow around your body, which in turn helps your muscles to get the oxygen they need. The result is healthy muscles that are not prone to tension.

18. Mindfulness can even help with HIV

This is one of the most staggering facts about meditation. It can help even help with HIV.

Your immune system uses "brain cells" that are called CD4T cells. These cells instruct the immune system about how to act when the body is under attack. HIV attacks these cells, which prevents the immune system from functioning properly, which leads to the symptoms of HIV. This can then lead to AIDS, the devastating condition that 40 million people currently suffer from.

Stress accelerates the decline of CD4 T cells. But researchers at UCLA report that mindfulness meditation stops the decline of CD4 T cells, which slows HIV.

19. Reduces viral activity, including cold and flu

Have you been suffering from cold or flu? No sweat. Meditation can help.

Researchers at the University of Wisconsin-Madison examined whether meditation or exercise was better at preventing cold and flu. They took two groups of people, gave one group mindfulness training and the other moderate exercise, and observed that *people in both groups* were less susceptible to cold and flu.

Another test showed that people who meditate have 76% less sick days from September to May than people who do not meditate. People who meditate also get rid of cold and flu quicker, at an average of five days compared to eight.

20. Improves energy levels

Meditation has been determined to raise energy for five reasons:

- It stops stress from sapping at your energy
- It boosts endorphins
- Promotes quality of sleep
- Boosts growth hormone and DHEA (see below)
- Improves brain functioning

21. Increases levels of Dehydroepiandrosterone

Dehydroepiandrosterone (DHEA), is an endogenous steroid hormone that is produced by the adrenal glands (gonads) and the brain, where it functions as a metabolic intermediate in the biosynthesis of androgen and estrogen sex steroids.

DHEA helps your body fight viral, bacterial and parasitic infections. It stimulates the thymus gland, helps prevents inflammation, and helps prevent depression and stress.

The good news is that meditation helps boost your DHEA levels, so you get all the benefits listed above. When you enter a deep meditative state, you naturally raise your

DHEA levels, and this helps with healing, relaxation, hormone regulation, and stress.

Dr Robert Keitch Wallace studied the levels of DHEA in meditators and non-meditators back in 1982 and found that meditators were biologically 12 years younger than non-meditators primarily because of increased DHEA levels.

22. Meditation reduces sweating

This is probably not the first health benefit of meditation to come to mind. People tend to think that meditation helps with stress, anxiety, depression, and other mental health problems, as well as relaxation and focus. Comparatively few people realise that meditation makes you sweat less. But it's a fact.

How can meditation make you sweat less?

It all goes back to points we've discussed so far. Meditation reduces breathing rate, heart rate and blood pressure. This helps your body to cool down. Meditating helps to control your body temperature and also prevents tension in your muscles. So, it stops the *causes of sweating*.

23. Reduces headaches and migraines

A study published in the journal Headache states that when you meditate you help prevent and relieve the symptoms of migraines.

Wake Forest Baptist Medical Center took 19 people with migraines and asked them to practice either standard medical care or eight weeks of MBSR (Mindfulness-Based

Stress Reduction). This MBSR therapy incorporated 30-minute meditation sessions and yoga lessons. The group that practised MBSR experienced, on average, 1.4 fewer migraines a month and had less severe headaches. Importantly, the length of headaches was significantly reduced, with headaches lasting on average 3 hours less in the MBSR group than in the group that had received standard medical training.

The study author announced that by practising mindfulness, the test participants "were able to have a sense of personal control over their migraines".

24. Offers pain relief

This is very similar to the point above but worth covering separately because, of course, there are many causes of pain.

25. Mindfulness reduces our dependency on medical care

A study in Quebec, Canada, showed that practising mindfulness and meditation leads to reduced cost of physician services because meditators do not need to visit doctors and physicians so frequently.

The study was specifically looking at medical costs, but nevertheless, I think this says a lot about how and why we visit the doctor and why meditation helps.

26. Reduces our need for pharmaceuticals

There are several reasons why people go on medication. And not all medication is truly necessary. You may have read the recent news reports about how doctors have been prescribing painkillers and anti-depressants often unnecessarily. But this begs the question: what makes people go on medication?

Often medication is prescribed as a placebo. And at other times people visit the doctor because of stress-related symptoms. At both these times, people are given medication for what is essentially psychosomatic problems. And as we have seen above, many of these psychosomatic symptoms can be relieved or cured with meditation. So, meditation gives people a viable alternative to medication in many situations.

27. Better sleep

Have you ever wondered how much more you would achieve if only you didn't need so much sleep? Anecdotal evidence reveals that people who have been meditating for a long time may, in fact, need less sleep than everyone else. This is backed up by Buddhist texts that say that for experienced meditators, just four hours sleep is the equivalent of eight hours to everyone else. That four-hour number might not be entirely accurate, however. According to one scientific study, meditators do indeed need less sleep but only by half an hour.

So, why would meditators need less sleep?

Meditation produces a mental state called "restful alertness" that is similar to the state we are in when we are asleep. So, if you practise meditation, your mind is at a state that is closer to sleep. Plus, "restful alertness" provides many of the same functions of sleep. When you're in the "restful alertness" state your body is already restoring itself and resting, so to an extent, you have already begun to perform the functions you perform when you're asleep.

28. Helps with insomnia

As well as reducing the need for sleep, meditation makes it easier to get to sleep in the first place. This is a direct continuation of the previous point. When you meditate you train your brain to enter the sate of "restful alertness", which is close to sleep. So, when you hit the sack, you are already closer to sleeping than most people, and it is, therefore, easier to drift off.

29. Improves vitality

Another excellent advantage of daily meditation is that it enhances vitality.

Vitality can be thought of as the trait of being energised and living in the moment with zest. It is a positive psychological trait that makes you get up and go and helps you to make the most of your day. This is directly related to what Eastern philosophies would call prana.

Prana flows through your body, keeping your organs energised and your brain alive. Prana helps you to live in the moment. But many things can interfere with the flow of prana. For instance, anxiety and depression can significantly block prana. This leads you to be closed off from the world and reduces energy levels.

By meditating, you clear your mind. This, in turn, helps prana to flow, which produces positive energy that, in turn, creates vitality.

30. Makes you better at sports

Meditation increases your reaction times, so you can hit that tennis ball faster or tell where the baseball is going to go. It also gives you an energy boost. Add to that the fact that meditation prevents muscle tension, increases confidence, makes you better at communicating, and helps you focus, and it is easy to see how meditation makes you better at sports.

31. Improves mind-body connection

One of the best things about meditation is that it heightens your mind-body connection.

At the deeper stages of meditation, your mind is very relaxed. This state of relaxation lets your mind open so that it is more sensitive to feelings in and around the body. Your thoughts silence, and you become much more aware of your physical body. You tune in to parts of your body you may never have noticed, like the rhythm of your breathing. This puts your mind in tune with your body, so there is more unity and cohesion in your being. This produces one of the deepest and most restorative states you can find.

Mental Health Benefits Of Meditation

As a meditation teacher, I am always inspired by stories of people overcoming anxiety, depression, and other mental health problems with meditation.

Take a look at the mental health benefits of meditation below.

1. Brain electricity

A study by the Norwegian Institute of Science And Technology showed that meditation improves the electrical activity in the brain.

Most of us have experienced those times when we simply zone-out, when we are restful and are not focusing on anything in particular. Those times offer your brain relaxation. But science has shown that when you actively practise an "open" meditation technique (when you are mindful of your environment without focusing on any one specific thing), you change electrical brainwaves that are associated with wakeful, relaxed attention.

2. Serotonin

Low serotonin levels are one of the leading causes of depression. Serotonin is a neurotransmitter that helps your brain pass information from one region to another. Almost all of your 40 million brain cells are influenced by serotonin. So it is easy to see why a lack of serotonin could cause severe psychological harm.

Meditation inhibits activity in the stress-production regions of the brain and increases activity in the regions that promote happiness. This raises serotonin development, which leads to a wide variety of psychological health benefits.

Mindfulness improves willpower

No one's perfect. And a lot of imperfections come down to a momentary lack of willpower. Whether you're struggling to quit smoking or can't quite find the energy to hit the gym, meditation can help.

3. Brain synchronicity

Your brain is divided into two halves, the right and the left. Between those two halves is the "corpus callosum". The corpus callosum is a band of nerve fibres that allow the left and ride sides of your brain to communicate with one another. This is important because both sides of your brain play different roles. The right side is for creativity. The left side is for rational think and logic. It's only by communicating with one another that those two sides form one powerful unit.

Meditation and binaural beats have been proven to enhance communication between the two brain hemispheres, which leads to more mental balance and better overall cognitive functioning.

4. Increases brain size

One of the fascinating benefits of meditation is that it increases white matter in the brain.

Yi-Yuan Tang, PhD, and a group of researchers at the University of Texas studied the effect of meditation on mind-body connection. They assigned college graduates either integrative mind-body training or a relaxation session. They took brain scans before and after 11 hours of these activities. The scans showed more white matter in the neurons around the anterior cingulate cortex, the part of the brain responsible for self-regulation, in the people who practised mind-body training. They also observed heightened love, compassion, happiness and relaxation.

5. Better reactions

Meditation improves performance on tests and reaction times. Scientists at the Department of Biology at the University of Kentucky tested whether meditation could help people to complete a psychomotor vigilance task. A group of people who were new to meditation spent 40 minutes meditating. They were then tested on the vigilance task. And all test subjects scored significantly higher after meditating. The researchers said that this showed a significant improvement in their reaction times.

6. Self confidence

One of the great personal advantages of meditation is that it makes you confident.

Many of us in the West have experienced moments of low self confidence. But did you know, low self-confidence is incredibly rare in Tibet. So rare, in fact, that when the Dalai Lama heard that low self-confidence was a problem here, he did not believe it. He then set out to cure the problem.

He believed that if people in the West started practising loving-kindness meditation, their low self-esteem would be cured. And he was right.

When you meditate, you become aware of the interconnectivity between all people, and you gain a powerful realisation that you are not alone. This inter-connection helps you to feel more a part of the world and significantly improves self-confidence. This is a significant benefit of meditation, given how important self-confidence is to our wellbeing.

7. Helps with anxiety

Dr. Elizabeth Hoge at the Center for Anxiety and Traumatic Stress Disorders at Massachusetts General Hospital tells us that meditation is one of the best ways of reducing the symptoms of anxiety. "People with anxiety have a problem dealing with distracting thoughts that have too much power," she explains. "They can't distinguish between a problem-solving thought and a nagging worry that has no benefit." Meditation, she says, helps people to distinguish types of thoughts in the mind so people with anxiety can control their "nagging thoughts" and reduce their anxiety.

8. Helps with depression

Meditation is one of the best ways of both preventing depression and treating depression. There have been very many studies into the effects of meditation on depression. One study suggested that if you meditate while doing vigorous exercise it will be one of the best possible treatments for depression. A study by the University of Exeter looked into mindfulness and stated that mindfulness is more effective than drugs at treating depression.

9. Postpartum depression

According to the Centers for Disease Control, between 11% and 20% of women suffer postpartum depression after having a child.

In 2015, Dr Dona Dimidjian [professor in the Department of Psychology and Neuroscience at the University of Colorado] published an article in the Journal of Consulting and Clinical Psychology in which she states that mindfulness can significantly reduce the risk of postpartum depression.

As well as helping with depression and anxiety, meditation helps with other mental health conditions, too. For instance, it is possible to use mindfulness meditation to stop OCD.

10. Addictions

There are lots of different meditation techniques that can help treat addictions and cravings. But research suggests that mindfulness might be the best.

Researchers at the University of Washington studied 286 people who have successfully completed a drug rehabilitation program. They assigned them either a course of mindfulness meditation, a conventional relapse prevention program or a 12 step program. Results showed the when mindfulness was used in rehab, the chances of success were significantly increased. Only 9% of the people who had used mindfulness relapsed, which is 5% less than the other two groups.

11. Anti-ageing

Could meditation even help slow the ageing process? Research suggests yes. And it is actually quite easy to see *how* meditation helps with ageing when you understand the process of ageing.

Stress, anxiety, depression, addiction, these all increase the ageing rate. And as we've already seen, meditation helps with all these things. So by creating balance and health, meditation helps to slow the ageing rate.

One study, published in 2013, found that as little as 15 minutes daily meditation immediately increased activity of the gene that creates telomerase, which is an indicator of longevity.

12. Youthfulness

The ageing process is largely caused by the breaking down of cells in your body. Your skin cells, for instance, grow old and get replaced by new ones, but it is difficult for your body to produce cells fast enough. This gradually makes your skin weaker, making you age.

When you meditate, you give your body a break so that it can focus on working on those core operations (like cell production).

We've also seen how meditation increases the length of telomeres in your body. Telomeres are indicators of longevity. If you want to know how long you will live, take a look at your telomeres under a very powerful microscope. The longer they are, the longer you will probably live. Good news is that meditation increases the length of telomeres.

We all know that stress is one of the worst things for ageing. The more stressed you are, the faster you will age. And the reason for that is because stress makes it harder for your body to function. And we have looked at how meditation produces relaxation and stops stress.

Put all this together, and you'll understand why meditation is such a powerful way of slowing the ageing process.

Cognitive Benefits of Meditation

If you're trying to boost your mind, you really should consider all the cognitive benefits of daily.

If, like me, you believe in exercising your brain, then meditation is a must. The more you meditate, the stronger your brain will become.

For proof, take a look at these cognitive benefits of meditation.

1. Helps you make smarter decisions

One of the benefits of meditation that is very well known in the East but still quite unknown in the West is that meditation helps you make better decisions.

Virginia Tech Carilion Research Center studied the effect of meditation on decision making. They found that meditators actually use different parts of their brains in decision making compared to non-meditators.

The study took 66 people and asked 26 of them to

meditate while the other were the control group. They played an "ultimatum game" in which one person is given $20 and asked to share it with someone. The receiver may then accept or refuse the money. If the offer is accepted, the participants get a sum of the money, but if it is rejected, they both get nothing. Essentially, this is a psychological game designed to test your decision making. So, what did the results show?

The researchers recorded the activity in each person's brain when they made these decisions. And the results showed that non-meditators mostly use their anterior insula, which is the part of the brain used in emotional disgust. The meditators did not use this part of the brain at all, and this tells us a lot about how meditators make decisions. The researchers say that meditators make decisions more rationally and less based on emotion than non-meditators.

2. Makes us act with more control and in a more constructive manner

When you allow your emotions to get out of control, they can affect the way you think and can lead you to make bad decisions and to act in harmful ways. Research has shown that when you meditate, you gain control over your emotions and can learn to act rationally despite those emotions.

The journal Current Directions in Psychological Science published an article by researcher Rimma Teper at the University of Toronto which proved that when you practice mindfulness you become more aware and more accepting of your emotions and that this, in turn, helps you to act with more self-control.

3. Makes us more balanced individuals

One of the general cognitive benefits of meditation is that it makes us more balanced. It does this by helping us control our emotions.

There is so much information constantly entering our brains that it can be difficult to remain emotionally balanced and to keep a healthy perspective on life. Meditation can help to balance the brain.

When you meditate, you create inner calm and peace. This allows you to see through many of the phenomena of the mind (such as thoughts and visualisation). Meditation essentially clears those mental toxins from the mind, so you are able to see straight and reason. This balances your emotions, so you are able to see things in a better perspective.

4. Improves emotional intelligence

Meditation can help you control your emotions and can increase emotional maturity.

"Emotional maturity" is a highly subjective thing, because what, precisely, is emotional maturity? Generally speaking, however, we can consider emotional maturity to mean you have control of your emotions, you are not reactive, you don't blame others for your problems, you are self-reliant, and you are a polite and reasonable member of society.

So how does meditation help with all that? Essentially, it comes down to mindfulness. When you meditate, you gain an understanding of your emotions, and this helps you to master them.

Edward Morler, Ph.D of Moreler International, tells us that a big part of emotional maturity is being in the now and letting go of the past. Meditation helps with this. When you meditate, you become aware of your thoughts and feelings, and you see them for what they are: unreal. This helps you to focus on the present moment and to make rational decisions not influenced by emotion.

5. Improves motor performance

One of the more interesting cognitive effects of meditation is that it improves motor performance and thereby helps us perform myriad different tasks, including sports.

Andy Rimol is a Princeton student and was captain of the basketball team. He wanted to test his theory that meditation made him better at basketball because it improved motor function. He believed that meditation would have long-term and immediate effects on perceptual-motor performance.

The results were clear. Meditators performed better at perceptual-motor tasks (these are movement-related skills). The meditators had far superior coordination. The test showed that meditation helps your motor skills both immediately and in the long term.

6. Effects of daily meditation on intelligence

How does meditation make you more intelligent? Six ways:

—Balances your left and right brain

—Makes your brain bigger

—Improves intuition and insight

—Improves memory

—Improves Emotional Intelligence (EQ).

7. Job satisfaction

Another interesting fact about meditation is that it increases job satisfaction.

Dr Ute Hulsheger and a team of researchers from the Netherlands studied the effect of mindfulness meditation on job satisfaction. As we have seen, mindfulness is very beneficial for controlling your emotions, and that's true at the office too.

The report, published in the Journal of Applied Psychology, asked 219 workers at service jobs, like retail and nursing, to write a diary twice a day for five days. They also rated their job satisfaction. According to their own reports, the people who practised mindfulness had higher job satisfaction and lower levels of emotional exhaustion.

8. Helps stop overthinking

It is a well-known fact of meditation that it helps you to stop overthinking. And most of us can appreciate how important that is.

Countless studies have shown that meditation helps you to stop thinking. However, I feel that this doesn't really need scientific proof. We meditators know full well how meditation stops your thoughts.

9. Focus and concentration

This is probably the most commonly known cognitive benefit of daily meditation: It helps you focus.

10. Improves Creative Thinking

Scientific research shows that specific meditation techniques will boost your creative thinking immediately, even if you have never meditated before.

Cognitive psychologists Lorena Colato and Dominique Lippelt at Leiden University conducted research and discovered that a brief meditation session could have a profound and lasting effect on the creative brain. However, this is only true for certain meditation techniques. After practising "open" meditation techniques (meditations in which you are receptive to your entire environment and to thoughts and sensations), your creative brain is significantly improved.

If you need to boost your creative brain, meditate on the entirety of your environment, sensations and thoughts (Open meditation

11. Helps us to learn and to remember

Whether you're studying to ace an exam or trying to

learn a new skill for work, meditation can help.

There are two parts of the brain that are highly active during memory storage and recall: the frontal lobe and the Hippocampus. These two regions are highly activated during meditation. Meditation acts like exercise for these regions of the brain, making them stronger. This in turns, makes you more able to memorise and recall information.

12. Helps you to remove bad habits

Let's be completely honest with one another. We all have some bad habits. After all, imperfections make us human. But there are times when you might like to get a handle on your bad habits.

Both mental and physical habits can interfere with your life. Nail biting, negative thinking, drinking. These bad habits get repeated over and over again until they are so ingrained in you that they happen on auto-pilot. The problem is that because you make these habits on auto-pilot, you often don't notice you're doing them. So how can you stop them?

The key is to practice mindfulness.

When you are mindful, you become more aware of what you are doing, and when you are more aware, you are more in control, which helps to stop bad habits.

Mindfulness gives you the ability to be aware of what you are doing. It makes you more conscious of your bad habits so that you can change them more easily.

13. Improves intuition

Everyone is naturally born with intuition. Intuition is the little voice inside that offers you advice and direction. But that little voice can be quiet, and you will miss it if you do not listen attentively. Thankfully, meditation can help.

When you meditate, and particularly when you practise mindfulness meditation, you silence your mind of unnecessary and unhelpful thoughts. That helps you to hear better, which in turn allows you to tune in to your intuition. When you are silent, you will hear your intuition. And the best way to find silence is with meditation.

Researchers at Massachusetts General Hospital in Boston showed that meditation increases the thickness of the brain's outer cortex, which is responsible for mental functions, including learning, concentration, and memory.

Researchers looked at longitudinal studies on the effects of people in Mindfulness-Based-Stress-Reduction therapy. The research shows that MBSR increases grey matter concentration in the left hippocampus, cingulate cortex, the temporoparietal junction, and the cerebellum. This suggests that MBSR improves learning, memory, emotional regulation, self-referential processing, and perspective-taking.

In another study published in the journal Consciousness and Cognition, it was revealed that just 20 minutes of meditation improves results on memory tests.

Because of the effect it has on these parts of the brain, meditation improves memory, both short term and long term.

14. Improves productivity

Do you ever wish that you could get more done at work? Do you ever feel that you would be much more productive if only you weren't distracted continuously? Meditation can help you to put your energy to good use so that you are more productive.

One study showed that eight weeks of daily mindfulness training could make employees (in this instance, they were human resource managers) less stressed and more able to focus on their jobs, which increases productivity.

15. Helps you see the big picture

When you focus too much on small details, you can get bent out of shape over nothing. For instance, if you are too concerned about a minor ailment, you might completely forget that you are 99% healthy person. Focusing on the 1% of you that isn't perfect will then lead to stress, which will cause more of you to become unwell.

When you can see the big picture, you stop worrying about those little things.

The problem is that sometimes momentary problems seem large simply because they are right in front of us. But meditation lets you see past the current minor problem so that you can appreciate the full, big picture. And that's a much healthier way to live.

16. Stops "Monkey Mind"

If you have been meditating for a while you have probably noticed those times when your mind seems to completely stop. You feel as though you're stepping out of a tight space into a vast open field. There's freedom and mental liberation. And your monkey mind stops.

" Monkey Mind " is a Buddhist term that refers an always noisy, ever-changing mind.

Buddhist philosophy has told us for millennia that meditation stops the monkey mind. Now, science has proven it.

In a study by IONS, PhD student Travy Brandmeyer studied 12 novices and 12 expert meditators and intentionally distracted them to see how their minds wandered. The results showed that experienced meditators suffer considerably less monkey mind than novices. But the researchers note that further studies are required to substantiate these findings.

17. Helps with problem-solving

One of my personal favourite cognitive benefits of daily meditation is that it's always there whenever you need a little helping hand. For instance, you can turn to meditation when you need help solving a complex problem.

In one study, a group of German psychologists asked volunteers to try to complete a complex problem-solving task before and after meditating. Before meditating most of the group struggled. But when they meditated, the researchers say, they were more able to think outside the box to find a solution. The scientists state that meditation helps you to solve problems in creative ways.

18 Improves overall intelligence by balancing brain hemispheres

Are you good at some things and terrible at others?

For instance, you're very creative but have zero logic? If so, it is probably because part of your brain is stronger than the rest.

Everyone naturally uses one half of their brain more than the other half (we have a dominant side of the brain). This causes an imbalance in the brain.

One of the scientifically proven benefits of meditation is that it balances the sides of the brain. This helps the brain to process information faster because it increases the rate of neural communication.

The result is better problem-solving skills, heightened creativity, improved focus and concentration, and better decision-making skills.

19: Improves brain wave patterns

Ever wanted to improve your IQ level? Then there's good news. Meditation can change your brain wave frequencies, which will boost your IQ.

Some brain wave frequencies are healthier than others, for instance, alpha, theta and delta. These brainwaves have been shown to correlate to improved brain functioning, heightened ability to learn, and increased creativity.

Science shows that meditating is one of the best ways of controlling brainwaves.

The research:

The Norwegian University of Science And Technology studied the effect of daily meditation on brain waves. The researchers asked a group of participants to practice a type of *open technique* called Acem. While the group were meditating, the researchers took EEG scans of the participant's brains. The results showed an increase in brainwaves that are conducive to a relaxed, wakeful state.

Relationship Benefits Of Daily Meditation

1. Helps with infertility

5% of couples experience primary infertility, which is the inability to have any children, or secondary infertility, which is the inability to conceive or carry a pregnancy to term.

Research shows that most cases of infertility are due to physiological or psychosomatic factors, which are usually identified in the woman. What upsets me is that 15% of people who experience this say it is the most depressing thing to happen to them in their lives. So clearly this is something we need to work to change. And thankfully meditation can help.

Stress is one of the leading causes of infertility. And

stress can prevent people from getting pregnant after they have been treated for a physical cause of infertility. At both these times, meditation can help with relaxation, which increases the chances of getting pregnant.

2. Makes us more responsible

An interesting fact about meditation is that it makes us more responsible. This is because of the effect daily meditation has on relationships and mood. Meditation makes you more empathetic, more compassionate, and more in control of your own actions. Hence, it both *motivates* and *enables* you to be more responsible.

A Harvard study confirmed that people who meditate are more likely to give up their seat for a woman in pain. Dr Hölzel, who conducted the study, said that people who meditate "may be more willing to help when someone suffers."

3. Makes us better listeners

Have you ever been listening to someone when you suddenly realise that you're not paying attention to what they're saying? We've all been in that position, haven't we? Thankfully, something meditation is good for is making you a better listener.

The Waisman Laboratory for Brain Imaging and Behavior at the University of Wisconsin-Madison studied the effect of meditation on listening skills in 2009. They found that when you meditate, you improve your attention and this, in turn, makes you a better listener. Even more surprising, it turns out that meditation is especially good at making you listen when you're not interested in what the other person is saying.

4. For couples

Writing for Psychology Today, Marsha Lucas, Ph.D stated that there are nine ways in which meditating improves relationships. They are:

- It helps you react better
- It improves emotional resiliency
- Improves communication
- Enables you to respond in more flexible, less stubborn ways
- Improves insight
- Increases intuition
- Increases morality
- Heightens empathy

5. Makes people less aggressive and less angry

The journal Consciousness and Cognition published a study that stated that meditation improves your body's response to anger.

Have you ever experienced those moments when you feel angry, your chest is tight, you're gritting your teeth, and you just can't help but spit it out and say the wrong thing? Imagine if you had more control at those times. You would be able to respond more appropriately. This study shows that meditation lets you do just that.

The study highlighted that one twenty-minute meditation session improves your body's response to anger by reducing breathing rate and heart rate, helping to balance blood pressure, and giving you more self-control. And in fact, people who have been meditating for a long time may exhibit no bodily response to anger at all.

6. Stops social anxiety

If like me, you have suffered from social anxiety at some point in your life, you will know that it can affect your lifestyle. But thankfully, meditation can treat social anxiety and make you more sociable.

Candance Pert [pharmacologist, neuroscientist and researcher at the National Institute of Health] and creator of Psychosomatic Wellness found that meditation releases endorphins that create positive feelings and cure social anxiety. Another study by Dr Sara Lazar compared the brains of meditators to non-meditators and found that meditators have thicker areas of their brain's cortex, especially in emotion processing areas. This showed that they were happier and more confident, and thereby less likely to suffer social anxiety.

7. Intimacy

Meditation makes you more intimate with loved ones because of the other benefits that we have looked at in this list. For instance, meditation makes you more confident, so you are more comfortable being intimate. Meditation also makes you more aware, so you can truly feel your lover. Meditation also helps you to relax and be in the moment, and it's easy to see how those qualities would help with intimacy too.

8. Loving Kindness improves tolerance and stops racism

Meditation makes you more tolerant of other people and can stop prejudices. And this is particularly true of Loving Kindness Meditation.

Alexander Stell, a doctoral student on the University Of Sussex' psychology degree program, says, "Some meditation techniques are about much more than feeling good and might be an important tool for enhancing intergroup harmony.

"We wanted to see whether doing Loving Kindness Meditation towards a member of another ethnic group would reduce the automatic preference people tend to show for their own ethnic group."

In his study, Stell took 71 Caucasian, non-meditating adults and showed them a photo of a black person. Half the group were asked to just look at the photo. The other half were asked to practise loving-kindness meditation and imagine sending out positive feelings to the black person in the photo.

The researchers studied the participants' prejudices using the Implicit Association Test, which asks test subjects to describe the people in the photo.

The research shows that after loving-kindness meditation, people are more likely to describe the black person in the photo in a positive way. The researchers concluded that Loving Kindness Meditation is a powerful way to end personal prejudices quickly.

9. **For love**

Buddhists advocate the importance of "universal loving-kindness", which is love for all people and animals. But naturally, this is not easy to achieve. The average person has certain prejudices, and even the most enlightened among us tend to have one or two people who we struggle to get along with.

Meditation, however, can increase your capacity for love. It does this in several ways. Firstly, it allows you to see past your prejudices by being mindful. It also helps you to accept other people, and especially their shortcomings. And it boosts compassion.

10. **Compassion and empathy**

One of the lesser-known and lesser-studied benefits of meditation is that it makes you more empathetic and more compassionate. But historically, this was one of the main reasons why Buddhist monks meditate.

Buddhists have always known that meditation improves empathy and compassion. And now, scientific research has proven that claim. In a study, a group of meditators heard the sound of a woman in distress while researchers studied their brains. The tests showed that meditators have heightened activity in the areas of the brain that regulate empathy and compassion.

11. Improves relations at work

It can be a challenge to maintain healthy and productive workplace relationships for one simple reason. Work is one of the most stressful environments. And when we are stressed, we become less receptive, less emotionally balanced, less empathetic, less compassionate, and less tolerant. That's precisely why if you have a bad day at work you might end up regretting something you say. But meditation can help.

Meditation helps you to relax at work. Take a 15-minute mindfulness break at some point in the day. It will remove stress, help you to relax, and restore you to your normal, tolerant, patient self. And then you will have positive workplace relationships, and you will be less likely to say something you end up regretting.

Yes, there are very many reasons to meditate, and different techniques offer different benefits. So let's now look at how to start meditating.

PAUL HARRISON

YES, YOU CAN MEDITATE WRONGLY

My mind was abuzz with excitement. Within months of first starting to learn meditation I had already journeyed through Chinese culture, Buddhism, Hinduism, modern spirituality, New Age, and so many other subjects that I felt the very world were a huge smouldering pot of philosophy and spirituality.

One morning after finishing a meditation session I happened to turn on the TV while eating a bowl of fruit salad. The cameraman was zoomed in on a string of brown beads wrapped around someone's wrist. The camera zoomed out to show that it was a mala, a string of beads that Buddhists and Hindus use to count breaths and mantras. The camera zoomed out further to show the old and wise brown eyes, the weathered face, the red robes, and the big childlike grin of the Dalai Lama. Below, a headline read, "Dalai Lama discusses the rise of meditation".

The TV interviewer was enquiring about the benefits of meditation when she happened to ask "And there are absolutely no risks from practicing meditation"?

I scoffed. *Silly interviewer. Of course there are no risks of meditation.* So I thought, because how could meditation possibly be of any risk? It's the healthiest thing in the world, isn't it?

The Dalai Lama's eyes narrowed and he raised his hand and said "Meditation is very powerful. It must be learnt properly."

The Dalai Lama continued to explain how when meditation is learnt in the East it is learnt alongside philosophy, history, and other aspects of culture. In the East, meditation isn't taken as a standalone practice but as one spoke in a wheel. Only when all spokes move as one can the wheel begin to turn.

In the West millions are learning meditation as its own thing, as a standalone. The Dalai Lama himself has stated that, "People need to learn more about Eastern tradition rather than proceeding to meditation too quickly. Otherwise mental and physical difficulties will appear". Yet millions of people excitedly hurl themselves into meditation, diving in at the deep end then desperately trying to learn how to swim.

For the vast majority of meditation techniques, it is imperative to learn and practice in the right way.

I wish I'd had someone to tell me to slow down all those years ago when I was starting out. I literally launched myself into meditation, practicing every single different technique I could get my hands on (and there were hundreds—we'll discuss the best of them a little later). I was just so excited to be practicing techniques that the old masters used, techniques that have been handed down through history.

It's hard not to get caught up in excitement once you start to discover all the different techniques and the myriad ways in which they can benefit you in your own life. But only fools rush in. The wise know to go steady.

That's why I think you and I ought to go over the basics now, before we start to learn the actual techniques. That way, once we get to the actual meditation techniques we'll know how to practice them safely and correctly.

So just what is the "right way"? What are the basic principles of meditation?

There are many thousands of meditation techniques, all of which use the mind and body in subtly different ways. However, there are some similarities shared across the spectrum of techniques. There are basic foundations on which the house is built. These are the essential bricks and mortar out of which any meditation regime should be constructed.

Firstly, it's important to set aside a special place for meditation, and it is better that this place be a specially designated *spiritual space*. Admittedly, finding an ideal space can be challenging. The numerous times I toured England on stage in theatre productions I often found it near impossible to find anywhere remotely "sacred". Staying at universities, hotels, motels, flats, in the van, and in the car, it's not easy to find a heavenly abode where you can tap into your inner Buddha. Sometimes you just have to make do. At times I'd run for miles through the streets—conveniently getting some exercise in—before finally finding a park, a pleasant view, or even just a bench on a quiet street where I could meditate. Not ideal; but it does show that you can always find *somewhere* to meditate if you look.

Hopefully you'll find it a lot easier to find a spiritual space than I did. Ideally, at least in the beginning, you'll find one single space that you can completely dedicate to meditation and nothing else.

If you have ever visited a nature reserve you will know why it's important to preserve certain spaces. You can feel the energy of a nature reserve the moment you enter it. It's pure, wild, natural; a beautiful space that immediately conjures feelings of freedom and tranquillity. The same is true for a meditation space. Over a period of time your meditation space will become a sanctuary filled with spiritual energy. You will enter the room and immediately feel purity, tranquillity, and warmth, because you have preserved the purity of the space.

Having a designated spiritual space is also highly reassuring. It's great to know that if you ever feel stressed you can enter your spiritual space and be free from it all.

Your spiritual space doesn't have to be a whole room, it could be a corner of a room or a part of your garden, or it could be a public space. At my home in Oxfordshire there is a brook at the bottom of our field. The brook is always quiet but for the gentle trickling of the water and the occasional rustle of wind in the trees. It is a spiritual space for me, a space where I can sit and feel free, where I can rebalance and heal. It's one of my many spiritual spaces.

A sacred space should be matched with a sacred time. When you make your time and space sacred, you begin to create a truly magical practice.

Routine is everything. When you know that at 6am you're going to get up, enter your meditation space, and meditate for twenty minutes, your mind becomes pre-programmed for tranquillity. You also form a very strong habit that will help you to continue to meditate even on those days when you don't really feel like it (and no matter how wonderful meditation is, there always will be some times when you feel like skipping practice).

When I was touring England doing The Canterbury Tales (I played the overweight, alcoholic miller, though I don't think it was typecast), I set the alarm for 5am every morning so I could meditate for at least 20 minutes. Because we were on tour it was impossible to have one designated space so instead I would take myself off to some field or park, practice yoga and meditate there instead— there's always a space and time worthy of meditation, no matter where you might be or how busy you might be.

Once you've got your sacred time and space set, condition yourself to begin relaxing at least five minutes before your meditation time, and outside of your meditation space.

When you enter your sacred time and your sacred space, you want to already be relaxed. You don't want to carry negative energy into those spaces. So, give yourself at least five minutes in which to relax before you enter your meditation space.

Once you do enter your meditation space, you'll want to check your posture. Good posture leads to good health and also to a relaxed, aware, and peaceful inner state. Make absolutely certain that you're relaxed and comfortable and that there is never any pain in your body.

Next, consider your breathing. Your breathing rate should be calm and slow. As you meditate your breathing rate will naturally slow down because you are relaxing. Your breathing may slow to a rate it's never been to before, both during practice and after. In 2003, Harvard scientists studied a group of ten meditators and discovered that their respiratory rates were much lower than non-meditators. This lower respiratory rate is indicative of lungs that are working more efficiently, and also of a calm and relaxed body and mind. So, be aware that your breathing rate will slow when meditating and also after meditating.

Finally, it's important to maintain the right mental attitude. The right attitude is one of nonjudgment.

It can be very easy to judge yourself as doing something right or wrong. After all, how many times are we told in our day to day lives that we're good / bad, right / wrong?

But in meditation there is no right and no wrong, there is simply what is. So, adopt a non-judgmental attitude, a peaceful and accepting attitude.

There is no right and there is no wrong. There is only what *is*.

These are the essential basics of meditation. They are the roots which you must plant if your spiritual self is to grow strong. By sticking to these simple rules you'll ensure a safe and successful meditation practice.

FINDING YOUR BEST MEDITATION POSITION

Your meditation posture is incredibly important. Not just for your body, but for your mind too.

Whether you're meditating sitting on a meditation chair, a mat, or the floor, you need to have proper meditation posture; otherwise you may experience knee and back pain. If you have a bad body position when meditating, you will put pressure on your spine, and this could potentially lead to spinal injury

This might not be a problem if you only sit to meditate for a few minutes, but if you're meditating for extended periods (which could be hours if you're at a Vipassana retreat), then you need to have the right posture. Even if you are lying down to meditate, you should ideally still adopt one of the proper positions. So, let's take a look at the best ones.

7 Best Meditation Positions

It is best to use one of the technical sitting positions *if you can do so comfortably*. So, let's take a look at these first.

1: Quarter Lotus

Quarter Lotus is a position in which your legs are gently crossed with feet underneath the opposite knee.

2: Half Lotus

Half Lotus is different to Quarter Lotus because one foot is on top of the opposite knee.

3: Full Lotus

Full lotus has both feet on the knees

4: Burmese Position

Burmese position is a more comfortable position than lotus. It is done sitting with both feet on the floor in front of the pelvis (not crossed).

5: Seiza

Seiza is a kneeling position, usually on a cushion.

6: Chair

Yes, it is perfectly acceptable to sit on a chair or cushion. A good chair will improve your seated meditation posture.

7: Shavasana

Shavasana is performed lying down with the arms and hands at the side of the body, legs a little spread.

8: Standing Up

One of the best meditation positions for beginners is standing up. This is a good option, especially if you have injuries of arthritis. Standing up will help you to focus and to feel grounded.

The Problem With Traditional Meditation Postures

Newsflash: No matter what any flexible yogi may try to tell you, it does not matter whether you sit with your legs crossed or uncrossed. The traditional meditation sitting position with the legs crossed could be doing more damage than good *if you find it uncomfortable*. Forcing yourself to sit crossed-legged could cause health problems. Sitting crossed-legged can increase blood pressure, cause knee injury, cause problems in other areas of the body as you compensate for lack of balance in your legs, and cause varicose veins.

Forcing your legs into a position they are not comfortable in is unsafe, especially if you have problems with your knees or other joints, or if you have a medical condition such as arthritis. Arthritic knees make it utterly impossible to sit for meditation in the lotus position.

Not only are these positions bad for your body, but they are also bad for your practice too. Forcing yourself into uncomfortable meditation sitting positions when meditating will impede your ability to concentrate. When you are uncomfortable, you cannot focus. If you sit in a painful way, you'll be distracted by the pain.

While it's true that Buddhist monks sit with their legs crossed, this is only because they are trained to do so and they find it comfortable.

Buddhist monks meditate in the lotus position because it creates a sense of stability. And science proves this. In one scientific study, researchers found that sitting with your legs crossed increases stability in the pelvis. This stability in the pelvis supports the spine and, importantly, creates a sense of grounding in the mind. When the body is stable, and still, the mind is more likely to be so. And that is why the best way of sitting for meditation is the lotus position. But this is only true if you can sit comfortably with your legs crossed.

Just because Zen monks sit in lotus position doesn't mean you have to.

So, if you cannot sit with your legs crossed and meditate comfortably, what are you supposed to do?

Actually, you have many options. Let me show you how to find the best position for your individual needs.

Finding Your Best Positions

1: Good Posture

Do you do yoga or tai chi? If so, you will know the feeling of intentionally adopting a pose. For instance, when you are in Warrior Position, you are in an energised, intentional, consciously aware position. There is a level of intent in the way you are holding your body. And that same intent must be present when you are meditating. It doesn't matter precisely which position you are in. But when you meditate, sit with intent.

2: Check For Stability

The primary reason Buddhist monks sit in the lotus position is that it creates a sense of stability in the pelvis and the spine. You can get that same level of stability in other positions. Whether you're in a chair, cushion or pillow, you can feel that level of stability when you sit correctly. When sitting to meditate, ask yourself: Do you feel stable? It should be a grounding stability that creates solidity in your body.

3: Tune-In To Your Mind

If you have followed steps one and two, you should feel a

sense of focus and stability in your mind. This is the final test and the most significant one. If you have good posture, you will feel focused in your mind. If your current sitting position is not meeting the criteria above, change position and run through those same three steps.

An Alternative Pose

In some instances, you will still struggle to sit comfortably for meditation. The good news is this: There are still ways you can meditate. One of the most straightforward solutions is to get a high-quality meditation chair, cushion or mat. Another option is to do a more active form of meditation.

Some meditations are not done sitting. For instance, Osho dynamic meditations [more on this later] offer a way to meditate while moving. These are perfect when you can't sit comfortably for long periods.

There many different ways how to sit for meditation and lots of techniques do not require you to sit at all. Therefore, if you've been finding your practice uncomfortable, try a different pose or technique.

Remember, the practice is mostly for the mind, not the body. While you might push yourself physically when you exercise, you shouldn't push yourself when you meditate. Chill. Go easy. Use the meditation posture that feels best for you.

Lying Down

Meditating in bed is one of the most popular ways to practice at home, because it's easier. Many people want to meditate lying down because it requires less effort. However, there is *supposed* to be effort involved with the practice. You wouldn't go to the gym and *not try* because you wouldn't lose weight.

And if your attitude going into mindfulness is not to bother then you won't get much out of it either.

Lying down is suitable for some meditation techniques, but not others. For instance, in Zen meditation, you must sit properly, traditionally in lotus position. This isn't about stretching your thighs. It's about the fact that when your body is properly balanced, you will focus better. Lounging induces a level of stress. It is a known fact that the heart rate increases when we are horizontal. And for some people, that increased heart rate could prevent them from relaxing and focusing.

Funny thing is, even though lying down to meditate is often not ideal, there are some specific meditation techniques that specifically ask you to do it. For instance, it is traditional to end yoga practice with a period of resting (usually an Emptiness practice). This is generally done in Corpse Pose (Savasana). However, this is a lot different to simply lying down to meditate. When we do this yogic practice, we've already warmed up the body (which also warms up the mind), and we are focused and energized from the exercise. That's totally different to merely crashing out on your mattress. If you have warmed up your body (and thereby your mind) and you are able to lie down in Savasana (not an easy pose to master) then yes, by all means, meditate lying down.

What if you need to lie down while meditating because you are too ill, or injured, to sit-up for an extended period of meditation? In this case, you could always try using a proper seat. However, if sitting down is just not an option, then yes, by all means, lie down. Before she passed away, my mother-in-law was unable to sit up because of a severe health condition. To meditate, she literally had no choice but to meditate lying down. Still, it is not ideal, and it is better to sit if you are able.

Of course, if you happen to be in bed anyway there is no reason not to be mindful. If you are meditating while lying down in bed on top of regular meditation, then this is really just a bonus, in which case you should go for it. Truth is, if you're lounging around anyway, you might as well do it mindfully.

The best position when meditating lying down is *Savasana*, an asana from yoga. To do this, start by lying on your back with your legs straight and arms resting at your side. Your hands should be approximately six inches from our body and your palms should face the ceiling. Let your body feel heavy on the floor Release your entire body, face, and eyes. Meditate in this position.

MALAS—THE ONE TOOL YOU NEED

There really aren't many items that you need to meditate. However, one tool that I do strongly recommend is a mala.

Meditation malas are necklaces and bracelets used for meditation. These traditional Buddhist items are so much more than just jewellery. They are one of the essential tools used in meditation. I recommend purchasing at least one mala.

Different types of meditation malas have special healing properties based on the particular material of the beads, tassel and the thread. That's why, when you choose your mala beads necklace, the first thing to consider is the material the beads are made from. You can find below a list of the different types of malas.

You will also want to consider the number of beads.

In the 8th Century BCE, monks started to use "monk beads" to help them count breaths during meditation. Because monks count breaths in cycles of 108, they created the Buddhist "108 bead malas"—one cycle around the necklace representing one cycle of breaths.

However, today you can also get small wrist malas that typically have 27 beads. So, you will also need to consider whether you prefer a mala necklace or bracelet when you choose mala beads.

The beads go by many names. Tibetan malas are traditionally called "moon and stars". Many retailers prefer to call them "lotus root", "lotus seed" and "linden nut". Or you can just call them "yoga beads".

The last bead on the mala is called a guru bead. This is a sacred bead that represents the connection between student and teacher and expresses gratitude and appreciation.

And there is also the tassel. A big part of the meditation beads' meaning is based on the tassel. The way the different pieces of the string come together to form the tassel is said to represent oneness, like each person on Earth coming together to create one collective unconscious. So, when you choose a mala necklace, make sure you also like the tassel and not just the beads.

When it comes to choosing mala beads to buy, your first choice will be the type of gemstone to get. Here are the meanings and benefits of the different gemstones:

Amazonite: for calm, alleviating fear and anxiety

Amethyst: for peace, stability and calm

Black Onyx: for alignment and connection

Carnelian: for abundance, prosperity and ambition

Calcedony: for stability, harmony and dreams

Citrine: for happiness and strength

Clear Quartz: for energy, creativity and clarity

Calmatian Jasper: for determination, strength and friendship

Garnet: for energy, chakras and balance

Green Aventurine: for new beginnings and prosperity

Howlite: for calm and third eye (Ajna chakra, more on this

later on)

Lapis Luzuli: for wisdom, intuition and third eye chakra

Moonstone: for intuition, dreams and energy

Obsidian: for protection and grounding

Ocean jasper: for relaxation, self-love and calmness

Pearl: for purity, innocence and imagination

Prehnite: for energy and spirit

Pyrite: for fire energy and vitality

Red jasper: for grounding, balance and healing

Rhodonite: for Yin, Yaang and love

Rose Quartz: for love, harmony and heart chakra

Rosewood: for protection and spirituality

Rudraksha seeds: for healing and guidance

Sandalwood: for calm and desire

Smokey Quatz: for grounding and stabilizing

Turqoise: for truth, grounding and protection

White jade: for potential, goals and success

Why There Are 108 Meditation Prayer Beads

There is a specific reason why there are 108 meditation prayer beads on a mala.

1: stands for God

0: stands for nothingness

8: stands for eternity

108 is an auspicious number. It's the same reason why we often do 108 sun salutations in yoga.

You will notice the number 108 throughout spirituality:

- There are 108 Mukya Shivaganas
- There are 108 energy lines that converge to form the heart chakra.
- There are 108 earthly desires
- There are 108 Upanishads (sacred texts)
- In astrology, if you multiply the 12 houses by the 9 planets, you get 108
- The sun is 108 x the diameter of the Earth. And 108x that diameter = the distance between the sun and Earth

How To Meditate With Mala Beads

Above we looked at how to choose mala beads. Now let's look more closely at how to use them for meditation.

The first thing to do is to remember the parts of the mala. Understanding the different elements will help you to use mala beads for meditation properly.

Meditation beads contain 108 beads, which are strung together with a piece of thread, and a single bead called a "guru bead", which is significantly larger than the others. The guru bead is essential because it is the marker that you use to mark the end of the necklace and the end of your meditation session.

As well as the guru bead, you may notice that your meditation prayer beads necklace also contains other large beads, usually spaced on every 27th bead, which is every one-quarter of the complete mala. Necklaces may have these beads placed halfway through, at the 54th bead instead. These are "spacers". When you get to the spacers" you should take a moment to check-in with yourself and refocus your mind if you're getting distracted.

There are specific ways to hold, wear, and meditate with a mala, as follows.

Holding The Beads

Firstly, never let your prayer beads touch the ground. If you do, it will deplete the healing energy from the mala. If you do accidentally drop your mala on the ground, you should cleanse the mala beads before wearing them again.

Do not let other people touch your mala beads because this can pass negative energy into the beads. If people do touch them, cleanse your prayer beads right away.

Meditation With Mala Beads

Now let's look at how to do a meditation with malas beads.

By learning how to use prayer beads for meditation you will be more able to focus when you meditate. The process of rolling the beads in your fingers is a gentle motion that helps to calm the mind and focus your attention.

Take a look at your meditation mala.

Notice that you have a tassel, which you will reach once you go all the way around your mala, which is usually 108 beads unless you have a bracelet, in which case there will be 27 beads. Then you've got a big bead that is called the "guru" bead. And there are 108 beads on the necklace. These are all the essential parts of your prayer beads necklace.

To use beads in meditation, hold them lovingly.

When you hold your prayer beads in meditation, you will want to hold them in your dominant hand with the tassel pointing towards you. You then start with the big bead, the "guru" bead, in your right hand. We move the mala when meditating by moving it on each breath or each recitation of a mantra. Move the beads using your thumb instead of your index finger because the index finger represents the ego. Keep meditating until you reach the guru bead.

You will want to coordinate your breathing with the mala when meditating. To do this, move the mala bead as you breathe in and you might like to count the breath too. The same thing applies when you use a mantra. For instance, if I'm meditating on "Om", I will breathe in, move the mala bead one across, recite "Om", breathe out, and then breathe in again and move to the next bead.

One good thing to do when meditating with beads is to make sure you calmly move the beads. If you try to rush your meditation, you will notice that you hold the beads too tight and move them in a violent way. Be gentle with them. Feel the smoothness of the beads and let that smoothness relax your mind

One of the most popular ways of using malas for meditation is when doing mantra recitation. When we are doing mantra meditation, we are meditating on sacred sounds such as "Om". Short mantras like Om are easy to count. Other mantras are very long, such as the Gayatri mantra. Keeping count of these is hard unless you have the proper equipment, i.e. a mala.

Not only do prayer beads help you to keep count, but they also help you to relax and focus on meditation.

When using prayer beads for meditation, we count in groups

of 108, with one full mala being 108 recitations (many types of mantra meditation also require us to chant specifically 108 times, so one full mala).

Instructions

1. Set your intentions. For instance, tell yourself that you are meditating to create inner peace or to send out love (choose a mala beads necklace that matches your intent)
2. Sit comfortably
3. Take hold of the mala in one hand and let it drop gently.
4. Touch the guru bead with the other hand
5. Each time you breathe in and out, move to a new bead of the mala
6. Keep going until you reach the guru bead (the end bead).
7. To take this further, choose a mantra to recite, such as OM. Recite the mantra once for each bead on the mala.
8. Keep going until you reach the guru bead.
9. Express thanks for the meditation and take a moment to contemplate.

How To Hold And Move Meditation Beads

There is a specific way to hold and move Buddhist prayer beads. Like so:

- Hold the prayer beads in your dominant hand with the tassel of the mala facing towards you

- The first bead (the one you begin on) is the one to the right of the guru bead

- Gracefully turn the beads in your fingers (without using your index finger, which is the finger of the ego) as you make your way to the next bead. Preferably turn the beads with your thumb.

- You should hold the mala beads in a controlled but gentle way.

- Feel the union between your breath and the movement of the prayer beads.

- You will eventually come full circle and find yourself on the guru bead. This is a time to pause and reflect. Sit still and express gratitude for your meditation session.

Wearing Meditation Beads

There is a right way how to wear meditation beads and a wrong way. If you chose your mala beads for healing purposes, all you have to do is put it around your neck or wrist. Simple. To get more out of them, you can even wear multiple malas at the same time. I love how this looks. You get different textures and colours to compliment your style, plus you get the multi-dimensional healing benefits of the different meditation malas. Make sure you choose mala beads that work well together if you plan on combining them.

Even though wearing meditation prayer beads is simple, there are a couple of things you should know.

For starters, you shouldn't let your mala beads touch the ground because this will interfere with the energy resonance. If you do accidentally drop it, you will want to cleanse it in saltwater. (You can read about how to cleanse mala beads below).

You might not want to let other people touch your mala beads either, because they can transmit their own energy to them that way. Whether you choose to follow these rules when wearing mala beads will depend on your own beliefs. So if you don't believe it matters then, hey, no sweat.

There are rules for wearing mala bracelets too. Most yogis believe they should be worn on the right wrist, although I do not follow this and instead wear them on the left (it's a matter of personal belief, after all). I honestly don't think wearing mala beads on the left hand is a problem.

Adding Dorje And Bells

While you're choosing mala beads, you might also like to consider Dorje and Bells. These are two short strings that contain ten small beads, which you can use for counting above 108. Most people will never require a dorje and bell. They are only necessary for very long meditation sessions. For instance, some types of mantra recitations that require you to recite the mantra very many times, sometimes into the tens of thousands.

How To Meditate With A Mala, Dorje And Bell

You use the dorje to count complete cycles of the mala when meditating. This way you know precisely how many recitations you have done because you have the full-mantra count (shown by the dorje) plus the bead of the mala that you are currently on.

Once you have moved the dorje up ten beads, you then have the bell counter. This counts 1000 recitations.

Between the mala, the dorje and the bell you can count up to 10,000 mantra recitations.

How To Cleanse Mala Beads

You'll definitely want to know how to cleanse mala beads because they will sometimes become impure, such as when you drop them or when someone else touches them.

Traditionally there is no prescribed time for cleansing mala beads. It's all about getting in touch with your intuition. If you feel that you should be cleansing your mala beads, you probably should. There will be observable energy in your being that tells you when it is time.

Feel your mala beads. Ask yourself: are they creating the right energy? If not, it's time to cleanse your mala beads.

Steps For Cleansing.

1) Sit outside and place your mala beads in the light of the sun or moon. The energy of the light will help to remove negative energy from the mala, purifying them.

2) Place your mala on the ground and burn dried white sage near it so that the smoke rolls over the mala.

3) While the mala is being cleansed, chant OM for 108 recitations.

4) Wash the mala with seat-salt-water. For best results, wash it in the ocean.

TECHNIQUES

GUIDED MEDITATIONS – DOING IT THE EASY WAY

Sometimes you don't need complicated dharma to follow and you don't want to invest time and effort into learning and practicing traditional meditation techniques; you just want the simple and easy answer, a way to relax and fast.

When I finished drama school I immediately wanted to get on stage in front of large audiences to play all the famous roles that actors dream about. Just one problem: auditions. Some find them easy. I'm not one of them. Auditioning was always a nerve-wracking experience for me. You head into an empty and silent theatre where there's just you and three complete strangers. Only they're not just *strangers*; they're strangers who could make your dreams a reality if you just put in the right performance. If you can hit that stage and be on fire for just five minutes, you'll get the role, else you're on your way home.

To get to an audition generally requires driving to the train station, taking a packed-out train to whatever city the audition is in, then taking a bus, and finally walking somewhere you've never been before. Nowadays I would be able to find the peace of mind on the train to practice breathing meditation, and then use the walk to do a spot of Zen Walking. But I was still new to meditation at this time and I didn't feel confident meditating in public. I needed an easier solution.

My experience at that time was similar to the vast majority of new meditators. They know they need to relax, but finding the time and space can be challenging so the easier the option the better. The absolute easiest option with meditation is *Guided Meditations*.

Guided meditations are often the entry point for newcomers to meditation. They're looking for a way to relax and unwind, perhaps a way to quieten their thoughts and feelings, something to help them overcome complications that have arisen in the mind. For myself en route to my auditions, my mind was racing. I was excited about the prospect of landing a great role, and nervous that I might screw the whole thing up. Quality acting demands a still mind, because you can't truly step into a character's shoes and adopt a character's thoughts and feelings until you've put your own thoughts and feelings aside. To do well in my auditions I needed a quiet mind. Guided meditations offered an easy way to get there. I'm sure you too can imagine many ways in which guided meditations would benefit you.

The attractiveness of guided meditations is their speed and ease. They're simply short videos or audio recordings that will take you on a meditative journey into tranquillity. They're quick, easy, effortless, and relaxing—everything you could want from 21st Century spirituality. Take a look at the following example and you'll get the idea.

An example of a guided meditation

Close your eyes. Listen to your breathing. Hear your breath coming and going, up and down, as tranquil waves stroking on a shore. See that shore. The skies above are blue. There's a gentle swooshing of the waves. The sun is warm on your skin. You feel the warmth spreading throughout your body, relaxing you. Your toes curl on the hot sands. The warmth spreads up your ankle to your knees, and continues up your body, right to the crown of your head. Your whole body is warm and relaxed, and your breathing is slow and gentle, matching the rhythm of the waves...

This is a classic guided meditation, a poetic and relaxing journey that leads you to relaxation and peace.

You can imagine how ideal this was for me en route to my auditions. I'm already sitting there in a train or car with music on. Why not just listen to a guided meditation? Simple.

Unlike other types of meditation, which require effort and commitment, guided meditations are premade. All you have to do is put them on. That's the benefit of them: If you don't have the time, energy, or mental strength to invest in traditional meditations, you can just put your feet up and listen to a recording, and it's all done for you. It's therapy on demand.

Guided meditations helped me to relax on the way to my auditions, and they help countless other people in similar situations. Nervous about a job interview? Got a business presentation to do? Just got home after a stressful day's work and want to put your feet up and escape for a while? Just take ten and listen to a guided meditation.

In all instances where you just want to relax quickly without putting any real effort in, guided meditations are great. But there's one all important pill to swallow with guided meditations: You have to accept the reality that they are nowhere near as powerful as traditional meditation techniques.

If you're looking to chill out, sure, put a guided meditation on.

But just know that *chilling out* is as far as those recordings will take you. We all love them because they require zero effort, but the fact that they require zero effort is also their downfall.

If you want to get fit and in shape you have to sweat. You have to put in serious effort to get the health and the body you want. And the same is true for your mind. If you don't truly exercise your mind you're never going to be mentally strong.

All in all, guided meditations are the equivalent of a trip to the beauty spa. You'll enjoy the time. You'll leave feeling relaxed. But it's a superficial treatment, a band-aid solution. It's not going to make your mind truly strong. You need genuine mental exercise to do that.

That's not a criticism of guided meditations. They're great for what they are: simple relaxation. But they are not substitutes for traditional meditation techniques.

The same is true for binaural beats, audiovisual media, and other meditation products. They're great products and some of them will definitely help you to unwind. But they are also severely limited.

Like a spa day, guided meditations should be used to relax, and they can also be used as an *absolute beginners'* entry-point to meditation. But if you want to take things further you have to be willing to put more effort in than simply pressing the *Play* button. If you want to get the most out of meditation, you have to learn how to meditate *properly*.

Let's take a look at the *real meditation*. Trust me, these are the ones that are going to change your life.

BREATH AWARENESS MEDITATION AND STILLNESS BREATHING

In the summer of 2004, I decided my girlfriend and I deserved to take a break and go on vacation.

My girlfriend's parents had passed away recently and she'd hardly had the chance to relax since, and I'd been working at a shareholder centre dealing with stock investors and quite fancied getting out of the old rut.

Spain was where my heart was at, and I knew my girlfriend would love Barcelona. The architecture is sublime, and tapas…? Catalonian puff pastries, those aromatic roasted veggies, paella, and Catalan style crème brùlèe? Yes please.

One day we were out for a stroll when we happened to pass the Plaza Monumental de Barcelona, which was the last bullring in operation in Catalonia. Now a museum, the Plaza exhibits the branding-irons and emblems of famous stock farms, along with the heads of famous bulls, a collection of posters from the past, old tickets, the suits of famous bullfighters and rejoneadores, and other items from the bullring's gruesome past.

Have you ever visited those barbaric execution camps known as bullrings? There, the toreros take to the stage dressed as glamorously as any Hollywood megastar. The bull charges out of the gate. The toreros wave their red cloth. The bull charges for them. And with a quick swing of the body the torero dodges around the bull, which then circles for another charge. The awful event continues until the poor animal is completely exhausted. And then the matador unsheathes his blade. It's a cruel sport, one we're fighting to put an end to. And it's the perfect representation of one of the crueller aspects of the mind.

Many people are controlled by the mind every bit as much as the bull is controlled by the torero. The mind waves the *red flags* of fear, desire, stress, and anxiety, making them charge and veer and stumble like the bull. The act continues, for some, until the end of their days. As the bull never finds freedom from the matador, some humans never find freedom from their own minds. They charge from desire to desire to desire, desperately dodging fears, trying to keep afloat through all the stress and worry. They grow tired, having aged. And then they look back on their lives and realise that they were the victims of their own minds.

It's one of the most common displays on Earth; people dashing about trying to make more money to afford bigger homes to keep up with the Jones', buying whatever latest gadget Apple and Google want them to buy, eating whatever mass media tells them to eat. These people are victims just like the bull. But unlike the bull, they have a way to escape. The bull will never control the matador, but we can control our minds. We just need to learn to stop all those thoughts, stresses, fears, and worries.

But how do you stop when there's so much going on and so much to do?

The best answer I've ever found to that question is breathing meditation.

Like the ocean, the mind is constantly tossing back and forth, waves crashing about, preventing you from seeing beneath the surface. But then one day the waves dissipate. The ocean becomes still. Suddenly the surface is clear and you can see within. Meditation's like that.

Meditation allows you to stop and to see what's happening within. And when you see within yourself, beneath your surface, it's as though you're taking your first breath, because you come to see life in a new light.

When you meditate, you see reality in newfound clarity. That's why meditation often leads to epiphanies, such as the epiphany I myself had the first time I meditated, when I realised what I'd never realised before: That I was dedicating myself to ending suffering.

It was a strange realisation at the time, because I hadn't applied to be a doctor, a counsellor, or another profession you'd typically associate with *ending suffering*. I'd been a singer and was then an actor. But yet I knew that it was true. I knew that all those times I took to the stage to entertain people, I did it because I wanted people to stop worrying, to stop stressing, to let go of everything that was on their minds, and to simply enjoy the moment. I wanted to make them laugh, sing, and be joyful for just a couple of hours, because that couple of hours was a fantastic catharsis. That's why every time a performance finished and the cast went right back to their changing rooms, I peeked out back and watched the audience members, seeing how their faces lit-up after a good show.

It's funny that so many people get caught up in the glamour and spectacle of the performing arts.
Because in truth, the performing arts—whether it's theatre, dance, music…--are about stories. They're about taking

people away from their own lives, from their own thoughts, for a couple hours so they can escape their own minds.

Stories are one of the oldest of all man's creations. Cavemen drew stories on walls millennia ago. Why? Perhaps it's because they knew that the mind needed silencing every now and again. Perhaps those ancient artworks were a form of therapy, a way to relax the mind. Perhaps they instinctively knew what Lao Tzu said, that mental impurities led to physical illness. Perhaps those stories on cave walls were how cavemen relaxed and healed their minds so they could maintain good health.

Long before science and medication came along, people were using stories as a way to relax and calm the mind. And where some medical practices have come and gone, stories have always stayed with us. There are very few things, next to breathing air, that we do as much as telling or reading stories.

Just think about the sheer amount of times you read or listen to a story. You wake up and put the news on, and you hear news stories. You talk to your friends and you hear stories about their recent events. You read a book. You watch a movie. You go to the theatre. You are always engaging with stories.

Some people think stories are mere entertainment. But if that's the case we must require entertainment literally 24/7, because we almost never stop listening to stories. Even when we go to bed we dream and our unconscious mind creates its own narrative and story.

If you ask me there's much more to stories than just entertainment. Stories are the absolute number one form of therapy. And I know for a fact that of all the hundreds of artists I've worked with over the years, the vast majority would agree. We all truly *need* stories for our wellbeing, for our health. That was why I personally got into the performing arts: because I recognised the powerful healing power of stories. And that was why I eventually got into meditation and became a meditation teacher, because I want to stop suffering, to help people to connect with the present moment and to find happiness and health. That's why I spend so long on my email, Twitter, and Facebook pages answering people's questions to help them, because I want to stop the suffering. But I only ever realised that the first time I meditated.

As powerful as my own personal epiphany was, I see equally powerful epiphanies in other people I teach meditation to. The first time they meditate and experience a true moment of inner clarity they come across a powerful realisation.

One woman I taught to meditate realised that she'd sabotaged all her relationships because she was afraid of abandonment (her father had left her when she was young). By teaching her meditation I helped her to overcome that sense of abandonment so she could have healthy relationships. She's now engaged to be married to the man she's been with for eight years.

A fifty year old man I taught realised that he was in completely the wrong business (law). He entered law just because he wanted to make more money than his brother. What he really wanted to be doing was fitness instruction. I helped him overcome his unhealthy competition with his brother so he could start on the fitness business he was passionate about. Now the owner of his own business, he's making more money than he ever did before, doing something he loves—and, yes, he's making more than his brother, though he's no longer concerned about his sibling rivalry.

Another male friend of mine suddenly realised that he'd spent 30 years chasing after a dream and in so doing had never really lived the true moments of his life. He is now dedicated to living in the present moment, and tells me he's done more living in the past year than he did in the 30 years he spend chasing his dream.

These are just a few of the many people who have seen within themselves using meditation. These people have all experienced the profound insight that meditation can offer. And you will to.

So, when you perform the meditation techniques that we're about to discuss, be prepared to experience a revelation.

The very first meditation technique that beginners should try is breathing meditation

Because the breath is the most ever-present function of both the body and the mind, it is the best place to begin meditation. Thich Nhat Hanh said it best: "Feelings come and go like clouds in a windy sky. Conscious breathing is my anchor."

By learning to breathe consciously we will give our minds an anchor, a way to remain earthed, a way to stay in the present moment instead of getting carried off in our thoughts and feelings.

EXERCISE: Breath Awareness Meditation

This is a simple but powerful technique that puts the mind back into contact with the breath, making us more aware of our body and our physical being, and also helping to focus and relax the mind.

Just follow these simple instructions.

1. **Sit comfortably with your eyes closed.** Give yourself a few moments to become comfortable and to relax. Focus your attention on the present moment—on sights, sounds and sensations. You'll notice that your mind slips between thoughts, "What's for dinner? Did I send that email?" etc. Ask these

thoughts to slow down so you can begin to see clearly.

2. **Focus your attention on your breath.** Observe your breath moving smoothly in and out of your body. Do not try to force your breath. The key is not to *control* but simply to *observe*. Be the person sitting on the shore of the ocean watching the waves coming and going. There is peace and tranquillity in simply observing.

3. **At times your mind will wander.** You may momentarily forget to focus on your breath. You may start to process thoughts, thinking about what you have to do next. Simply bring your mind back to the moment, back to the breath. Be like the buoy that bobs up and down on the waves but remains fixed by its anchor.

4. **Let go of thoughts and feelings. Allow yourself to observe your thoughts and feelings but do not *attach* to them.** *Attaching* to a thought is essentially seeing it as *you*. For instance, when thinking *I have to make dinner* we tend to associate with the *I* and we tend to believe that we really *do* have to get up and put the stove on. Non-attachment is *observing from a distance*. We see the fact that there is a thought, but we don't allow it to affect us. We simply say "That is a thought *and nothing more*".

5. **Continue like this.** Over time you will observe many things about yourself and about your mind, including the three states of impermanence (anicca), dissatisfaction (dukkha), and non-self (anattā)—the states we discussed in our introduction to different types of meditation. When you discover something about your mind, simply *observe* it. Don't dwell on thoughts, don't argue with them, don't reject them, simply *observe* them.

When most people first practice breath awareness meditation they are amazed how difficult it can be just to focus the mind.

YOUR BEST MEDITATION

The average person spends most of their days in a whirlwind of thoughts and feelings. It can feel quite unnatural, at first, to halt that whirlwind and to sit in silence. But you'll find that as soon as you do sit in silence your mind relaxes, your body lets go of tension, your spine elongates, and your posture improves. These are physiological signs that meditation is working. You may also notice that you yawn and that your brain suddenly feels very "open". These are all good signs.

When practicing breath awareness meditation, the mind follows the breath, breathing up and down, up and down, like the rhythmic motion of a bird's wings, up and down, up and down. There is constant motion. We breathe in, moving the wings up, then out, moving the wings down. By focusing on the up and down of our breath we connect to the present moment. But the mind is always moving.

What's better than moving is to exist in stillness, to be outwardly active but inwardly still, like the flight of the common swift.

> *The swift hovers in the air without moving its wings. Likewise, the mind can hover on the present moment, existing in a state of stillness, an effortless presence.*

The swift flies by holding its wings still and drifting on the wind. It can even sleep while floating in the air. The mind can do likewise. The mind can be completely still, drifting along on the present moment, never moving, simply soaring as though on the wind.

To achieve this state of *stillness in motion* that allows the mind to float on the present moment, practice the art of *Stillness Breathing Meditation*. This ancient technique produces mental stillness by focusing the mind on the moments *between breaths*. There is not up or down. There is pure stillness.

EXERCISE: Stillness Breathing Meditation

1. Begin in the same fashion as you did with the Breath Awareness Meditation—sitting comfortably, permitting yourself a few moments to relax, and then beginning to focus on your breath.

2. Begin to observe the moments between inhalation and exhalation, and vice versa, the moments of stillness. Observe what you find between breaths–a stillness; a settling point. When the mind rests on this stillness it becomes like the wings of the swift: stillness in motion.

3. Continue to meditate on the stillness between breaths. Remember to release thoughts, feelings and sensations as you did with the Breath Awareness meditation.

4. Aim to achieve complete mental stillness, the mind drifting effortlessly on the present moment, as the swift floats on the wind.

If you are new to meditation, practicing these techniques once a day for twenty minutes will give you a great sense of inner peace and relaxation. It will allow you to live in the present moment without having to battle your thoughts and feelings. This will make life easier as you'll be spending less of your mental energy on controlling your own mind.

MINDFULNESS MEDITATION

My personal life was developing as rapidly as my spiritual life. I had broken up with my girlfriend after she decided to start seeing someone behind my back. Single, I decided to make the most of my newfound free time. I returned to Oxford and spent my every waking moment training in either meditation or art. I suppose you could say I transcended time at this period. Between studying spirituality, reading Shakespeare and ilk, practicing classical acting techniques, and also writing for contemporary magazines, my focus was spread throughout time.

I auditioned for absolutely every role I could and finally managed to score roles in Chaucer's The Canterbury Tales and The Marriage Of Figaro. I packed my bags and headed off on tour with a brilliant ensemble of actors and artists.

That summer our tour headed to the Edinburgh Fringe Festival, that spectacular menagerie of performing arts. In between shows I'd head out for runs around Edinburgh's sumptuous fields and hills, meditating and practicing yoga where and when I could. That whole summer the sky was clear of clouds and my mind was clear of thoughts. I was reminded of just how alike the sun and the mind are. Both are energy centres.

The sun creates heat and light. The mind creates awareness and consciousness. The beams of the sun radiate outwards, spreading light onto all they touch. The mind radiates consciousness, which illuminates our world. Without the sun we wouldn't see and we wouldn't be alive. So too with consciousness; without it we wouldn't see and we wouldn't be alive (or at least not awake). But just as the rays of the sun can be blocked, dimmed, and transformed by clouds, so can consciousness be blocked, dimmed and transformed by thoughts and memories. Too many clouds block the sun. Too many thoughts block the mind. Clear away the clouds and you're left with a beautiful, bright day. Clear away the thoughts and you're left with a beautiful, awakened life.

As with the sky, the mind always has some degree of *cloudiness*. Right now, for instance, a part of your mind will be focused on reading this book. But, if you're like the average person, your mind will also be thinking thoughts, momentarily visualising things, perhaps carrying on conversations with yourself, multitasking, and performing many other tasks and operations that are *not* "reading this book".

Those thoughts, feelings, internal dialogues, and other mental *noises* are like the clouds preventing the sun from reaching the ground. They're obstacles that are preventing your consciousness from reaching out to external reality.

Imagine all those mental distractions dissipating until your entire mind is focused on this book. That would be one act of mindfulness, which can otherwise be termed *"present mindedness"*. Or, to put it another way, imagine opening the *Task Manager* of your computer (the application that lists all the different programs, services and operations that your computer is carrying out). Mindfulness would be the equivalent of turning off all the superfluous services and operations so your computer (or your mind) is focussed on just the one thing.

It's an incredibly simple concept to grasp. It's simply *doing what you're doing, living in the present moment,* and *being aware of the present moment*. It's something that we should already be doing and *would* already be doing if it wasn't for the fact that society and modern technology encourages mindless behaviour. TV, the internet, video games, cell phones...most of us are staring into a screen for a considerable portion of the day, not living out in the real world. That's one reason why people have become more mindless in modern times. Fifty years ago, when people spent more time on one thing and led slower lives that weren't completely bombarded by screens and a plethora of information, mindfulness would have been a nice *boost* to your health. Now it's a necessity. In an era when we have to fight just to get an hour to relax outside and to live in the moment, we need a tool to help us preserve our minds and to stay focused on reality. That tool is mindfulness, the practice of non-judgmentally living in the present moment.

EXERCISE: Mindfulness Meditation

1: Sit comfortably with good posture

2: Notice your legs. Cross your legs if it's comfortable to do so

3: Make sure your spine is in natural alignment

4: Place your upper arms parallel to your upper body. Let your hands drop onto your legs. Make sure you are relaxed.

5. Focus on the sensation of your breath moving through your body; how your breath enters your nose or mouth, then into your chest and so on. Choose a focal point (I like to focus on the sensation of the breath between my upper lip and nose).

6. Your mind will wander. That's fine. Just gently return to focusing on your breath.

7. After twenty minutes of breathing, gently open your eyes and tune in to your environment. Notice sounds. Notice how

your body feels. Notice how you're relaxed. Take a moment to experience that moment of relaxation. This will help you to recall the feeling of relaxation the next time you need to.

Mindfulness Meditation Is Powerful

I've witnessed the power of mindfulness hundreds of times in countless different situations. I've seen mindfulness get people through depression, overcome stress, and cure many mental health problems, and I've also seen mindfulness transform people's working lives, family life, and social lives.

One of the more interesting people whom I've taught mindfulness meditation to was a professional gamer. He played in video game tournaments throughout North America. He's a truly talented guy. He's so talented that he routinely makes it to the top 8 in tournaments (this is out of hundreds of people). But he always used to get nervous when he was close to winning a tournament.

The problem, we discovered after a lot of conversation, was that he was too aware of how much it would mean for him to win. He'd get close to winning when he'd become too excited or too nervous to focus. He'd make a mistake, and then he would lose. It happened over and over again.

I taught my friend mindfulness so he could stay in the present moment, so that when he was playing he'd just be playing, nothing more. He stopped thinking about winning and simply played the game. This empowered him to play his regular game while in the finals of a tournament. And that, in turn, led him to accomplish what he'd wanted for so long: to stop being second and start being first.

That's just one of the more fun examples in which mindfulness has helped someone. Obviously that example is about performing. Mindfulness helps you to stay focused so you can do whatever it is you need to do without being distracted. I'm sure you can readily apply that to your own life. After all, who couldn't use more focus? Imagine being able to focus your mind 100% on the work you're doing instead of having to constantly *weed away* those distractive thoughts and feelings. Imagine being able to just live in the actual moment 100% of the time. It would simply make life so much easier.

But not only does mindfulness make life easier and help you to focus on whatever it is you're doing, it also offer myriad health benefits.

A partial list of the proven health benefits of mindfulness would include:

- Slows down your breathing rate (this helps breathing for asthma and other conditions)
- It lowers the rate at which we consume oxygen.
- It raises blood flow to the heart
- It helps us to become more tolerant
- Improves our physical relaxation
- It is excellent for people suffering from high blood pressure
- It improves our exercise tolerance
- Reduces free radicals, which equals less tissue damage
- Improves skin resistance
- Lowers our risk of getting cardiovascular disease
- Improves the air flow to the lungs = better breathing
- Slows the aging process
- Makes us better at sports events

- Improves the endocrine system
- Over a period of time meditation helps us return to normal healthy weight
- Helps the immune system to relax
- Is of benefit to electrical activity in the brain
- Meditation lowers the levels of blood lactate and thus helps cure anxiety attacks
- Is of benefit to diseases including arthritis and allergies
- Helps lower the symptoms of pre-menstraul syndrome
- Meditation decreases muscle tension
- Helps with post-op healing
- Boosts the immune system
- Reduces viral activity

INTRODUCTION TO BUDDHIST METHODS

The majority of meditation techniques come from Buddhism.

Dig into ancient texts and you'll find the very heart and core of meditation. It's in the classics like the Bhagavad Gita, the Vimalakirti Sutra, and the Pali Canon, that you'll find the roots of meditation. Like the trunk, branches, and leaves of a great tree, meditation has grown over countless years, but its roots are still anchored in the ancient texts, among the fertile soil of ancient Eastern culture.

In the classic language of Buddhism, meditation is referred to as bhāvanā and jhāna/dhyāna, which respectively mean "Developing into existence" and "a deeper awareness of oneness". Put those two terms together and you'll discover the principle belief and purpose of Buddhist meditation: Developing the existence of oneness. Buddhist meditation is all about cultivating the mind to realise the truth: that we are one with the universe and all in it. This is what Buddhists refer to as *enlightenment.*

Enlightenment: *In Buddhism, enlightenment is the ultimate purpose of meditation. Enlightenment can be thought of as* *meaning "Release from the self".*

The general aim of Buddhist practice is to liberate the self from the ego so we can achieve oneness. But different schools of Buddhism achieve this through different techniques.

For instance, Theravada Buddhism (a specific school of Buddhism) incorporates more than one hundred meditation methods, the majority of which revolve around mindfulness. Contrastingly, the Tibetan tradition uses over a thousand different visualisation meditations. This is why if you ever attend a Buddhist school you'll be taught techniques that correspond to the teacher's style of Buddhism. The Dalai Lama, for instance, teaches Tibetan Buddhism, where the hugely popular author and teacher Thich Nhat Hanh teaches Zazen (Zen).

There are, however, many similarities between the different Buddhist schools. One of the major similarities lies in the *three essential characteristics of the Buddha's teachings*. Visit the temples of the different schools of Buddhism and you'll hear most teachers discussing three types of training: Virtue (which they call "sila"), Meditation (Samadhi) and Wisdom (panna). These three types of training are the pathway towards enlightenment, and each one is essential.

Buddhists believe that these virtues and ethics cannot be separated from meditation. If you're to truly learn Buddhist meditation, you must learn the philosophies and principles behind it. Those philosophies and principles are told through the "Noble Eightfold Path", which is the "way" towards enlightenment. The *path* is broken into eight sections: Right understanding, right thought, right speech, right action, right livelihood, right effort, right mindfulness, and right concentration. When learning Buddhist meditation in the traditional way, students will also learn these eight paths. The

"Dharmachakra"; an eight-spoked wheel that represents the Noble Eightfold Path.

But of course most people are not interested in dedicating themselves to the Buddhist "path" or to "enlightenment". Rather they are interested in taking the many wonderful Buddhist techniques and meditations and using them to improve their health and to help them live their lives without stress or pressure.

Let me show you how you can use Buddhist meditation for everyday life a little later in the book. You'll discover how to use Buddhist meditations to create happiness and joy, to live in the moment, to boost your health and to improve your overall wellbeing

ANAPANASATI

Buddha said this meditation technique bears "great fruit" (meaning great benefit) when practised regularly. It is an essential Buddhist meditation, a type of mindfulness meditation.

Anapansati (pronounced "An-a-pan-a-sah-tee") trains the mind to stay calm and balanced. The word Anapanasati means "mindfulness of breathing". So, it is a method in which we are mindful (consciously aware) of the breath.

Anapansati is one of the most popular techniques used in Zen Tianati, Theravada, and Tibetan Buddhism. It was initially taught by Buddha more than 2500 years ago. The original instructions are found in the Anapanasati sutta.

In the 6th Century BC, Buddha instructed his followers to go into the forest, sit under a tree, and mindfully observe how the breath flows through the body.

Good advice.

Spend ten minutes sitting under a tree watching your breath, and you will become very relaxed and calm.

That's traditional Anapansati. Anapanasati has evolved over the years. Today it is not just a Buddhist practice but a medical and scientific practice too. Science has proven that there are many benefits of Anapanasati meditation technique, as the Buddha advised originally in the Anapanasati Suta.

You can use this method any time you would like to relax,

calm the mind and focus.

EXERCISE: Anapanasati

1: Choose A Relaxing Place To Sit: Proper space is important because it helps you to relax. Your area should be quiet and peaceful, which is why Buddha instructed his monks to go into the forest in the Anapanasati Sutta. It is easy to get distracted, so make sure that there are as few distractions as possible. You should also consider lighting. The area should not be too light nor too dark, and it should be a comfortable temperature. You don't want to be shaking or sweating profusely when you meditate.

2: Choose A Posture: I always recommend doing Anapansati seated and in a good cushion. But it is possible to do Anapanasati meditation technique in various positions. You can do it lying down, standing, or sitting. You can use whichever pose you're happiest with. Just makes sure you have good posture.

3: Relax: Make sure your mind is relatively calm before continuing. You might like to count breaths, stretch your body, or just take a few moments to let go.

4: Focus On Your Breath: You may find that counting your breaths helps you to concentrate. If so, count an inhalation AND exhalation as one count (Breathe in, breathe out, count one. Breathe in, breathe out, count two etc.). If you find that you are struggling to concentrate, count your breaths up to ten and then start over. Alternatively, move your focus to a different part of your breathing, a part that appears more apparent. You can count for the entire session if you wish, but this is only for beginners. Once your mind is fully focused, maintain that focus for a minimum of five minutes. After this, you may wish to adapt your technique depending on your reason for practising.

If you are meditating to develop an understanding of yourself, you may wish to observe your thoughts. If you are aiming purely for focus, keep concentrating on your breathing. You may also use visualisations and other techniques at this point.

5. Advancing

Now that you know how to do Anapanasati meditation technique, you may wish to vary it, depending on your reasons for meditating.

Here are some of the best ways to adapt the basic Anapanasati meditation:

Focus on the entirety of the breath. Imagine the breath as one. There is no in or out there is just breathing. Meditating on the oneness of breathing helps develop inner stillness.

Focus on the energy behind the breath. There is an energy, or a lifeforce, behind the breath. When you meditate on this, you will find what I term Infinite Creativity—the most elemental part of ourselves. When you connect with this part, you will find immense freedom and power.

Meditate on the connection between mind and breath. You will find that how you breathe alters your mental state and vice versa.

Mindfulness: Observe your thoughts to discover the truth of yourself.

Impermanence: Notice how each breath is different, how body and mind continually vary. We are like liquid—always moving—and yet we may be inwardly still.

Try humming or reciting "Om." This will tune your mind-body into the frequency of the sound.

6. Development Through The Four Tetrads

Traditional Anapanasati meditation progresses through four tetrads. These stages of Anapanasati are not for beginners. If you are a beginner, practice Anapanasati meditation only so far as mindfully observing the breath. Once you have gained practice, progress through the following stages.

7. First Tetrad: The first tetrad is simply mindfulness of breathing (physical sensation) and noticing whether the breath is long or short. This then leads to mindfully observing the breath through the whole body. We then use this to relax the body.

8. Second Tetrad: At this stage, Anapanasati becomes more of a contemplative meditation technique. This stage of Anapanasati is all about feelings and emotions. Because the mind and body are relaxed, we will experience the feeling of rapture (piti). The second stage of Anapanasti is to observe these feelings mindfully. The Anapanasati sutta recommend maintaining mindfulness of breath while also observing these feelings. Mindfulness of breathing is used as the anchor, so we do not get drawn into emotions and lose ourselves.

Like Thich Nhat Hanh said, "Feelings come and go like clouds in a windy sky. Conscious breathing is my anchor".

We use the breath to keep the mind anchored while we mindfully observe our feelings. You will notice that the mind tries to avoid negative feelings and is attracted to positive emotions. Once we are aware of this process, we can label them as craving (the more wanting more positive feelings) and aversion (the mind wanting less negative feelings). We can then stop this perpetual to-ing and fro-ing.

9. Third Tetrad: The third tetrad deals with emotions and with the mind. Because we have learned to stop reacting to our experience, we can be more inwardly calm and happier. The next step is to observe how the mind is filled with joy. Our more joyful mind is now more still. This leads to heightened concentration.

10. Fourth Tetrad: This tetrad is all about freeing the mind by using reflections. In this tetrad, we reflect on the impermanence of experience and the continually changing nature of thoughts, feelings, emotions, and sensations. This is done by mindfully observing how these elements change as we meditate.

Benefits Of Anapanasati Meditation Technique

Spiritual Benefits

Buddha said in the Anapansati Sutta that it is a vital stage on the path to enlightenment. Buddha taught in the Anapanasati sutta that this technique would develop the Seven Factors of Enlightenment: Sati (mindfulness), Dhamma Vicaya (analysis), Viriya (persistence), Piti (rapture, which essentially means that you are joyful and enthusiastic), Passaddhi (serenity), Samadhi (concentration), Upekkha (equanimity), And finally, Anapanasati leads to freedom from suffering.

Health Benefits

- One of the best techniques for relaxation
- Increases serotonin
- Improves communication between hemispheres of the brain

- Improve reactions
- Prevents depression
- Prevents anxiety
- Anti-again for body and mind
- Lowers heart rate
- Helps balance blood pressure
- Lower risk of cardiovascular disease
- Improves airflow to lungs
- Improves immune system
- Helps with PMS symptoms
- Decreases muscle tension
- Improves energy flow
- Reduces headaches and migraines
- Improves motor performance
- Increases productivity
- Increases focus
- Stops "Monkey Mind" (a controless, restless, scattered mind)
- Makes you more intelligent

ZEN

Zen is a school of Mahayana Buddhism that is heavily influenced by Taisom. That's why there are many similarities between methods like Zazen and traditional Daoist meditation techniques. One of the primary focuses of this school of Buddhism is Mindfulness.

The majority of Zen meditation techniques focus on increasing mindful awareness. They also incorporate specific postures. For instance, in Zazen meditation, which is a traditional seted practice, we use specific seating positions along with the hand positions called mudras.

There are many different Zen meditation exercises. It is worth practising each of them because they offer unique benefits. The walking method called Kinhin, for instance, will give you different benefits to seated Zazen meditation technique.

One of my favourite books on Zen meditation is Zen Training: Methods And Philosophy. In it, author Katsuki Sekida says, "Zen training is a means of enabling us to live our ordinary lives supremely well."

The key to living supremely well is mastering your mind, which is what these methods are all about. So, how do you do it? It's best to begin with the postures and positions because these are so vital to the practice.

How To Do Zen Meditation

It is traditional and beneficial to use proper seating position, hand gestures (mudras) and other body positions when practising meditation. Here is a guide to adopting the right position for the body so that you can practice properly.

Positions: Sitting, Kneeling, Or Standing

Zen Meditation techniques us specific sitting positions and standing positions, specifically, Burmene, half-lotus, and Seiza, which we looked at in the section on Meditation Positions. In Zen, these sitting positions require a cushion called a zafu. This is a particular type of cushion that helps you maintain proper posture while also being comfortable.

A zafu is essential for both body and mind because if you do not have a comfortable posture, you will find it very difficult to focus. And without focus, the exercises simply will not work. A good cushion will elevate the hips in such a way that the knees are lowered to the floor, which is a stable and comfortable position conducive to focus.

An alternative is to stand. To do this, stand straight, place your feet shoulder-width apart, position your heel inwards a little, place your hands on top of your belly with the right hand held over the left, make sure not to lock your knees.

Positions For The Rest Of The Body

Eyes: One of the differences between Zen meditation techniques like Zazen and other forms is that the eyes are kept open. This is to stop you from drifting off into a daydream. The right way to use your eyes is to focus on nothing but instead softly guide your gaze to one meter in front of you on the floor. Your eyes should be half-open. You may also choose to position yourself in front of a wall or some other object so that there are no distractions.

Neck And Head: In Zazen, the position of your neck and head is critical. If your neck and head are in the wrong position for extended periods, you could suffer a spinal injury. To combat, position your head and neck like so: Keep your neck straight, pull your chin in a little, imagine that your head is gently rising towards the ceiling (but do not force it). Make sure that you are balanced and comfortable. You should be able to maintain the position without effort. Your teeth should be together lightly, an your tongue should be against the roof of your mouth.

Hands And Arms (Cosmic Mudra): Zen uses a specific mudra called the cosmic mudra, in which one hand is cupped on top of the other with both palms facing upwards and the hands held a little in frton of the chest (when standing) or on the lap (when sitting).

State Of Mind: If you perform the other parts of Zen meditation technique correctly, your state of mind will naturally follow. Without the right state of mind, you will not get the health benefits of Zen. When it comes to attitude, acceptance is vital, as it always is in Buddhism. You will naturally have thoughts come to your mind when you meditate, as you do with other methods. Let these thoughts exist; do not repress them, fight them, or cling to them, but rather let them rise and fall as they will.

Breathing: When doing Zazen meditation, breathing technique is fundamental. The right breathing here is a little different to what you might have experienced with other methods. And it is imperative to get it correct. To breathe correctly, sit in the right posture (see above). Then, breathe quietly in through the nose with your mouth closed. The breath must be relaxed, and should come in long, calm inhalation and exhalations that are never forced. The focus is on the exhalation.

The Right Room: Distractions are the enemy of good practice. The fewer distractions, the easier it will be to concentrate, which is why Zen monks often meditate facing a wall. However, you do not need to be facing a wall. You can sit comfortably wherever you like. But be aware that the more relaxing your room is and the fewer distractions there are, the more successful your pratice will be.

EXERCISE: Zen Meditation

This is the primary Zen meditation. When doing Zazen, When you begin, you should have an idea of how long your session will last. And you should have done everything to make sure that you will not be distracted during that time.

1) Set an alarm for the end of your session.

2) Find a comfortable space somewhere you can relax and where you will not be distracted.

3) Place your zafu or zabuton in a comfortable spot. If you are choosing to face a wall, you will need to place the zafu about a metre in front of the wall so that your eyes fall to the bottom of the wall when you meditate.

4) To begin, relax. You will find it helpful to practice breathing methods for a few minutes.

5) Close your fist with the thumbs tucked inside the fingers, and move your hands so that the back of your hands touches your knees with the digits up.

6) If you would like to show respect to Buddha, you can do gassho. This is where you adopt the Anjali Mudra and bow to show your devotion to Buddha.

7) Adopt the cosmic mudra ("Hokkaijoin") and check your posture (see above).

8) Begin focusing on your breath and particularly on your exhalation.

9) Count to 108 breaths.

10) I like to go into a Vipassana practice now (see *Vipassana*)

Benefits Of Zen Meditation

The benefits of Zazen include: improved focus, improved sleep quality, a more peaceful mind with less negative thoughts, improved intuition, and development towards enlightenment.

Many of these benefits have been proven. Brain scans reveal that Zen meditation can help free the mind of distractions, which could be beneficial for ADD, ADHD, anxiety and other mental health complications.

Giuseppe Pagnoni [neuroscientist, Emory University in Atlanta] conducted research into Zen meditation techniques. The team compared 12 people with experience of Zazen with 12 people who had never tried it. Participants were asked to focus on their breathing while distinguishing between real words and gibberish on a monitor. The research revealed that Zen led to different activity in the "default network" of the brain, which is linked to mind-wandering and spontaneous thoughts. Zen meditators brains returned to normal faster after each word than the non-meditators did. This, Pagnoni states, shows that "meditation may enhance the capacity to limit the influence of distracting thoughts," Pagnoni said. This, researchers state, could mean that Zen meditation helps with conditions caused by distractive and disruptive thoughts.

ZEN WALKING: ENLIGHTENMENT IN YOUR FEET

Beauty surrounds us, but usually we need to be walking in a garden to know it. -- Rumi

There's something distinctly cathartic about walking, isn't there? You put your runners, boots, or sandals on and head out the door, and you immediately feel a lift in your chest, an expansion, a freedom. A long walk through a beautiful countryside is one of the purest of joys.

Having landed in Toronto and moved into my new home with Jeannie in Hamilton, who turned out to not be the psychotic madwoman I'd feared but the beautiful angel I'd hoped for, I was eager to explore my new home.

Our city has a bit of a bad rap on account of the fact that it's a steel city full of factories. But it's really a diamond in the rough, because surrounding all the concrete is a gorgeous natural landscape that has more waterfalls than anywhere else in the world, a picturesque harbour, and many hidden footpaths to explore.

Personally I love to indulge in a trek along the escarpment by our house, where I'm writing this. Some part of my abdomen seems to fill with light and sing with joy when I escape the urbanity and surround myself— almost pen myself in— with the tall rising trees and the surging rush of the waterfalls. The footpath leads down and around to Lake Ontario, that majestic body of water that seems to stretch out infinitely as though to tell us all that nature will always endure despite mankind's efforts to the contrary. There I'll take the path around the lake until my legs grow tired and my mind fills with more appreciation for home.

My walk, as with most long walks, is like an old friend: reassuring, always there. Hippocrates said "Walking is man's best medicine". He has a point. A good walk uplifts body, mind and soul. But there is a way to make walking even more serene and therapeutic: by meditating while you walk.

Numerous spiritualities and religions incorporate walking techniques. "Circumambulation"—an overly longwinded word that simply means "to move around a sacred object"— is practiced in Christianity, Islam, Judaism, and many other religions. For instance, in Romania at Easter priests will walk around the temples singing hymns. By moving the body slowly the mind also slows and enters a trance-like state in which there is nothing but the walk and the sacred object around which we're moving.

Scientists also advocate the importance of walking for both physical and mental health. Recent research has shown that a walk in a soothing natural environment may in fact change the way the brain works and thereby help to improve mental health.

It's a known fact that people who live in urban environments are more prone to stress, anxiety, and depression. Specifically, those who live in the city and have no access to natural environments are most prone to mental health disorders. But simply taking a walk around a park can help significantly to lower levels of stress hormones.

Research shows that walking in a natural environment helps to prevent brooding, morbid rumination of thoughts and stresses that can prevent us from living in the moment. This brooding is one of the chief precursors to depression and it is alarmingly more common in city dwellers. Brooding, or "morbid rumination" is strongly associated with a part of the brain called the *subgenual prefrontal cortex.* The research shows that as little as a 90 minutes walk around a quiet leafy park helps to reduce activity in the subgenual prefrontal cortex, meaning less brooding, less stress and depression, and better mental health.

Clearly, walking is a fantastic activity when it's done in the traditional way. But we can make walking even more cathartic, enjoyable, and relaxing simply by combining walking with meditation. We can practice "Zen walking".

Zen Walking is predominantly practiced in Zen, Chan Buddhism, Korean Seon and Vietnamese Thien. Monks will use walking meditation as a way to get the body moving in between periods of seated meditation. Traditionally the monks will walk clockwise around a sacred space while holding their hands in a specific position. The position has one hand closed into a fist while the other hand grasps the fist. This hand position (or "mudra") is called *Shashu*.

Mudra: *A mudra is a body position that has an effect on the energy in your body. Many mudras use just the hands, some use the entire body.*

With their hands in Shashu position, Zen monks will walk slowly around the sacred space, consciously focusing on the movement in their legs. This leads to greater consciousness of body, and a heightened mind-body connection. It also helps to ground focus on the present moment, as the mind is consciously focussing (being mindful of) the movement of the body.

> **"After a day's walk everything has twice its usual value." —George Macauley Trevelyan**

EXERCISE: Zen walking meditation

1) Find a path of approximately 40 foot in length.

2) Place your hands in Shashu position. Make a fist with one hand. Now lightly grasp that fist with the other hand. This is the Shashu mudra.

3) Begin to walk up and down the path.

4) While walking, meditate on the sensation of movement in your feet and legs. Also be aware of how your mind instructs your body to move. If you look closely you will feel the connection between intent and action. Meditate on that connection.

5) It is traditional to keep your gaze down and to not focus your gaze on anything. But if you're a beginner you might like to also meditate on your surroundings. Smell the air, enjoy the colours of your garden or walking space, use your senses to explore the environment.

6) When you reach the end of the path turn and repeat

7) Find an easy pace, neither too fast nor too slow. It is important to walk at the pace that you most feel the mind / body connection. Sometimes (when stressed, for instance) this pace will be fast. Other times it may be slow. Generally the longer you spend Zen walking the slower your walk will become.

8) Focus your attention on your body and the sensations in your body.

9) Allow your attention to enter your feet and lower legs.

10) Feel the movement of each step and the way it feels in your feet. Feel each movement in taking a step. Be aware of the raising of the foot, the leg swinging, the foot returning to ground and then the other foot taking over.

11) If you find it helpful, count each step. This can help you to stay in the present moment.

F.A.Q's About Zen Walking Meditation

I tend to receive a lot of questions about Zen Walking on the Facebook and Twitter pages. So, to help you out I've created the following Frequently Asked Questions segment.

How long do you need to practice to see benefit?

The more you practice the more benefit you will see. But of course, time is limited. You don't want your meditation practice to interfere with other activities you have going on in the day because then you will feel compelled to rush once you finish your walk (which is counterproductive). Personally, I find twenty minutes to be a good length of time, but anywhere between ten minutes and an hour is fine.

Should you increase the speed of walking while you practice?

You'll naturally find a good speed as you practice. It's best not to think about how fast you are walking, but rather to focus on the meditation itself. As you relax you will likely slow down more, simply because you are more aware of the process of walking itself.

Where are some good places to Zen walk?

Aim for places free of distractions. Nearby parks and footpaths can be good. Provided you will have the peace to genuinely get into the meditation, anywhere is usually fine. Naturally, it goes without saying, that roads should be avoided.

But I don't have the time!

One of the questions I get asked the most as a teacher is "How do you find the time to meditate?" Many people live very busy lives. Finding time is not easy. Thankfully it is possible to incorporate meditation into your everyday life without losing too much time.

Zen Walking is an exercise which you can practice without losing time. Though Zen Walking Meditation is usually practiced in a meditation garden, it doesn't have to be. If you are on your way to work and know a safe route away from roads, you can leave ten to twenty minutes early and practice Zen Walking Meditation on the way to work. The same applies to all other times when you are travelling. Simply leave a little early and take a safe route (avoid roads!).

Another great exercise is to go for a Zen Walking Meditation with the family or with friends. You're probably used to chatting away with family and friends, but spending some quiet time together and going for a walk is another great way of bonding. You'll find that you feel much closer to friends and family after a walk together.

Zen doesn't have to take up much time. Monks may meditate for hours every day, but that doesn't mean you have to. Simply look for some ways to incorporate meditation into your everyday life. Trust me, no matter your lifestyle you can find time for meditation. If you don't think so, please read my new book: Zen And Now; it will show you precisely how to meditate wherever you are, whatever you're doing.

SAMATHA

**Calmness is the cradle of power. –
Josiah Gilbert Holland**

Spiritual desolation. That's where I was in the summer of 2010. Having temporarily split up with Jeannie, entered an impromptu relationship that quickly headed south, and ended up living in a motel room with coffee stains down the walls in a country where I had no one I knew well enough to call on, my mind cracked and I suffered the most painful period of my life.

I headed home on British Airways with a mind full of *avidya*. And it turns out that Lao Tzu was right because no sooner had my mind strayed than my body became ill—I developed severe skin problems down my legs that looked like the skin was rotting. My life soon became a cycle of visits to the doctor and a counsellor. Sleepless nights and nightmarish days; that was my life at the time.

Only, of course, every single part of the pain that I felt at that time was created by my mind. Because it would later turn out that absolutely *none* of what I feared was actually true. I had feared I would never get back with Jeannie. She'd proven me wrong about that within a few days. I'd feared that the problem with my legs might be permanent, maybe they might even need amputating. In fact it turned out that the problem with my legs was a case of severe eczema. I feared I had depression and would be put on meds. Turned out it was what the psychologist called an "Extreme Stress Reaction".

Absolutely none of my fears were true. Everything that I had gone through was a lie. How often is that the case? How many of us go through pain and suffering because we create unrealities in our minds?

Of course it all seems obvious in hindsight. When I look back on that period of time I find it hard not to shake my head at myself because of course none of those stresses were real. I went through all that pain for nothing. But then it's easy to see reality when you're calm. It's a lot harder when you're stressed.

That's why one of the two core mental disciplines that Buddha taught was *Samatha*, which essentially means calmness—the other is Vipassana, which means insight.

Buddha knew that Samatha, calmness, helps us to see reality clearly and to not allow the mind to create all the nightmarish visions that it can sometimes create. Put simply, Samatha helps us to "keep a grip on reality".

The best understanding of the term Samatha comes from direct translation. Samatha is Pali for "calm", and can also be expressed through the Tibetan term Shyine, which means "peace" and
"purification". If you put together those three terms, calm, peace and purification, you get the gist of what Samatha meditation is all about. It's about calming the mind to produce inner peace which leads to purification.

In traditional Buddhism, Samatha enables the mind to concentrate (which in Pali is "Samadhi") which leads the mind to being absorbed by the object of concentration (which is called Dhyana), which in turn leads to insight ("Vipassana") and finally what Buddhsits call "Liberating Wisdom" (Panna).

We cannot get to Dhyana, Vipassana, or Panna without Samatha. We need calmness to allow us to focus, which leads to insight and wisdom.

Calmness is first, and calmness is Samatha.

Samatha: *Buddha taught that morality and mental calmness are the first steps on the path to enlightenment. Without calmness and morality we cannot achieve insight, wisdom, or enlightenment.*

I imagine every single person on Earth can immediately grasp the truth of what the Buddha taught. Without calmness we are hugely ineffective. I know that I myself, in my younger years, was about as calm as a Great White in a bloodbath. I can vividly remember my "angry years". They happened after I broke up with the girl I was with in Birmingham—though not *because* of that breakup, more because the urbanity of my new home was beginning to chill my rural heart. I began to think that I didn't have time to meditate, which led me to temporarily abandon my spiritual quest, retiring my collection of Thich Nhat Hanh and Chopra books to their shelves to gather dust. Over time the business and noise of my job and the city led my mind to become unstill. Anger took hold. I'd explode over practically anything. I'd get angry over the slightest of grievances. Someone cut me up on the road? That's a middle finger. Someone looked at me funnily? That's a cause for confrontation. I started listening to *Nu Metal,* abandoning Mozart and Tchaikovsky for Slipknot and Metallica. I became a headbanging metal-head with a pension for late nights, cigarettes and alcohol.

During that time I could never focus. And that lack of focus led to me wasting countless hours, getting noting done fast. I knew that before I could achieve anything at all I would need to develop calmness.

Thankfully I had my knowledge and experience of meditation to fall back on. I returned to practicing meditation, beginning with basic mindfulness and breathing meditations. That practice enabled me to restore my mind to calmness (Samatha). That calmness led me to concentration (Dhyana) which led to insight (Vipassana) which finally led to wisdom (Panna). But it all started with calmness, with Samatha.

Samatha Meditation is really a more exotic term for "concentration meditation". It's meditation that involves focussing on one specific object—traditionally there are forty meditation objects used in Samatha, you can find a list of them below.

When you focus your mind on one object you build your concentration levels, the same way a gymrat builds bulk by lifting weight over and over. At first when you begin to focus your mind on an object your mind will wander, just as a muscle may tremble under a barbell, quivering before finally giving in and dropping the weight.

Most of us aren't accustomed to focusing absolutely on one thing, so our levels of concentration are fairly weak. The mind struggles to concentrate and soon brings up thoughts and distractions, like debris being churned up in a river. The mind brings up noise and the focus is lost. That's the first time. Over time, with practice, the noise and the debris is cleared. Then the mind, as the water, runs pure, allowing you to continue to focus for long periods of time.

After several months of practice your mind will have become significantly stronger. Eventually, your levels of focus will become so strong that when you concentrate on an object you feel as though you are one with it; you are not aware of the difference between the meditation object and yourself because your mind is so keenly focused. This is what Buddhists call *Jhana*, "fixed mind".

The Buddha taught that there were five stages of Jhana, with the meditator moving up through the stages sequentially. At the highest state of Jhana, when the mind is completely fixed on external reality, the practitioner is said to be freed from desire, lust, hatred and other mental impurities. The result is complete happiness and serenity.

In the ancient times there were some practitioners who used Samatha as a means to gain supernormal powers like clairaudience. They believed that when the mind is so absolutely attuned to an object it is able to receive messages from that object. For instance, when focussing absolutely on another person the meditator would hear their thoughts. At the highest level of Jhana the mediator is left two choices: use their power for their own good or for the good of others. Only by using their power for the good of others can the meditator truly defeat Dukkha, suffering, from their mind.

Eliminating Dukkha is the ultimate aim of Samatha meditation.

Through continual practice we learn to accept and to perceive the reality of physical, mental and spiritual pain. This sense of acceptance then allows us to overcome the pain. "Dukkha" and "Suffering" are Buddhist vernacular. Today we are more likely to say that meditation allows us to overcome negative thinking, depression, anxiety, stress, and all other mental pain, as well as helping to alleviate the symptoms of wounds and illnesses.

It is worth noting that Samatha meditation should be practiced in a relaxed way. Most of us aren't used to focusing our minds absolutely on one thing. If you ask your mind too much too soon you could cause harm, as the weightlifter tears a muscle when lifting too heavy a weight.

Demanding yourself to focus on one object for an hour is like demanding your legs to run a marathon the first time you put your running shoes on. Injury will occur. That's why it's imperative to train your mind gradually. I've personally made the mistake of trying to focus too hard too soon before and I know from first hand experience that you're only setting yourself up for a migraine.

So, go slow. Meditation should be practiced gradually. Try to focus on your object for around five minutes the first time. Then after a week you can try ten minutes and so on. But don't start by demanding yourself to focus for such a long period of time that you strain your brain. Be wise. Your mind is your best friend and most important ally. Treat it as such.

EXERCISE: Samatha

1: Sit comfortably with good posture.

2. Become aware of your breath. Take ten mindful breaths to relax.

3: Focus on your meditation object As you focus, allow thoughts and feelings to come and go as you will. When you get distracted, gently return your focus to your meditation object.

4: Observe the space between your mind (your conscious awareness) and your meditation object. Now move your conscious awareness so that it is inside your meditation object. Your mind and meditation object should be one.

5: Continue to return your conscious awareness to your meditation object, aiming to achieve oneness. Stay focused on your object for twenty minutes.

Here are the forty Samatha objects to meditate on

Traditional Samatha meditation includes the following forty meditation objects. Many of these you will most definitely not want to actually meditate on (you'll see what I mean!). This list is simply for educational purposes.

Ten "Kasinas":

The kasina are visual objects that you can directly meditate on. These are:

Earth,

Water,

Fire,

Air,

Blue,

Yellow,

Red,

White,

Light,

Enclosed-space.

Ten "kinds of Foulness":

These are ten meditations that involve meditating on decomposing corpses. In the time of the Buddha it was common for corpses to be disposed of in carnel-grounds, which meant it was relatively easy to find a corpse and meditate on it. Today in Thailand teachers advocate meditating on visions of your own body in these various states, though this should only be attempted by advanced meditators as this can be quite disturbing.

The bloated,

The livid,

The festering,

The cut-up,

The gnawed,

The scattered,

The hacked,

The bleeding,

The worm-infested,

Skeleton

Ten kinds of Recollection (Anussati):

Anussati means "recollection," "contemplation," "remembrance," "meditation" and "mindfulness."
*These meditations involve devotional practices, like recollecting the sublime qualities of the Buddha (which could equally be Shiva, Jesus Christ, or your own deity—remember, this is **your** meditation to do as you personally see fit). They also include meditative attainment, such as the ability to recollect past lives.*

Recollection of the Buddha (the Enlightened One),

Recollection of the Dhamma (the Law),

Recollection of the Sangha (the Community),

Recollection of Virtue,

Recollection of Generosity,

Recollection of Deities,

Recollection of Death,

Mindfulness occupied with the body,

Mindfulness of Breathing,

Recollection of Peace.

Four Divine Abidings:

Loving Kindness,

Compassion,

Gladness,

Equanimity.

Four Immaterial States:

The base consisting of boundless space,

The base consisting of boundless consciousness,

The base consisting of nothingness

The base consisting of neither perception nor non-perception.

The One Perception: the Perception of Repulsiveness in Nutriment. *This refers to being mindful of the negative or less attractive aspects of food and drink, including the procurement of food, food in its unprepared state, and the secretion of food and drink. This meditation is used to make the individual aware of the negative aspects of desirable flavours, which helps to overcome cravings and thereby leads to healthy, mindful eating and drinking. In layman's terms, once you're aware of where a burger comes from, what it's made of, how it feels in the stomach, and what it looks like when secreted... well, you're less likely to eat that burger.*

The One Defining: the defining of the Four Elements.

A Modern and Practical Way To Practice Samatha Meditation

Naturally, not all of the 40 objects of meditation are objects you would like to meditate on. Decomposing corpses? No thank you. Let's contemporise and get real.

Essentially Samatha meditation involves focusing on a positive object that elicits a positive response.

For instance, breathing is calm and centring. When you meditate on your breath you calm and centre your mind.

Running water is free and flowing. When you meditate on running water you free your mind and create flow.

Blue skies signify liberation. When you meditate on a clear sky you liberate your mind.

Focus on an object with a clear positive trait and you will a) develop your concentration, and b) mentally absorb the positive quality of that object.

You can choose to focus on any positive object you like. Some of my personal favourite objects to meditate on are: stars, the sky, candles, water, my cats, my breath, my body, positive mental qualities (like love and kindness) and nature.

Feel free to choose your own positive objects. But I will strongly recommend that among your meditations you include meditations on your body, your breath, physical movement, a calming sound, and positive mental images. The body and the breath are particularly important as they anchor your mind and enhance your mind-body connection.

Once you've chosen your object to meditate on, sit comfortably and with good posture, give yourself a few minutes to relax, then begin to focus your mind on the object. Observe the object through your senses. Hear it. See it. Smell it. Taste it (if applicable). Touch it. Be one with it.

Meditate on your object for no less than 5 minutes and preferably for 20 minutes. This will calm your mind and allow you to absorb the positive qualities of the object.

Your mind is infinitely adaptable. Nourish your mind with positivity and it will grow like the branches of the Bodhi tree.

LOVING KINDNESS MEDITATION

"Like a caring mother holding and guarding the life of her only child, so with a boundless heart of loving kindness, hold yourself and all beings as your beloved children." – Guatama Buddha.

When aggressive sharks attack humans, nearby dolphins will rush to the person's aid, risking their own lives to save the human. It's a natural part of the dolphin's compassionate and loving spirits. It's also part of the reason why dolphins are one of the most loved animals in the world: because we all recognise the essential *goodness* in their nature.

I always feel that compassion is truly the most important thing in the world. Without it we'd have obliterated the world and blown each other to pieces eons ago. It's like the Dalai Lama said, "We can live without religion. We cannot live without human kindness". It's a statement very many people agree with and feel passionate about. At the end of the day, what's humankind worth if we cannot be loving and kind to one another and to this beautiful world we all inhabit?

We need compassion to survive, but the funny thing is it's often those people who have been pushed to the brink who become extremely compassionate. Honestly, I swear, there's a direct correlation between going through rough times and developing compassion. The evidence is all throughout history. Jesus Christ, Buddha, Ghandi, Mother Theresa… the vast majority of people we consider saints lived troubled and difficult lives. And the same is true for we mere mortals. I know that I, personally, was changed forever on account of the various hardships I've been through. The self-inflicted turmoil I went through when I had my "Extreme Stress Reaction" in 2011, when I was forced to move back to England and to rebuild the tattered ruins of my life, lit a fire in me, a desire to do whatever I could to help people avoid the emotional turmoil I myself had faced.

After my Extreme Stress Reaction I dedicated even more to meditation, and I began TheDailyMeditation.com. My intent and passion with TheDailyMeditation.com is to empower people to use meditation to end suffering so they can enjoy happy, peaceful lives. My compassion was born out of my trouble, and the same is true for others who follow similar paths: We want to help others avoid suffering.

If you follow our newsletter, you'll notice that I often post about love, compassion and kindness. That's because I personally believe that love, compassion, and kindness are three of the most important traits in the world. And not only are they important, they're also win / wins.

When you're compassionate and kind you help another person, but you also help yourself too.

To illustrate that fact, consider charity work. I've personally been involved with charities numerous times over the years —mostly for animal charities. Every time I do charity work I feel fantastic: fantastic to help out, fantastic that I'm capable of being of benefit the world in what small way I can, and fantastic that I've spent my time doing something important. That's a personal win. And the animals and people I help win too. They win by being giving charitable donations that help to keep them alive and to maintain their wellbeing. They win. I win. Everybody wins. And it's all because of basic human compassion, or *loving kindness*.

Loving Kindness (called "Metta" in Pali) is benevolence, friendliness, friendship, good will, kindness, and love. It is one of the ten *pāramīs* of the Theravāda school of Buddhism, and the first of the four sublime states.

"Parami: The term "Parami" is Pali for "Perfection".
There are ten perfections: Generosity, Virtues, Renunciation, Insight, Effort, Patience, Honesty, Determination, Loving Kindness, Equanimity.

Buddha taught his followers that Metta would help them to develop the four sublime states of Equanimity (Upekkha), Metta (Friendliness), Compassion (Karuna) and Joy (Mudita).

Of these four states, Metta (friendliness) comes first. Loving Kindness (Metta) Meditation first develops warm feelings towards others. This in turn leads to compassion (Karuna) as we develop heightened levels of empathy--feeling happy for the successes of others and compassionate for their suffering. This then leads to Appreciative Joy—the appreciation of the good fortune of other people. Finally, we achieve Upekkha, equanimity, the state in which we extend love and kindness to all living beings.

Upekkha: *A state of equanimity (mental calmness) that is part of the process towards enlightenment in Buddhism.*

In order to cultivate "Metta" or compassion you can practice several different meditation techniques, of which "Loving Kindness Meditation" (or *Metta Meditation*) is generally considered the most important.

Buddha himself practiced Loving Kindness Meditation every day. He would spend all morning meditating and reciting mantras. Then, towards the end of the Buddha's meditation sessions he would come to Loving Kindness. He would sit down to meditate, focusing first on his breath, and then extending thoughts and feelings of compassion, love and kindness to himself. Then he would look around him at the villagers and monks and would imagine sending out positive feelings of love and kindness towards them. Finally he would look for some way to help his community, and would immediately set out to do it.

As well as being an essential part of Buddhist practice, Loving Kindness also offers many realworld benefits.

In the Pali Canon (an ancient Buddhist text), it is said that Loving Kindness Meditation helps us to sleep well, to wake well, to avoid nightmares, to be closer to other people, to feel a sense of emotional protection, to feel closer to others, and to develop concentration

These beliefs are backed by scientific research. Richard Davidson, a neuroscientist and Director of the University of Waisman Center, conducted research involving fMRI scans of monks who had been meditating for many years. The research revealed that Loving Kindness has a profound impact on the brain as it significantly heightens our compassion for others, and also heightens levels of joy, happiness and contentment

Further research has also shown that Loving Kindness Meditation:

- Reduces stress
- Balances blood pressure
- Reduces risk of cardiovascular disease
- Promotes positive feelings
- Improves empathy and compassion
- Helps eliminate the symptoms of depression
- Reduces the symptoms of anxiety
- Improves social wellness and social intelligence
- Removes negative feelings and emotions like loneliness, jealousy, and loss
- Improves brain function
- Reduces migraines
- and Increases grey matter volume

One of the most important benefits of loving kindness meditation is the fact that it helps us to love and feel compassionate not just for other people, but for ourselves too.

One girl I taught Loving Kindness Meditation to was struggling to accept the fact that she had allowed herself to put on a lot of weight. She was once beautifully healthy, but she'd gone through severe stress and had been comfort eating, which led her to put on 100lbs. She could handle the fact that she was overweight. What she struggled to accept was the fact that she had allowed herself to ruin her health. She felt angry towards herself, and guilty too, and that anger and guilt was manifesting in depression.

With Loving Kindness Meditation I was able to teach her to accept what she had done and to forgive herself. Once she had gotten over the past and had found self love once again, she found it relatively easy to return to her healthy habits and to lose weight. It was just getting over that hurdle of forgiving herself and accepting the errors she'd made. As soon as she'd forgiven herself and moved on she started exercising and eating healthily again. Now she's even fitter than she had been previously. She's a shining example of the power of self love and a reminder of the fact that once you accept and love yourself you will naturally want to act in ways that will promote your own wellbeing.

Once we have achieved self love, the next stage of Loving Kindness Meditation is to extend our loving kindness towards others, beginning with those close to us, those people whom we love and respect. This helps us to feel and to act positively towards the people in our lives. For instance, I once taught a married couple facing divorce to practice extending loving kindness towards each other. They both spent twenty minutes a day extending loving kindness towards one another. This helped them to accept the weaknesses and errors of the other, which led to a very healthy relationship. They're still together today and are now happier than ever.

Once we've extended loving kindness to people close to us, we move on to neutral people (people we know but feel indifferent towards). This includes colleagues, people we know but rarely speak to, and people about whom we simply feel indifferent. When we practice loving kindness towards these "neutral" people we begin to feel much closer to them. This in turn leads us to act more positively towards them, which often leads to new friendships and relationships.

Finally we come to the most challenging part of loving kindness. In this part we extend loving kindness towards those people towards whom we currently experience negative feelings. For instance, a lot of people don't get along with their neighbours—tragically; your neighbours can be some of the best friends and most helpful acquaintances you have. But after a few years living next door to one another, with all that noise and the fact that they put up that ugly fence, it can be easy to fall out. By practicing loving kindness you can learn to see each other in a positive light, which cures any animosity and restores the positive relationship.

This final part of Loving Kindness can also help to cure seriously unhealthy relationships as well and emotional suffering.

I'll give an example from my personal life. About a decade ago my father had been on business down in Portsmouth, England. He was walking back to his hotel when two men ran down the road. One of the men pulled a knife out of his pocket. He slashed it down my father's face. Then they ran. My father, bleeding severely, managed to crawl into the nearest building, which happened to be a restaurant. By some miracle there happened to be a doctor eating in that restaurant when my father crawled in covered in blood and near death. The doctor managed to wrap the wound up to help control the bleeding for long enough for the ambulance to get there.

I don't mention the story because of the miracles that seemed to be working together to keep my father alive. Rather I mention it because at first I had an extremely negative reaction to what happened. I (rightfully, perhaps) hated those two men who had attempted to murder my father. I felt mad at society too, which I felt had "let it happen". But I knew that I could not allow those two men to destroy my state of mind. They'd done more than enough damage already. So I practiced Loving Kindness Meditation. I imagined sending compassion towards those two men who had so harmed my dad. And in so doing I managed to forgive them and to move on. This wasn't an overnight process. It took practice. But now those two men are no longer a stain harming my mind.

When I talk about those two guys now everyone says "You must want to kill them". I could want to do that if I let myself. It would be easy, I suppose. But that would only lead to damage. Instead I've chosen to understand that they're the unfortunate result of an imperfect society. They themselves are almost definitely victims of some sort of suffering. You don't act that way unless you're truly hurting inside. So they're victims themselves. And instead of hating them, I figure it's better to try and understand them and where they come from, and to help cure their hatred and anger so things like this stop happening. In my mind that's just a healthier and more positive way to be. But I'm only able to be so positive towards those guys because I've been practicing Metta Meditation. So, how do you do Loving Kindness meditation? Let's take a look.

EXERCISE: Loving Kindness Meditation

1: Find somewhere quiet where you will not be disturbed for ten to twenty minutes. Sit, lie down or stand up, making sure you have good posture.

2: Focus on your breath: Focus on your breathing for a few moments to quiet and calm your mind. You may do this by using either of the two breathing meditations we discussed in the previous section.

3: Send loving kindness to yourself: Imagine seeing yourself happy and smiling. Now imagine sending out feelings of love and kindness towards yourself. Also imagine those same feelings being returned to you.

4: Next, think of five positive things about yourself, five things to love. Now think of five ways in which you enact self love (perhaps you are kind to yourself by eating healthily, by giving yourself peace when you need it. . . think of ways in which you are kind to yourself).

5: Finally, say to yourself the Loving Kindness Meditation words: "May I have loving kindness. May I have strength, peace, love and success. May I also have the strength to overcome all obstacles."

6: Repeat with someone close to you: Bring to mind someone close to you (family / friend) and repeat the process. Imagine the person happy. Imagine sending them love. Imagine them sending love back to you. Now think of five things to love about that person. Next think of five ways that person shows loving kindness to you.

Now say the Loving Kindness Meditation words "May (name of person) have loving kindness. May they have love, peace, strength and success. May they also have the strength to overcome all obstacles)."

7: Now repeat the process with a neutral individual

8: Now repeat with a hostile individual

9: Return to the beginning and repeat.

Always remember the sacred loving kindness script: "May (name of person) have loving kindness. May they have love, peace, strength and success. May they also have the strength to overcome all obstacles)."

The benefits of Loving Kindness Meditation

Believe it or not, this simple meditation technique is truly powerful. Here's a look at some of the many health benefits that Metta Meditation offers.

Increases positive emotions / Decreases negative emotions

In 2008, positive psychologist Barbara Frerickson conducted research that showed that practicing loving kindness meditation (metta) for seven weeks led to increased love, joy, pride, contentment, awe, gratitude, and hope. These positive emotions in turn lead to increased mindfulness, increased sense of purpose, a decrease in illness, and an increased sense of social connection.

Increase vagal tone

A study in 2013 showed the effect of loving kindness meditation on emotions, and revealed that loving kindness meditation affects the vagal tone, a physiological marker of wellbeing. This in turn shows that loving kindness meditation can help us to heal physically and emotionally.

Decreases migraines: The positive emotions and stress reduction created by loving kindness meditation leads to less migraines. Research conducted in 2014 Tonelli studied the effects of metta meditation on people who suffer from migraines, and observed a significant decrease in migraine frequency in those who practiced the meditation technique.

Helps Chronic Pain

In 2005 research (by Carson et al.) studied the effect of metta meditation on people with chronic lower back pain. They showed that the reduction in stress led to less severe pain.

Helps Post Traumatic Stress Disorder

In 2013 research (by Kearney et al.) showed that practicing loving kindness meditation for 12 weeks leads to less severe symptoms in post traumatic stress disorder patients.

Helps Schizophrenia

A pilot study conducted by Johnson in 2011 researched the effects of metta meditation on individuals suffering from schizophrenia spectrum disorders. The results showed that meditation led to decreased negativity, increased positivity, and therefore was instrumental in recovery.

Boosts Emotional intelligence

The brain evolves based on the activities we perform (based on Neuroplasticity). Regular practice of loving kindness meditation leads to increased compassion and thereby teaches our brain to be more socially intelligent.

Increases Gray Matter

In 2013, Leung et al. showed that loving kindness meditation leads to increase gray matter in the areas of the brain related to emotional regulation.

Helps Respiratory Sinus Arrythmia

Another important benefit of loving kindness meditation is

that it relaxes the body. This results in several physical benefits. Ten minutes of practice, for instance, leads to increased cardiac control, slow and more relaxed breathing, and helps with respiratory sinus arrhythmia.

Decreases telomere length

Stress has been scientifically proven to decrease the length of telmores, which are genetic materials that are a marker of aging. In 2013, Hoge et al. proved that loving kindness meditation led to longer telomeres and thereby slowed the aging process.

Improves Social Value

Practicing loving kindness meditation makes you a more socially valuable person. In 2011 Leiberg et al. showed that loving kindness led to increased compassion, which in turn motivated individuals to behave in a way that was beneficial to society.

Boosts Compassion

One of the most important aspects of Buddhism is compassion for all life. So perhaps it's not surprising to hear that research conducted by Jones & Hutton in 2012 showed that loving kindness meditation significantly increased compassion.

Heightens Empathy

A study in 2013 showed that loving kindness meditation also leads to increased empathy.

Makes you less biased

In 2014 Kang, Gray & Dovido showed that six weeks of loving kindness meditation led to less bias against minorities. This suggests that communal practice of lovingness kindness meditation would lead to the cessation of racism and other prejudices.

Increases Social Connection

This is the one benefit of loving kindness meditation that you will notice above all others. Loving kindness meditation makes you feel much more connected to the people around you. This was proven by research conducted by Kok et al in 2013.

Reduces self criticism

Part of practicing loving kindness meditation is extending thoughts of love and kindness towards yourself. This leads to less self criticism, which in turn raises self esteem and can help to cure depression and negative thoughts. This was proven by research in 2014 by Shahar et al.

It works in small doses

In 2008, Hutcherson proved that just 10 minutes of loving kindness meditation was enough to provide the benefits listed above.

It lasts

Finally, the benefits of loving kindness meditation will endure. In 2011 Cohn et al showed that 35% of participants who practiced loving kindness meditation had improved emotions for 15 months.

KARUNA MEDITATION: NOURISHING THE SOIL OF COMPASSION

If you want others to be happy, practice compassion. If you want to be happy, practice compassion. – Dalai Lama

Many of the most beautiful moments in history have stemmed from the fertile soil of compassion.

During the Holocaust, German industrialist and spy Oskar Schindler was a member of the Nazi party. Originally working as an informant, Schindler purchased enamelware and ammunitions factories, originally intended to be a profit-making venture. It wasn't long before Schindler used his assets to protect Jews from execution. He employed 1200 Jews to work in his factories in order to keep them safe. Then, as pressure from the Nazi's continued to mount, he began to bribe members of the Nazi SS to keep the Jews from being executed. By the end of the war Schindler had spent his entire fortune in protecting the Jews in his factories, despite the fact that the Nazi's were breathing down his neck every step of the way. His love and kindness is a prime example of the beauty of compassion. And it also led to one of the most touching movies in history in Schindler's List, a flick which will move even a cold stone to warm tears.

Abraham Lincoln was another man who embodied compassion, bringing about the abolishment of slavery in America. Martin Luther King, Ghandi, Mother Theresa... the list goes on. Take a look back through the history of the world and you'll find that it's not the ultra wealthy or the glamorous celebrities we remember. It's the people who sacrificed themselves to make a difference in the world. It's the people who embodied the most important of traits: compassion.

The Pali term for compassion is "Karuna", a word close to the heart of Buddhism and Jainism. In Theravada Buddhism, living through Karuna (or living through compassion) is seen as the key to attaining great happiness in life. It's easy to imagine how Lincoln, Martin Luther King, Schindler and ilk must have felt a tremendous depth of warmth deep down knowing that they were singlehandedly changing the lives of thousands, if not millions of people. No wonder so many religions and spiritualities place compassion above all other traits.

In Buddhism, compassion is considered one of the four "divine abodes" (Brahmavihāra). The other three are loving kindness (Mettā), sympathetic joy (Mudita) and equanimity (Upekkha). These "divine abodes" are considered so essential to the spirit that it is believed to be impossible to achieve enlightenment and become a bodhisattva without achieving a very high degree of Karuna (compassion).

Jainism holds compassion in equal reverence. In Jainism, Karuna is one of the four reflections of universal friendship, the others being amity (maitri), appreciation (pramoda) and equanimity (madhyastha). These four reflections are used in Jainism to stop the influx of karma.

In Christianity, compassion is represented through the love of Jesus Christ and his death at the cross in atonement for our sins. Though the word "Karuna" might be alien to Christians, the western term "compassion" seeps through every page of the Bible.

And in Taoism, the Tao Te Ching speaks of "Three Treasures", which are virtues of the utmost importance. They are *Humility, Frugality, and Compassion*.

> **"I have just three things to teach: simplicity, patience, compassion. These three are your greatest treasures." – Lao Tzu**

In modern society, compassion speaks for itself. Simply think of the people whom you hold in highest regard. More than likely they are all extremely compassionate, caring, and loving people. We may feel a level of respect and sometimes even jealousy towards the rich and famous. But reverence is reserved for the compassionate, for brave soldiers who protect countries, for volunteers who risked their lives to help out at ground zero at the Twin Towers on 9/11, for the brave souls that travelled to Asia to help save those stricken by the tsunami, for the caring folk that journeyed to New Orleans to save people in the aftermath of Hurricane Katrina. Those are highest of the high, the most noble of the noble, the divine; and their good deeds are all fuelled by the fires of compassion.

> **"Soldiers who protect countries. Volunteers who help out at 9/11, Hurricane Katrina, the tsunami... They are the highest**

of the high."

As a show of ultimate Karuna, or compassion, Bodhisatva's (enlightened ones) vow to lead all sentient beings away from suffering towards the attainment of enlightenment.

It isn't just spiritualities and religions that tout the importance of compassion. Science does too. There are a great many proven health benefits of a compassionate mind.

For starters, science has proven that being compassionate does make you happy. Research conducted by the National Institute of Health shows that the brain's pleasure centres are activated when we perform acts of kindness. But you really don't need the scientific research to know that. Simply perform one act of random kindness. Hand a homeless man a meal and you'll feel a surge of warmth and joy in your heart that will make you feel fantastic for days. Spend a few hours talking to a lonely elderly person and you'll feel more valuable because you've made a big difference in their life. Pay people compliments and you'll notice you can't help but turn your lips up into a kindhearted smile. It's as though compassion were a natural elixir.

Sadly all too many people try to make themselves happy by being generous *to themselves.* But science has proven that this simply isn't as effective as being generous to other people. One scientific study that was published in the journal Science showed that people are on average happier when they spend money on someone else rather than on themselves.

But you might think, *I need to spend money on myself, looking good isn't cheap!* Think again. Science has proven that compassion is one of the most attractive traits in the world. We are naturally attracted to people who are kind, and not just people who are kind to *us* but people who are kind *in general.*

If everyone stopped spending so much money trying to make themselves look good and spent more trying to help other people, not only would we all be happier but we'd be less lonely too.

I don't know about you, but personally when I look back on the 38 years of my life what I'm most proud of, what let's me sleep easy at night, what holds my chin up, and what makes me say to myself "Hey Paul, you're alright" are those things I've done for other people. Giving so much of myself to help my family get through my dad's drinking problem; being there for friends at times when they were at rock bottom and sometimes even near suicide; helping raise money for charities to help people and animals who are in need; and of course teaching meditation to help people find peace and happiness... those things mean more than anything. And given that you're reading this book and are therefore clearly interested in spirituality and wellbeing, I'm willing to bet that you too are a compassionate and loving person, and that every time you look back on the good deeds you've done you for feel damn proud—and with good reason.

Kindness and compassion will make you happy, will boost your sense of self worth, and will even make you more attractive to other people. And your compassion will also help others. Indeed, any act of compassion that you perform will be as contagious as a common cold. We know that thanks to Jonathan Haidt at the University of Virginia, who conducted research into the affect of kindness on group mentality. He showed that people feel happier when they see other people being kind. A subsequent study by UC San Diego showed when people witness acts of kindness they're more likely to be kind themselves. So, your one act of kindness will make both you yourself and other people happy, and it will also lead other people to be kind too. This rising kindness will then spread like wildfire and before you know it the world will be alight with the warmth of compassion and kindness.

In case you somehow aren't taken by the idea of universal happiness, you might like to know that kindness and compassion have also been proven to make you live longer. Many studies have shown that compassion makes you more resistant to illness and helps you to live a longer life.

And it isn't just good for physical health but mental health too. If you ever suffer from anxiety or depression, do this: Be outrageously kind and compassionate to someone. Just do something really, really nice. Science suggests that your one act of compassion could lift you out of a funk.

Finally, if you're thinking "I'd be a lot kinder and more compassionate if only I had the time," guess what? Science has shown that being kind and compassionate actually makes you feel as though you have more time.

So be kind. Be kind to people. Be kind to nature. Be kind to animals. Just be kind. Because when you're kind, everyone wins.

So let's get started developing our compassion. We can do so by practicing Karuna meditation, which is best when done *after* Loving Kindness.

Loving kindness is like the soil on top of which we build the flowers of compassion. So, practice Loving Kindness Meditation first. Then, when you're ready, try the Karuna technique below.

EXERCISE: Karuna Meditation

1) Find somewhere quiet where you will not be disturbed. Sit with good posture in a comfortable position.

2) Take a few moments to do a body scan meditation, focussing on the sensations in your body. You may also do a breathing meditation before continuing.

3) Bring to mind people who have been unfortunate. Begin with the people for whom you feel the most sympathy. Remember that sincerity is everything in the Karuna meditation technique.

4) Bring to mind one particular individual who has been suffering and whom you would like to help. Wish this individual freedom from their suffering. Wish for them to be happier, healthier, more fortunate, and more successful.

5) You may find it beneficial to speak out your wish for this person. For instance, for someone who is ill you may say, "May they become healthy and strong" or for someone who has been unfortunate with money, "May they find financial security, richness and prosperity." These lines are just examples—express your sincere compassion in the words that feel right to you.

6) If you feel any conflicting emotions—for instance if you feel judgmental towards the person— be mindful of your feelings but do not dwell on them. Simply observe them (if you struggle to do this, you'll find Vipassana and Mindfulness very helpful).

8) Get in touch with the feeling of compassion. Be mindful of it. How does it feel in the body and the mind? Are there any obstacles in the way to true compassion? Be mindful of all that is happening within.

9) Compassion is a feeling, an energy in the body and

mind. Connect with that inner energy of compassion. Meditate on it. The more you meditate on the energy of compassion, the more that energy will grow inside of you, making you more and more compassionate, developing your levels of Karuna one step at a time.

VIPASSANA MEDITATION: HOW TO SEE THE WORLD WITHIN YOU

"A moment's insight is sometimes worth a lifetime's experience."—Oliver Wendell Holmes, Sr.

Do you ever feel as though you're at the mercy of unseen elements? Do you ever act in ways that surprise you, ways you don't understand? Do you continue to live out a life that somehow doesn't feel quite right for you? If so you may be the victim of unconscious aspects of your own mind.

It's one of the unfortunate facts of life that the majority of us are controlled by thoughts and memories that are buried so deep in the mind that they never see the light of day—or rather, the light of *consciousness*.

A couple years ago I was helping a young Canadian guy to overcome shyness. For as long as he could remember he'd been painfully introverted. He couldn't even think about talking to someone without feeling a tightness in his chest. And on those precious few occasion when he was able to speak to someone, he'd become raspberry red and mumble in a way that he said was "like Kenny from South Park".

He'd experienced these same phenomena nearly every time he spoke to anyone. But the bizarre thing was that he had absolutely no clue *why* he was so shy. He knew he needed to talk to people. He knew *how* to talk to people. He simply could not do it.

Usually when someone has an emotional complication that they're aware of but don't understand it's the manifestation of unseen inner turmoil. Something deep down in my friend's mind was making it impossible for him to open up to people. Something within himself was preventing him from being social. The only way that he would ever overcome his shyness was to first become conscious of what was happening beneath the surface of his own mind.

Thankfully, there is one ancient and powerful meditation technique that can empower us to see deeper into our own minds. It's one of the oldest forms of meditation in the world: Vipassana.

Vipassana was born far back in the 6th Century, during the time when Mahayana Buddhism was expanding through the East from India to South East Asia. India had seen an economic boom from the money that Romans were bringing through the country as they made their way to Asia to buy luxurious goods. Trade routes between Burma, Java, and India meant that Asians were put in direct contact with Indian culture. Buddhism, along with the Pali and Sanskrit languages, Indian literature, and meditation, were all brought from India to Asia.

South East Asian empires, which at the time were extremely powerful, began to adopt Buddhism and to create Buddhist architecture and art. The empire of Srivijava in Indonesia adopted Mahayana and Vajrayana Buddhism and became a great centre of Buddhist learning, the emperor supporting over a thousand Buddhist monks at his court. Beautiful statues of bodhisattvas were created along with the temple of Borobudur, the largest Buddhist structure in the world, which is still viewable today.

It was against this backdrop of Buddhist expansion that Vipassana meditation was created, but most of the teachings on Vipassana were lost. Then, in the 1700s, a Burmese monk named Medawi began to teach and write about Vipassana. Medawi was deeply set against the Burmese attitude. The Burmese considered meditation unimportant, believing that it was impossible to reach enlightenment. Medawi was passionate about restoring the Buddha's teachings and wrote over thirty books. His words and wisdom caught the attention of Burmese king, Bodaw-hpaya, who gave him a title and endowment. Medawi mastered Vipassana and taught many other students. Through the line of teaching Vipassana reached Ledi Sayadaw U Ñanadhaja, who would become one of the most famous and influential Theravada Buddhists in history. When western colonialism collapsed in Burma and Sri Lanka, Theravada Buddhism was rejuvenated and reformed and Buddhist literature became immensely popular. One of the most popular texts at the time was "The New Burmese Method of Vipassana", otherwise known as the "Mahasi Method", which was the culmination of the Vipassana teachings, written by Mahasi Sayadaw U Sobhana. This book became the root of what is now considered modern Vipassana meditation.

The term itself, "Vipassana", literally means "insight into true reality". In a nutshell, Vipassana meditation is about seeing into the true nature of things—most importantly, seeing into the true nature of the mind. Specifically, Vipassanaa was used to make monks conscious of the impurities of the mind, impurities which Buddhists call the Three Marks of Existence.

The Three Marks of Existence are Dukkha (suffering), Anatta

(non-self) and Anicca (impermanence). By practicing Vipassana meditation, Buddhists learnt to become conscious of these three "marks", and thereby to weed them out of their minds like thistles in a garden. Today, Vipassana is used to purify the mind, which leads to general wellbeing and positive behaviour. Though the practice is deeply seeped in Buddhist tradition, it can be practiced by Buddhists and non-Buddhists alike.

Contemporary Vipassana is a way to "see into the true nature of your mind" so that you can perceive reality clearly. This helps to create mental balance and clarity of perception, or what Lao Tzu called "Right mind", which leads to right action —action which benefits us in healthy and positive ways.

Less a technique and more a *style*, Vipassana incorporates many different practices, ranging from breathing meditations to body scan and other exercises designed to create *pure perception of reality.*

For instance, we may practice Vipassana for emotional wellbeing. This would entail using meditation to see the pure reality of an emotion. For instance, when feeling sad we wouldn't simply say "I feel sad", we would meditate on the sensation of being sad, discovering precisely what the *reality* and nature of sadness is. If you do this (and I recommend you do the next time you feel blue) you'll discover that emotions are really a combination of physical sensations, visualisations and imaginings. Sadness typically manifests as a trembling of the lips and a *dampness* of spirit, together with visualisations of the root cause of the sadness (for instance, if we've just broken up with someone we will see their face and that will create the sadness). By being aware of this true reality of our emotions we gain understanding, and with understanding we gain power over our emotions.

For my shy friend, whom we were discussing previously, I

believed Vipassana would help him to see the truth about what was happening every time he tried to talk to someone. I taught my shy friend to practice Vipassana so he could become aware of what was happening in his mind, confident that once he understood the true nature of his shyness he would gain power over it.

He practiced several different Vipassana techniques, of which *body scan* and *mindfulness of the internal workings of his mind* were the two most important. Then one day he came to me and told me that he'd suddenly realised what was going on. He had perceived the true nature of his shyness.

He explained that his parents had been very strict and had almost always punished him for speaking out of turn. That had led him to becoming very quiet and to feeling anxious every time he needed to speak. He never really thought directly about his parents punishing him, but every time he wanted to speak he'd feel a tension throughout his jaw and his front teeth would clamp down on the tip of his tongue—clamping on the tongue is actually a classic body language gesture that people make when they're nervous of talking, the teeth clamping down to stop the tongue from moving, making it impossible to speak.

At the same time he was performing these unconscious body language gestures he would see a very subtle, almost unperceivable image of his parents in his mind's eye. This was the reality of his shyness. Those three things—the image of his parents, clamping on his tongue, and tension in his jaw—*were* his shyness.

Vipassana made him aware of what was happening. His mind was automatically creating fear and that fear was expressing itself physiologically through the clamping of his tongue between his teeth, the tense jaw, and the vision of his parents.

By being aware he was quite quickly able to change. We

decided that he should begin by focussing on not clamping down on his tongue. That made him more relaxed when he wanted to speak. After a few days without the clamping he started to speak (just gradually at first). He continued to practice Vipassana for months, gradually changing and being liberated all the while, like the butterfly emerging from out the chrysalis. Now, today, he is completely cured of shyness and is actually a confident speaker. He's also a perfect example of how Vipassana, or "insight into the true nature of things", can be immensely empowering.

To change something, you first need to become aware of what it is you need to change. Vipassana gives you awareness of your mind so you can change your mental habits.

To understand the true power of Vipassana you first have to grasp the complexity and power of your own mind. Your mind controls your reality. Your entire world is carried with you in your mind.

As Zen master Thich Nhat Hanh said, "You carry Mother Earth within you. She is not outside of you. Mother Earth is not just your environment. In that insight of inter-being, it is possible to have real communication with the Earth, which is the highest form of prayer."

When you look within, you often see much more than you do simply looking without. That's why Vipassana is so powerful: because it guides you from the superficial nature of external reality to the oceanic depths within. Once you take control of those inner currents, you take control of the entire ocean of being.

EXERCISE: Vipassana

1: The Buddha himself said that Vipassana meditation is best practiced under a tree in a forest or in a similarly peaceful environment. You can practice Vipassana meditation at home if you prefer, but do make sure that you have a peaceful space to meditate.

2: Vipassana meditation is best practiced while sitting with the legs crossed in lotus position. But if you find this position uncomfortable, feel free to adopt any position in which you are comfortable and in which you will not need to fidget. If you have back pain, for instance, you will find it much better to sit on a chair or to lie on a bed, either of which is fine.

Whichever position you opt for, it is important that you have good posture. This helps energy to flow naturally through the body and also helps to create mental stability and focus.

3: Once you are sitting down, close your eyes. Breathe in and focus on your abdomen. Do not attempt to control your breathing, but rather breathe in a relaxed manner. As you breathe, focus on the sensations in your body. Focus on the rising and falling of your abdomen as you breathe.

4: Aim to be aware of the entire breathing process. Reach down with your mind and feel the sensations arising in your abdomen. Hold your focus locked on the breath in the abdomen. Breathe in and breathe out with both body and mind. Body leads and mind follows.

5: Come to understand the breathing process as one movement. We usually understand our breathing as a process of three steps. We breathe in, pause, and then breathe out. But the process is one and so should the focus be. Don't focus on in-breath, pause, out-breath. Be mindful of the entire process as one movement. At the same time, don't force your mind. The focus should be natural and relaxed and there should be no mental strain. Rest the mind on the present moment.

6: It can be challenging to maintain focus for extended periods. If your focus wanders, offer your mind support. You can do this by saying to yourself, "My breath is rising... rising. Pausing. And now falling." Describing the movement of your breath in this way will help you to maintain focus.

7: If your mind creates thoughts, simply tell yourself, "I am thinking" and then re-aim your mental focus on your breathing.

8: If your mind wanders don't judge yourself. Don't say "I'm not focusing enough." Though we try, it is impossible to maintain focus 100% of the time. Even the most advanced meditator experiences some moments when the mind wanders. Simply guide the mind back to the rising and falling of your abdomen.

9: There will be times when a specific noise or distraction draws your attention. For instance, if you're meditating at home when the doorbell rings your mind will immediately jump at the sound. This is one example of an *intrusive event*. These intrusive events lure the mind. We immediately lose focus and instead of focusing on breathing we pay attention to the event. Be mindful of what is actually happening when you are distracted. In the instance of the doorbell, mindfully observe the event and label it as a sensation—e.g. mindfully observe the sound and label it "Sound." This helps your mind to recognise the nature of external stimuli. Having observed and labelled the sensation, return your focus to your breathing.

10: At times you will also notice sensations that occur in the body. Perhaps you feel an itch in your legs, or a tingling at the back of your neck. Label these sensations by describing the way the sensation feels. If you feel a warm air moving over your wrist, for instance, mindfully observe that sensation and say "warm movement." This is just an example.

11: Mental sensations such as thoughts and imaginings can

also be labelled. For instance, if you see an image in your mind, label it "Mental image." Describe the precise reality of what the thing is. If you imagine hearing a sound, say "Imagined sound" and so on. Don't attach *unreality* to any mental phenomena. If, for instance, you visualise the face of a friend in your mind's eye, don't say "That's my friend's face" because, of course, it *isn't actually your friend's face,* it's just a mental image, so label it as such. This process is immensely helpful. Most people are constantly being deceived by their mind. They come to think that the things they see and hear in their mind are real. Just by saying "Mental image" or "Imagined sound" you train your mind to understand the true nature of mentally constructed information.

12: There is a specific way to end Vipassana meditation. It is important to not just open your eyes and immediately go about your ordinary day. Instead, open your eyes slowly, telling yourself "opening, opening." Then, when you begin to choose what to do next, say "Intending, intending". Then slowly and mindfully begin to go about your day.

13: It is best to continue the Vipassana process for the whole day. This doesn't mean that you have to literally continue meditating for the whole day. Rather, when going about your day, be mindful of what's going on inside of you. Do one thing at a time. Should thoughts enter your mind, label them in the manner described above. This helps to cultivate insight and mindfulness in your day to day reality.

Vipassana is all about insight. The insight you create is awareness into the true nature of reality. The process of observing and labelling helps the mind to realise what is real and what is a mental construction, which sounds as though it should be immediately obvious but is actually quite complicated. Simply think about the last time a thought made you unhappy. For instance, of all the times I think about my father the majority of times the thoughts are positive: his smile, his comforting presence, his generosity, the silly way he said that absolutely everything was "Just perfect". But sometimes my thoughts are negative; sometimes they're about his drinking and the emotional pain my family went through. The moment I begin to think about my father's drinking I feel a sinking in my gut, which is a sign of approaching sadness. Had I not practiced Vipassana I would likely dwell on that sadness and allow it to affect me. But thanks to Vipassana, thanks to *insight,* I'm able to say "That feeling is just a sensation. It doesn't mean anything." I'm able to quell the onset of sadness before it takes hold of me.

Practice Vipassana and you'll gain powerful insight into the true nature of reality and the nature of your own mind. That insight will empower you to liberate yourself from the trappings of the mind. Emotions, painful thoughts, stress…they will melt like butter in a pan against the warm light of pure perception.

Dhyana Meditation : Overcoming The "Self" And Finding Oneness

All things are linked with one another, and this oneness is sacred – Marcus Aerilius

Whether practicing meditation as a spiritual practice or as an entirely practical thing, it's important to start with Samatha. Samatha calms and focuses the mind, allowing you to concentrate. Once you're able to concentrate properly, you can then begin Vipassana, which will produce insight and allow you to take control of your mind. Having calmed and taken control of your mind, you will then be prepared to advance to the next stage: Dhyana.

Dhyana is oneness meditation and is one of the most advanced stages of practice. If you've been following along with the meditation techniques in the book so far, and you've been successful at each of the techniques we've tried, then you'll be ready to move on to Dhyana.

Dhyana meditation is a Hindu and Buddhist practice that may have begun with Buddha or may have begun prior to Buddha, in Hinduism. Historians aren't actually sure precisely when Dhyana meditation was born. But many believe that Dhyana was first mentioned in the Hindu text the *Upanishads*.

It's in the Upanishads that you'll find the conversation between Prince Arjuna and Lord Krishna that we were discussing earlier. In Upanishads, Krishna advises Arjuna to "fulfil his Kshatriya duty as a warrior and establish Dharma", which led to the development of Hindu dharma. Many historians believe it was in this conversation between prince Arjuna and Lord Krishna that Dhyana was first mentioned. In the conversation, Dhyana meditation is a synthesis of Hindu and Yogic practices. As such, Dhyana meditation is important in yoga,

Hinduism, and Buddhism.

Many believe the term Dhyana was first mentioned in the discussions between Prince Arjuna and Lord Krishna, which is depicted in the Hindu classic the Upanishads.

Dhyana literally means "Deeper awareness of oneness". The term "oneness" has spiritual and religious overtones primarily because it is so closely associated with Buddhism and Hinduism. But in truth oneness needn't be spiritual at all. In fact, regardless of your spiritual or religious beliefs, you will almost definitely have experienced at least a few moments of oneness in your life.

One of the most powerful feelings of oneness I personally ever experienced was during the London Marathon (I ran in support of the Blue Cross, an animal charity in the UK). There are many beautiful sights to take in during the course of the 26 miles (42 kilometre) race. But one particular sight will always stay with me. At mile 6 a sharp descent leads you down to the Cutty Sark, the famous ship from the 1800s. It's here that the three different runners' paths converge. Thousands of runners come together like birds gathering into formation as one giant flock; tens of thousands of runners all heading down the same road. It lights a fire in the belly. I distinctly remember the feeling of lightness in my legs as I ran down that hill, the wind in my hair, the salt of sweat in my eyes. The moment was everything. There was no *me,* no *self*, no thoughts, no separation between myself and the thousands of other runners. It was a moment of complete oneness.

I would later experience another moment of profound oneness, during the death of my old cat, Tibby. She was 19—remarkably old for a cat. She had been weakening and weakening. Her old eyes were barely open. My mother and I knew that Tibby was close to death from the shallow gasps of breath and the film over her eyes. Tibby had always been my mother's cat. They spent so much time together. They truly were very close family. Just before Tibby drew her last breath she fought a little and with her last gasp of energy managed to crawl up onto my mother's lap. That was the very last thing she did: taking a seat on my mother's lap, choosing to die with the person she'd spent all her life with. It was a truly beautiful moment. At the time of Tibby's death I was not myself. I experienced a moment of profound oneness with her, a feeling that those old grey whiskers were my old grey whiskers, that those tired eyes that were gently falling to quietude and rest were my own eyes. Looking up, I saw my mother sitting perfectly still, statuesque; and it was as though my own spirit was intertwined with hers.

Moments of oneness are divine. They can take your breath away, uplift your spirit, quell all fear and sadness, and forge memories that last forever. And beyond their emotional and spiritual potency, moments of oneness can also offer valuable down-to-Earth, practical benefits.

Consider, for example, the benefit that oneness can have on your everyday work. If you're one of the millions of people who work in a less than ideal working environment (*I'm definitely one of them*), then you're probably well aware of the amount of effort it takes just to focus, and the amount of time you waste on unnecessary distractions. Phones, voices talking, your own rumbling tummy, stresses that are on your mind… it all adds up to prevent you from being able to work effectively. Imagine if you were able to shut off all that noise so that the only things that exist in the world are you and the task you're trying to achieve. Imagine how much more you'd get done.

When you achieve complete oneness—when you become one with an object or task—you'll find you're a million times more effective and also significantly happier because you're able to dedicate your entire mind to one thing at a time.

You can achieve that state of oneness through Dhyana meditation, a practice in which you train your mind to become one with the object, person, or task of your choosing.

To better understand how Dhyana meditation works, imagine yourself as having three points. The first point is the origin. This is the very core from which your consciousness stems. It is like the sun. It is the creator.

The second point is your mind body. Here you may be aware of thoughts, feelings and sensations.
These thoughts, feelings and sensations are like clouds that prevent the sun from breaking through.

The third and final part is reality itself. If you are meditating on an object, on your breath for instance, this third part will be that object. In a breathing meditation the third part is the breath. Likewise, in a candle meditation the third part is the candle.

In Dhyana meditation you are only aware of points 1 and 2. You are aware of the origin of your own consciousness, and you are aware of the object on which you are meditating.

By removing the second point (the thoughts and feelings that muddy our perception) we put consciousness in direct contact with the object of meditation. This is Dhyana: oneness.

EXERCISE: Dhyana meditation

1: Choose a relaxing object to meditate on (you can use your breath or a physical object or an object you are visualizing in your mind).

2: Dhyana begins like most other meditation techniques. Take a moment to relax your mind and to focus.

3: Detach. Allow the mind to be still, and you allow your consciousness and the object of meditation to fuse together as though they are one.

4: Where Dhyana differentiates itself from other meditation techniques is in its *directness*. Usually, when we're meditating we meditate via the senses. When meditating on the breath, for instance, we usually meditate on the *feeling* of the breath coming and going. When meditating on a candle we meditate on the *sight* of the candle. When meditating on music we meditate on the *sound*. We're meditating *via our senses*. But Dhyana does not involve the senses. It involves only the mind itself. The mind is focused on the resting place, on the origin, on "the centre of being".

5: Achieve stillness. When meditating in the traditional sense there is a sense of *direction*. If you are inwardly quiet and investigate what happens when your mind focuses on an object, you'll see that the mind generally *reaches out* for that object, as though you're positioning your consciousness on the object. This is not the case when practicing Dhyana. In Dhyana the mind is still. It's as though the object of meditation is merging with the mind at the centre of origin, rather than the mind reaching out for the object. This is a subtle but very important difference, because it is effortless. Meditation involves concentrated effort to focus on an object. Dhyana is effortless focus, a focus of stillness.

In Dhyana we are made one, absolutely, with the object. We are not the person sitting at the edge of ocean watching the waves. We are the waves themselves. We are not the meditator. We are the object.

Do not sit at the edge of the sea watching the waves. Aim instead to become the waves themselves.

HINDU & YOGIC MEDITATION

Hinduism and yoga go hand in hand. In fact there's an interesting debate about whether yoga is a Hindu practice—mostly because yoga was first mentioned in the Hindu spiritual text The Upanishads.

Hinduism is the world's oldest religion and was one of the most important factors in the creation and development of meditation.

Many of my acquaintances often debate among themselves as to which religion, Hinduism or Buddhism, actually created meditation (it's a fascinating conversation). Some argue that Buddha was born a Hindu and was familiar with Hindu practices, so therefore the practice of meditation derives from Hinduism. Others argue that meditation as we know it was not created until the beginning of Buddhism and is therefore a Buddhist practice.

Either way, there are a great many similarities between Hindu and Buddhist meditation techniques, but also some important differences.

In Hinduism meditation is called Dhyana or Jhana. If you have ever spoken to a Hindu meditation teacher you will likely have heard them discussing how to use Dhyana to cultivate oneness; to heighten awareness of body, surroundings, and senses; to obtain self knowledge; and to achieve "mokṣa", which is the highest achievement, the liberation of self from the perpetual cycle of death and rebirth.

In Hinduism, meditation first appeared in the classic text the Upanishads, a collection of dialogues between Hindu sages and their students, in which the sages discuss meditation as being "deeper concentration of the mind" and leading to "great self knowledge and liberation from the illusion of Maya, the illusion of the material world".

It's quite interesting that the sages should discuss meditation in this way, as liberating the mind from the illusion of the material world. Although we here in the West in the twenty-first century might have a slightly different view of precisely what the material world *is* and what "Maya" or "illusion" is, we can all identify with the idea of being bound to and slave to the ever-changing material world.

The material world (and the illusion thereof) is one of the biggest causes of stress and suffering. We feel stressed when we are out of a job, for instance. There's no financial security. We worry that we won't pay the bills. We fear we may default on our mortgage. But have you noticed that in all these statements ("financial security", "worrying about bills" "fearing defaulting on the mortgage") there are two elements: there's the mental state (fear, worry, etc.) and then the physical reality (money, mortgage, bills, etc.). We trick ourselves into believing that a physical thing (the job) will alleviate the mental state (stress, worry, etc.) where in actual fact they are two completely separate things.

The mind creates the illusion that the mental state is somehow tied to the physical state (that getting a job will quell stress). But this simply isn't the case. After all, how many people feel stressed even once they've secured a high paying job? Once we have that high paying job the mind then tricks us again, saying "The stress will now go once I've been promoted". But the stress never goes. It never goes because the mind is tricking itself into believing that a physical reality will heal a mental reality, when the two are actually separate. That is illusion. When Hindus meditate the chief purpose of their meditation is to achieve self knowledge and self realisation by liberating themselves from such illusions. Of course, I've given a very modern example here, but the general principle has remained the same for thousands of years. It's one of the many ways in which ancient customs are applicable to modern lives, one way in which those sacred texts that were written thousands of years ago are still relevant in the twenty first century.

One of the most important of classic Hindu texts is the Bhagavad Gita, a narrative that shows a dialogue between Pandava prince Arjuna and his guide and charioteer Krishna.

In the Gita, Arjuna is faced with a duty to fight the righteous war between two opposing sides, the Pandavas and the Kauravas. Krishna advises Arjuna to "fulfill his Kshatriya (societal) duty as a warrior and establish Dharma." It is this dialogue that introduces the Dhyana Yoga system, the Hindu meditation system that synthesises Dharma (the Hindu order) with Bhakti (faith and worship).

Meditation in the Hindu tradition begins with "Dharana", a technique in which the practitioner focuses the mind and sight between the eyebrows. This develops concentration. While focusing on this fixed spot energy enters the mind. This energy gradually builds and the focus intensifies, leading to meditation and the state called Samadhi, a point of extreme concentration.

Unlike most other forms of meditation, when practicing meditation in the Hindu tradition, the practitioner is not aware of the fact that they are meditating. They are only aware of their own existence and the object on which they are meditating. This creates a powerful sense of oneness. It is a beautiful and powerful experience in which nothing exists but the individual and the object of meditation, fused as though they are one.

There are many different types of meditation in the Hindu system. One of the most important is mantra meditation, which involves the recitation of specific words or sounds.

If you visit India during a religious celebration, such as Krishna Janmaashtami (the festival which celebrates the birth of Krishna), you will hear Hindus reciting mantras throughout the night, showing devotion.

The specific mantra that is recited is dependent on which god is being worshipped. It is believed that by reciting mantras to the gods Hindus not only show their devotion but also receive specific blessings. Some mantras are said to create wealth, some longevity, others happiness, and so on. There are even mantras for finding lovers and for paying off debt.

It is believed that these mantras work one of two ways. The first way is the strictly spiritual way, the idea that reciting mantras from ancient religious text will conjure specific real-world outcomes. The second way is more scientific and practical and revolves around energy resonance. Different sounds occur at different frequencies. Therefore, when you produce a specific sound in your body you change the frequency of the energy of your body (and also the energy in your mind). Different energies create different physical and mental states. So in effect you can influence your body and mind by reciting mantras of varying frequencies.

But mantras do not have to be used expressly for worship or for specific ambitions. They can also be used for pure relaxation. Indeed, mantras are one of the best entry points to meditation, because the act of reciting the mantra gives the mind something to focus on, which helps us to stay with the meditation as opposed to being lost in distractions.

Stemming from Hinduism are the meditations found in yoga.

There are a great many yogic meditations, which date right back to 1700 B.C. These meditations aim to create enlightenment and self knowledge, and they form just one part of a much larger discipline.

A complex discipline, the classic yoga system involves rules of conduct (yamas and niyamas), physical postures (asanas), breathing (pranayama) and contemplation (pratyahara, dharana, Dhyana, samadhi). Today, yoga is typically viewed as a physical exercise, but in truth it is a very deep spirituality that involves both physical and mental exercises along with beliefs and principles.

To properly perform yogic meditations, it's important to understand and to use the full yogic system. However, there are many yogic techniques that can be adapted for a more practical (and easier) use. For instance, yogic meditations include Trataka (focusing intensely on a small point to bring energy to the Third Eye, as we looked at in our discussion of Closed meditations), Nada (meditating on sound) Tantra (which, despite what Sting might have told us all, has little to do with sex and more to do with contemplation), and Pranayama (breathing). Many of these techniques can be used readily by newcomers, but others are dependent on more advanced knowledge—for instance, you may have heard of the term "Kundalini yoga", which deals with the *kundalini energy* said to be dormant in the body.

Let's take a look at the most popular and best meditations from Hinduism and yoga.

MANTRA MEDITATION

A mantra is a sacred word or sound usually in Sanskrit that is believed to produce spiritual, psychological, or physical benefits to the person who utters it. In this way, they are comparable to spells, incantations and prayer formulas, though there are significant differences.

Meditation mantras have existed for more than 3000 years.Over the years, we have seen the growth of Hindu, Buddhist, Jainist, and yoga mantras, and today there are also self-improvement *affirmations*, which work in similar ways.You can find concepts similar to mantras in Japanese Shingon, Christianity, Zoroastrianism, tantra and Taoism.

The exact meaning and definition of a mantra varies depending on the specific culture or spirituality that we're looking at. For instance, tantra mantras are considered sacred, where some other fomrs just use relaxing sounds.Not only are there mantras in different spiritualities, such as Buddhist mantras and Hindu ones, but there are different *types* too. There are musical mantras that are chanted and that use exact musical measurements.

Kundalini mantras, for instance, often involves specific musical notes. And there are fundamental one-syllable mantras like Om ("Aum") which is one of the Buddhist meditation mantras beginners may have heard of, and is one of the primordial sounds. There are 108 primordial sounds that are used.

Some masters state that meditation mantras are thoughts that have magical or spiritual powers.

For instance, in *An Outline Of The Religious Literature In India*, J. Farguhur states meditation mantras are religious thoughts or prayers that have supernatural powers. And in Heinrich Robert Zimmer's *Myths and Symbols in Indian Art and Civilization*, meditation mantras are defined as verbal instruments that produce certain qualities or traits in an individual's mind.

One of the most hotly debated questions about mantras is this: do they meaning anything, or are the words meaningless?

When we use meditation mantras, are we saying anything specific?

Some masters will tell you that the precise sounds do not mean anything and that a mantra's function is musical in nature, that the power of the sacred sounds comes from resonance, rhythm and metres.

Other masters say that meditation mantras are precise mental instruments with precise meanings.

What is universally agreed, however, is that meditation mantras have a meter, rhythm and melody that is essential to their purpose. In other words, *you cannot just repeat a meditation mantra over and over; you have to use them musically.*

Another view says that meditation mantras mean absolutely nothing and that the sounds are similar to the utterances in folk music where singers make sounds that evoke certain feelings but which ultimately do not have any linguistic definition. Instead, what is important is the sound quality. This is the explanation offered by Frits Staal in *Rituals And Mantras: Rules Without Meaning*.

The important take-away from this is: *When you use meditation mantras, as well as pronouncing the words correctly, you must also use the correct musical qualities. Why?* Because the meaning of mantras is usually not as important as the sound and feeling that they evoke.

The auditory faculty of human beings has evolved to include certain constants that create the foundations of our auditory composition. Those tiny little bits of sound (syllables, grunts, etc.) have been with us for millions of years. And they have helped us to make sense of the world.

Just like birds sing to tell each other about the weather, we have used utterances to communicate with one another and to become informed about the world around us. Sound works through echoes. A ball hits the wall of your house; soundwaves pass around the environment bouncing off of objects until we interpret them. That's basically how sound works. And it's out of these echoes that our speech was born.

In his book *Harnessed: How Language and Music Mimicked Nature and Transformed Ape to Man,* neuroscientist Mark Changizi posits that the major phenomes of speech have evolved to resemble the sounds of nature. You can hear this when you speak. Think about specific words, like "crash", "honk, and "giggle", and you can hear the sound of the event itself in the word. In other words, they are onomatopoetic. Some languages are more onomatopoetic than others. Sanskrit, which happens to be the language that most mantras come from, is a very onomatopoetic language. Most classic mantras come from Sanskrit, so they too are very onomatopoetic. Therefore, when we use meditation mantras, we hear echoes of nature

The Four Koshas

When we talk about literal meaning and sound quality, we are really talking about *kosha.*

There are four koshas (levels) of a meditation mantra.

Literal meaning: This is the primary level. At this level, we understand the meaning of the sound as though it were any other word.

Feeling: This is a more subtle level at which we feel the meaning.

Inner awareness: This is the level at which we experience the sound inwardly.

Soundless sound: This is the deepest and most profound level of a mantra.

When you perform Japa (recitation of mantras), you aim

to pass from the primary level to the deepest level, to take the mantra from its literal meaning and to journey with it to soundless sound, the deepest level.

There is a science to meditation mantras.

These primordial sounds create echoes of nature in the body.

A fascinating fact about sounds is that the sounds themselves reverberate in the mind and body. So when you speak, you are creating physical events in the body and mind.

So, if mantras are based on the sounds of nature, and when we create vocal sounds, we produce physical events in the body, then logically when we recite a mantra (Japa) we create a physical event that is an echo of nature in the mind and body.

The third aspect of mantras is meditation. Meditating on mantras puts our consciousness inside the sound, or to put it another way. It puts consciousness inside the echo of nature.

Put all that together, and you realise that when you perform meditation mantras, you create a physical echo of nature in the body and mind. You then place your consciousness inside that echo of nature by meditating. Your entire being is now being affected by the sound. And that is where their power originates.

Best meditation mantra for beginners

OM

The absolute best meditation mantra for beginners is "Om", which is pronounced "Aum".

This entire sound is a sonorant and it does not feature plosives or fricative—it is an entirely "open" sound. Make the sound now, and you will see what I mean. Because Om is entirely sonorant, it is entirely "open".

Vocal sounds resemble nature. "Crash" resembles a crash. "Honk" resembles a honk. What does "Om" resemble? Formlessness. There are no sonorants and no fricatives, so the sound is empty. When we recite "Om", we create an echo of formlessness in the body. We then place our consciousness inside it by meditating. And the result is to return us to the point of formless existence. When we meditate on the open sound we clear the mind and return to our purest form.

Hindu Meditation Mantras for Beginners

The history of meditation mantras begins with Sanskrit words used in Hinduism. These originated during the Vedic period when writers and gurus became fascinated by poetry, which they saw as divine and inspiring. This poetry formed the foundation of mantras.

This passion for poetry and sound led to a 500 year period in which meditation mantras were written and recorded. If you've ever wondered where mantras come from, it is from this 500 year period.

The meditation mantras were diversified during the period of the Hindu Epics when they were adopted by Hindu schools. Meditation mantras then evolved through the Tantric school. This school taught that each mantra represented a deity, which is how many still think of them today. In the Vedic tradition, meditation mantras were not just recited. They were used together with ritual acts. For instance, when practising Bagalamukhi mantra, which is used for protection, the ritual is to wear yellow clothes and a yellow rosary and to offer flowers to the deity Bagalamukhi. This is just one example of a ritual act used in a mantra.

Meditation mantras evolved further through Buddhism and Jainism.

Buddhism and Jainism stemmed off from Hinduism, and the split caused major changes in the evolution of mantras. Hindus began to use mantras as a way to ask the gods to help them, for instance, to save them from illness. And later Hindus used them to transcend past the perpetual cycle of life and death. This led to different types of mantras, including anirukta (not enunciated) upamsu (inaudible) and manasa (not spoken but recited in mind) as well as chants and spoken mantras.

In the Tantric belief, the universe is comprised of sound, and the supreme (para) creates the universe through the word, Shabda. The universe is comprised of different frequencies and levels of sound. In Tantra, mantras are essential, and again there are different types, which are marked by their length and structure. For instance, mala mantras contain a very long chain of syllables, where bija mantras are only one single syllable that ends with a nasal sound that is called anusvara. These sounds relate to different gods, with dum being Durga, gam being Ganesha, and so on. These bijas are used in different combinations, which leads to the creation of longer mantras. In the tantric tradition, it is believed that meditation mantras give a person supernatural strengths

In many Hindu meditation mantras, it is necessary to repeat the sound a certain number of times. This is called Mantra Japa, which refers to mantras that are repeated a specific number of times, often 108 and usually with the aid of a meditation mala/rosary.

Examples

Gayatri Mantra: Used for invoking the universal Braham.

ॐ भूर्भुवस्वः | तत्सवितुर्वरेण्यम् | भर्गो देवस्य धीमहि | धियो यो नः प्रचोदयात्

Oṁ Bhūrbhuvaswaha Tatsaviturvarenyam bhargo devasya dhīmahi dhiyo yo naḥa prachodayāt

"Let us meditate on that excellent glory of the divine Light (Vivifier, Sun). May he stimulate our understandings (knowledge, intellectual illumination)."

Pavamana

असतोमा सद्गमय | तमसोमा ज्योतिर् गमय | मृत्योर्मामृतं गमय || asato mā sad gamaya, tamaso mā jyotir gamaya, mṛtyor māmṛtaṁ gamaya.

"from the unreal lead me to the real, from the dark lead me to the light, from death lead me to immortality.

Shanti

Oṁ Sahanā vavatu

sahanau bhunaktu

Sahavīryam karavāvahai

Tejasvi nāvadhītamastu

Mā vidviṣāvahai

Oṁ Shāntiḥ, Shāntiḥ, Shāntiḥ.

"Om! Let the Studies that we together undertake be effulgent;

"Let there be no Animosity amongst us;

"Om! Peace, Peace, Peace.

Buddhist Meditation Mantras For Beginners

You have probably heard or read Buddhist meditation mantras before. If you look at old Buddhist art or items, you will notice that the Buddha holds malas (beads) and that there are little decorative fences around the piece. These "fences" and beads are symbolic of Buddhist meditation mantras that have been around since the time of Guatama Sidhartha.

Because they are rarely mentioned in the sutras, the common belief is that Buddha Shakyamuni's dharma system did not include mantras. But the system does include the Heart Sutra mantra "OM, Gate, gate, paragate, parasumgate, bodhi, Swaha". And historians state that the Buddha taught protective dharanis or charms to hermits in the forest who lived in isolated places. And that was the beginning of Buddhist meditation mantras —they were used as protections for the mind (as a fence protects land, a mantra protects the mind).

In Buddhism, meditation mantras are believed to be divine and it is important to have reverence for Buddhist mantras if they are to work. Because Buddhist meditation mantras have to be *believed* in order to work, many modern scientists determine that they work as placebos, that their magic is the magic of the mind and that because the mind believes it is being healed it will indeed be healed.

In Buddhism (and most similar faiths) mantras are comprised of one or more syllables. Most Buddhist meditation mantras relate to one specific deity and are used as a way to express devotion to that deity. The essence of both the deity and of the mantra is contained in the seed syllable, also called the "bijas". Sanskrit "A", for instance, contains the essence of the Heart Sutra.

Buddhist meditation mantras usually work by emptying the mind, then visualising the seed syllable, then letting the visualisation grow into the form of the deity related to that seed.

The most famous bija or seed syllable is Om, pronounced "Aum", which I previously mentioned is the best meditation mantra for beginners. Om is the universe and all that is, all that was, and all that ever will be.

The letters of Aum also represent specific things:

A = alret

U = dreaming

M = asleep

And then there is the silence that followed the mantra, which is used to represent emptiness.

Visualising Om, Ah and Hung

"Om ah hung" is a Buddhist mantra for mental health.

One of the most important mantra techniques in Buddhism is a technique in which we recite Om, AH, and HUNG while visualising those syllables at the head, throat and heart. At the same time, we visualise receiving a guru's Body, Speech and Mind. In this technique, the three syllables are different colours.

Om Mani Padme Hum

Om Mani Padme Hum is a mantra that is used to invoke the blessings of Cenrezig, the embodiment of compassion. You can read much more about the meaning of this Buddhist mantra via the link above.

Shakyamuni

Oṃ muni muni mahāmuni śākyamuni svāhā Om muni muni mahamuni shakyamuni svaha

OR

Om muni muni mahamuni shakyamuniye svaha

Guatama Sidhartha is also called the Shakyamuni Buddha, who is the sage of the Shakyan clan and the first person to achieve enlightenment.

The meaning of this Buddhist meditation mantra is "Om wise one, wise one, greatly wise one, wise one of the Shakyans, Hail!"

Amitabha

Oṃ Amideva Hrīḥ

This is the mantra of the celestial Buddha, Amitabha. It is the best meditation mantra for protection from dangers and for overcoming obstacles. It also boosts loving-kindness and compassion.

White Tara

Oṃ Tāre Tuttāre Ture Mama Ayuḥ Punya Jñānā Puṣtiṃ Kuru Svāhā

White Tara is associated with longevity. This mantra is usually chanted with a specific person in mind. It is the best meditation mantra for breaking through limitations.

Green Tara

OM TARE TUTTARE TURE SOHA

The Green Tara is the best meditation mantras to use to overcome emotional, mental, and physical blockages. It is also a mantra for good relationships.

Medicine Buddha

Tayata Om Bekanze Bekanze Maha BeKanze Radza Samudgate Soha

The Medicine Buddha mantra is recited for success. It is also the best meditation mantra to use to stop unhappiness and suffering.

Manjushri

Om A Ra Pa Ca Na Dhih

This is a wisdom mantra and the best meditation mantra for memory, writing, debating and similar tasks.

Vajrapani

Om Vajrapani Hum

This is the best meditation mantra to stop hatred.

As you can see from the meanings of Buddhist meditation mantras, in the Buddhist tradition mantras are used mostly to develop positive mental traits and to connect with Buddha.

Some of the meanings of Buddhist mantras are similar to the meanings of Hindu ones. Where Buddhist and Hindu mantras differ is that there are far more Hindu mantras, and Hindus also use mantras for many more reasons than Buddhists do. In Hinduism you will find mantras effective to almost all personal and health problems, where Buddhists have less mantras and they are used for only a select number of reasons.

EXERCISE: Mantra Meditation

1. Find the mantra you would like to recite and make sure you understand it fully. You should know what it is used for, which deity it represents, and if there is a certain rhythm or musical meter that you should use. Naturally, you should also make sure that you know how to pronounce the mantra accurately.

2. For some meditation mantras, and particularly Hindu ones, there might be a specific ritual to perform before or during the mantra. Make sure to check this.

3. Meditate for a short while in order to clear your

mind.

4. Begin to recite the mantra with the right musical tone and rhythm.
5. For some mantras, and especially Buddhist mantras, you will also use visualisation techniques.
6. Continue for a full round of mantra repetition. For many mantras this is 108 repetitions.
7. As you progress you should move through the four koshas (you can read about the four koshas above)
8. This is the basic process of meditation mantras for beginners. However, the specific mantra you are using may have additional instructions.
9. Sit still for five to ten minutes to relax.
10. Express thanks for the mantra and the deity, if there is one.
11. You can take this further by doing Bhakti, which we will look at next.

BHAKTI MEDITATION

The self is all. And the all is selfless.

Once you have calmed and focused your mind with *Samatha meditation* and learnt to be one with an object through Dhyana meditation, you will be prepared for Bhakti, a style of meditation based on a movement within the Hindu faith.

The Bhakti movement began in the 7th Century at a time of great social change in India, when Hinduism was reformed from its old caste-based system towards a system focused on individualism.

Traditional worship of God was becoming outmoded. In its place came the Bhakti philosophy that God should be loved and respected as a close friend or lover. The poet-saints championed a variety of new philosophies, moving against rituals, ceremonies and idol worship towards more of an individual expression of love and devotion. They advocated the use of art as a means of devotion, which led to the creation of many songs, poems and chants being used to express love of god(s).

The term "bhakti" literally means to "show devotion and love to". This is achieved by focusing the mind on the object of worship and becoming one with that object in a marriage formed of love and devotion. Traditionally, the objects that were worshipped were the gods Vishnu and Shiva.

In order to remain in contact with God, nine types of devotional practice were used:

1) Sravaṇa (listening to scriptures and stories)

2) Kīrtana (praise which is actually ecstatic singing)

3) Visnoh smaraṇa (remembering or "Fixing the mind" on God)

4) Pāda-sevana (rendering service)

5) Arcana (worshipping an image)

6) Vandana (paying homage)

7) Dāsya (servitude)

8) Sākhya (friendship)

9) Atma-nivedana (complete surrender)

Meditation is considered one of the most important practices on the Bhakti path and the absolute best way to achieve oneness with God.

Today, Bhakti is still practiced to develop oneness with God, but in the West the technique has been adapted to allow for a more generic use. You don't need to be devoted or a worshipper in order to practice Bhakti meditation, and you also don't have to be a Hindu or Buddhist, or even religious. For my five cents, if a technique helps you to live a healthier and better life, you should use it, regardless of what religion you are and what you do or do not believe in. After all, we're all one, right?

Bhakti is a wonderfully healthy and positive technique that began in Hinduism but which has subsequently evolved over the past 1300 years. Having been used to create oneness with God(s), it can now be used to create oneness with any object that is highly positive and sacred or spiritual in nature.

The core idea behind Bhakti meditation is that when you become one with an object you will absorb the positive qualities of that object into your own mind. Buddhists, for instance, will meditate upon the peaceful, loving, and enlightened nature of the Buddha. They will make themselves one with the Buddha, and in so doing will gain insight into the nature of the Buddha and will develop the positive qualities of the Buddha in themselves. Christians may do likewise with God or Jesus Christ. And so on. Naturally, if you're religious you'll know your god(s) and will most likely want to meditate on them. But if you're non-religious you might like to practice Bhakti by meditating on your choice of positive person, creature, or object. If, for instance, you are a lover of water and appreciate the way in which water flows so freely and powerfully from one place to the next, you might like to sit beside a river and meditate on the flowing tide. You will find this immensely liberating.

I personally love to practice Bhakti by meditating on the elements. I might sit beside a waterfall and meditate on water, or light a candle and meditate on the way that bright amber light shines its energy in all directions and without shadow. This makes me aware of how I can be compassionate and loving to all, without the need to take sides or harbour prejudices.

Exercise: Bhakti Meditation

1: In order to practice Bhakti successfully it's imperative to practice Samatha and Dhyana first. These will calm and centre your mind, creating the necessary focus and inner peace needed for Bhakti.

2: Once your mind is calm and centred, choose a subject on which to meditate. Choose a subject that is highly positive and which contains traits that you would like to have in yourself. For instance, if you would like to develop your sense of freedom you might like to meditate on a clear blue sky.

3: Traditionally, you would now create a meditation space which is dedicated to your deity / subject. You would fill this space with images, sculptures, candles relaxing features, and other items that will help you to relax and to connect to your deity.

4: Once your space is set and you've chosen your deity or special object, sit comfortably and with good posture. You should feel stable, relaxed, and comfortable. Proper physical alignment will help your energy (chi / qi / life force) to flow through your body freely.

5: Close your eyes and focus on the space between your eyebrows (your third eye). You will feel a build-up of energy in this area.

6: Ask your deity / subject to become one with you.

7: Meditate on your subject in the traditional sense, by simply focusing on your subject. Then, once you feel that you are in contact with your deity / subject, imagine becoming one with them. Imagine there being no distance between your consciousness and the subject. You are merging to become one.

8: Continue to meditate on your subject for up to twenty minutes.

9: At the end of the Bhakti session, thank your deity / subject for coming to you. Open your eyes. Sit still for a few moments, gradually returning to your normal state.

What to meditate on

The subject of your meditation should reflect the trait you

wish to develop in yourself.

If, for instance, you would like to develop your sense of compassion, you might like to meditate on Ghandi or Buddha. If you wish to be more in touch with your body you might mediate on an athlete or on your own body. If you would like to become calmer and more peaceful you might choose water or a clear blue sky.

It's up to you what subject you choose to meditate on. But here are a few ideas along with the traits they represent.

Water	Freedom and power
The night sky:	Eternity and wisdom
Ghandi / Buddha / Mother Theresa	Compassion and kindness
Silence	Stillness
Death	Death is a complex subject but generally when you meditate on death you develop your appreciation of time and your humbleness.
Cats	Playfulness (not all meditation subjects have to be serious)
Trees	Wisdom and patience
Waterfall	Power (I personally like to meditate at Niagra Falls, of which the truly wonderful classical composer Gustav Mahler said "At last, Fortissimo!" I guess he appreciated the power of the Falls as

	much as I do).
Bird song	Joy
Your own reflection / visage	Self awareness
Angels	Hope and compassion
Gemstones	Different gemstones reflect different traits and characteristics
Colours	Different colours reflect different mentalities and emotions. Green, for instance, reflects nature and health, where black represents power and authority, and yellow represents happiness. Meditate on the colour that reflects the trait you'd like to develop.
Your own breath	Meditating on your own breath will calm and centre you.

There are infinite subjects on which to meditate. Ask yourself what trait you'd like to develop. Find a subject that reflects that trait. Then meditate on it. Ask the object to become one with you. Then you will absorb the qualities of that object.

If the idea of *absorbing the positive qualities of an object* seems a little too magical for you, consider the case of a baby or a young child. Children and babies learn extremely quickly, far quicker than adults do. They learn from the people and objects they come into contact with. This process of learning (or mental *absorption*) would continue into adulthood if it weren't for the fact that we humans develop mental rigidity.

Scientifically speaking, an adult has a more developed prefrontal cortex that is packed full of memories. Every time an adult does something or sees something they refer to those memories and look at how something was *previously* rather than how it is *now*.

For instance, if when growing up a child is spoiled and made to believe that the world revolves around them, that mentality will often continue into adulthood because the prefrontal cortex is continually using memories from childhood to inform the adult of who they are. This prevents new information from readily entering the brain. Conversely, kids have less developed prefrontal cortices and can therefore absorb new information quicker and can also perceive the world from an open perspective rather than thinking "This is how things *are* because memory tells me it's how things *were*". To the adult New=Old. But to the child there is only New.

If only we could open our minds so that we were seeing things precisely as they *are* and not how they *were*. If only we were *mindful* of the present moment. If we were mindful of the present moment, rather than always seeing things as they *were* we would be able to absorb new information. And that, of course, is where meditation comes in.

When you practice Bhakti meditation you are in an extremely *open-minded* state. Your entire mind is opened to the object of meditation. That clears the dam known as memories from the river of consciousness, allowing new water (or new information) to flow downstream to the brain. Move the memories out of the way and see things in the clear light of the present moment (as we do in meditation) and we restore our brain's adaptability.

And that is why when you practice bhakti meditation you absorb the positive characteristics of the object you're meditating on.

CHAKRA MEDITATION

"The Way is not in the sky. The way is in the heart." - Buddha

In Indian traditions, the Chakra system is the system of energy that flows throughout the body.

The chakra system works like water. Prana (the sustaining energy of life) moves through rivers called Nadi towards energy centres called chakras, which operate like wheels (the term "chakra" literally means "wheel"). Those wheels facilitate the operation of vital organs in the body and also correspond to different mental characteristics, some chakras being associated with spirituality and creativity, others with compassion and self love, and so on.

Different religions and spiritualities have different theories regarding the number, order, and position of chakras in the body, but the conventional agreement is that there are seven primary chakras in the body and that they are all located at various points on the spine, ranging from the crown of the head to the pelvis.

Meditating on each of the chakras helps to stimulate the flow of prana, or life force, around the body, which loosens and frees the body and mind, boosting wellbeing and helping you to stay healthy and vibrant.

The overall chakra system is important to holistic wellbeing, and it is believed that by balancing the chakras an individual will enjoy high levels of wellbeing both mentally and physically. But as well as being important to overall health, each of the independent chakras contains nerves, energy, and major organs that are essential for psychological, physical, spiritual, and emotional health. These organs and nerves rely on the steady flow of energy in order to stay healthy.

Each individual chakra is associated with its own vital organs, bodily functions, and mental characteristics. The crown chakra, for instance, is associated with spirituality, consciousness, and inspiration. By meditating on the energy of a chakra you will stimulate the chakra and free the energy within, which will in turn lead to development of the associated characteristic. So by mediating on the crown chakra you will become more spiritual, more conscious, and more inspired.

At times the chakras become blocked, either by illness or by emotional suffering or psychological disorders. People who are depressed, for instance, may have a blockage at their heart chakra or crown chakra, which is preventing them from being emotionally balanced. By meditating on their chakras they can free prana, which will energise their body and mind and return them to health.

THE SEVEN CHAKRAS:

Root Chakra:

The root chakra is at the spine's base and is associated with the colour red. The Root Chakra relates to our connection to our family and fellow humans, as well as to Earth and nature. This chakra's mantra (sound) is "LAM".

The Sacral Chakra:

The Sacral Chakra is situated a little above the navel and is orange. The Sacral Chakra relates to our inner child and our sense of spontaneity and creativity. . This chakra's mantra is "VAM".

The Solar Plexus Chakra:

The Solar Plexus Chakra is associated with yellow and extends from just below the heart to the navel. The Solar Plexus Chakra is related to our "internal parent"—our self esteem; ego; "shoulds"; and our sense of individuality. This chakra's mantra is "RAM".

The Heart Charka:

The heart chakra is situated in the centre of our chest and is associated with green and pink. The heart chakra—as you might expect—is linked to love, confidence, trust, compassion and also inspiration. This chakra's mantra is "YAM".

The Throat Chakra:

The Throat Chakra is associated with blue and is at the base of the throat. The throat chakra is linked to speaking, truth responsibility, surrendering to the divine, decision making, and personal authority. This chakra's mantra is "HAM".

The Brow Chakra (also "The Third Eye"):

The Brow Chakra or Third Eye Chakra is in the middle of our forehead and is associated with indigo. The brow chakra / third eye chakra is related to vision, divine understanding, wisdom, intelligence and intuition. This chakra's mantra is "AUM".

The Crown Chakra:

Naturally, the Crown Chakra finds its position at the top of our heads. The Crown Chakra is associated with violet and pure white light and is related to our connection to the Higher Power, living in the moment, devotion, inspiration, Source, integration of the Whole, and higher alignment. This chakra's mantra is "ANG".

Exercise: Chakra Meditation

Chakra balancing meditation has been used for thousands of years. This wonderful technique brings higher energies of light and love to our chakras, which in due course will heighten our vibrancy rate and bring Light to our energy field. This leads to the purification of the body for complete mental and physical health.

1) Before beginning, it's important to know the colours of the chakras, as discussed above.
2) Begin by sitting comfortably somewhere you will not

be disturbed. Make sure your back is straight.

3) Breathe slowly in a relaxed manner and make sure your breath is being drawn deep into your body.

4) Feel your breath moving up your spine as you inhale and down when exhaling. Focus on this movement for a moment before continuing.

5) Beginning with the root chakra, imagine the root chakra's colour. Feel the energy gathering in the Root Chakra. When you feel that you have correctly visualised the Root Chakra, begin to chant the chakra's sound (which you can find in the descriptions above). Meditate on the colour and the sound for a few moments, then move up to the Navel Chakra

6) Continue this process up through the seven chakras. Once you finish you may stop or proceed back down the chakras, vividly visualising the colours as you go, as well as recognising the feeling associated with the chakra.

When used frequently, this chakra balancing meditation will promote health and wellbeing. It will help fight depression naturally and promote positive feelings and inner peace. It will also heighten your spiritual development.

THIRD EYE MEDITATION

To truly see, you must first open your eyes—all three.

The third eye is the mystic eye that is said to be the seat of divine insight. But, somewhat ironically, we are still trying to gain insight into the exact position and function of the third eye. Humans have believed in this mysterious element of their physiology for millennia, as is proven by the fact that ancient artworks show humans and monsters with three eyes. But just where exactly is the third eye and what exactly does it do?

Hindus offer the oldest answers to the third eye conundrum. They have long believed that the third eye is located in the middle of the forehead just a little above the eyebrows. Meanwhile, Theosophists believe the third eye is connected to the pineal gland, the pea-sized conical mass of tissue behind the third ventricle of the brain, which secretes hormones in some mammals. They believe that millennia ago humans had an actual physical third eye that was atrophied during the evolution of man. This is somewhat backed by the fact that reptiles and amphibians do have a third parietal eye. They use that third eye to sense light, for help navigating, and to regulate their circadian rhythms (the physical, mental and behavioral changes that follow a roughly 24-hour cycle).

And the *scientific belief* is that the third eye is indeed the tiny pinecone-shaped pineal gland, and that one of the functions of the third eye, or pineal gland is to secrete melatonin, a neurohormone, while we sleep.

> *Science has yet to uncover all the functions of man's third eye. But we do know that reptiles and amphibians have a third* parietal *eye used to sense light and for navigation.*

Did you know*: Theosophists believe that humans used to have an actual physical third eye located in the forehead?*

Given the fact that the pineal gland is no bigger than a piece of sweet corn, you might wonder just why so many cultures and religions throughout time have been so fascinated by it. But it turns out that size is no indicator of importance, because the pineal gland fills an incredibly important role in our survival and wellbeing. Or at least, we know it is important not to *disrupt* the pineal gland. Scientific research suggests that when you disrupt the pineal gland's chronobiological connection to the 24 hour cycle of light and dark you will not only be disrupting your ability to perceive, but also increasing your chances of contracting illnesses and diseases, including cancer. On top of this, research conducted by Vanderbilt University has shown a correlation between circadian disruption and obesity, diabetes, and heart disease.

Pinealophiles (those who religiously believe in the third eye) hammer home the horrors we're doing to ourselves by disrupting our pineal gland, our third eye. They gesticulate that an age of always-on technology, artificial light, and inconsistent sleep periods have damaged our genealogical ability to protect our health. No wonder so many fantasy, sci-fi and horror books and movies portray the impact of a disrupted pineal gland, nor why so many psychologist, mystics, and spiritualists are advocating the importance of turning off your devices!

So, despite its size the third eye is a truly vital part of the human body. And that, perhaps, explains why so many cultures and spiritualities have been obsessed with the third eye for so long.

But for all we do know about the third eye, there's plenty more waiting to be discovered.

Jimo Borjigin is professor of neurology and physiology at the University of Michigan and a pioneer in visualisation of the pineal gland's melatonin secretion. Speaking to Alternet.org, Borjigin states, "We still lack a complete understanding of the pineal gland. Numerous molecules are found in the pineal exclusively at night, and we don't know what their functions are."

We haven't come too far since four centuries ago when Rene Descates called the pineal gland the "principal seat of the soul". We are still somewhat at the mercy of speculation. Pretty much the only thing we know for next to certain is that artificial light affects the pineal gland and leads to increased chance of contracting cancer. Itai Kloog, a researcher at Harvard University School of Public Health, states, "We've proven beyond a doubt that artificial light is a risk factor. Light at night contributes to higher risk of developing hormonal cancer."

So, science, Buddhism, Hinduism, Chan (a relative of Zen) and many more groups and spiritualities advocate the importance of training the third eye, and most of those spiritualities agree that meditating on the third eye chakra leads a person to connect with the vibration of the universe and to gain access to insight and intuition.

Given the ubiquitous belief in the importance of the third eye, it seems fair to say that no matter what your faith or spirituality, whether you're a non-believer, a Hindu, Buddhist, Christian, or a devout scientist, or anyone else, you will almost definitely benefit by recognising the existence of your third eye and by practicing techniques designed to exercise your third eye, of which the most popular and most powerful is the Third Eye Meditation technique.

Here are some ways in which Third Eye Meditation might help you (based on traditional Hindu and Buddhist belief):

- It helps to treat anxiety and depression by making us more aware of our thoughts
- It helps us to understand people by making us more in tune with others. This is why psychics use this technique so often.
- It helps with business as it promotes deeper understanding of reality.
- It helps your relationships as it allows you to understand others better.

EXERCISE: Third Eye Meditation

1) Find somewhere quiet and peaceful where you will not be disturbed. Make sure you are comfortable. Then proceed with the following steps slowly.
2) Breathe deeply through your nose. Hold momentarily then exhale through the mouth. Relax.
3) Relax the face. Feel the relaxation extending to the body.
4) Gradually relax more and more.

5) Focus your attention between your eyebrows. Become aware of your third eye, the energy in the centre of your forehead. Feel it opening and radiating light. Notice the light travelling outwards from your Third Eye in 360 degrees.

6) Let go and release any negative or disruptive thoughts.

7) Continue to relax

8) Allow the sphere of light in your forehead to open. Observe the light radiating.

9) Continue to relax your body. As you do so, be aware of the sensation of your body becoming lighter and lighter.

10) Allow your third eye to open, continuing to relax.

11) Ask for divine help to open your third eye.

12) Allow the light to flow through you, out of your third eye.

13) Ask your Higher Self to fill you with pure white light. Ask for the light to fill you throughout, entering every place in and around you.

14) Ask your Higher Self if there is a message about you opening your third eye. Be still for a couple of minutes and allow any message to appear.

15) Notice if there are images or thoughts or visions arising in your third eye.

16) Once you have experienced the third eye for long enough, take your time and gradually bring your awareness back to the present place and time.

17) Say (aloud or in your head) "I am fully present in this moment, here and now."

18) Take a deep breath, stretch, and express thanks for your third eye meditation.

YOGA BREATHING METHODS

You might be surprised by the sheer number of breathing meditation techniques that yoga, Buddhism and other systems offer. There are hundreds. Some are ideal for beginners, some less so.

While you do not need to know all the different methods, you certainly do need to know the basics.

As a meditation teacher, I am continually alarmed by the number of new meditators who do not know proper breathing meditation technique.

Not only is proper breathing imperative to meditation, but it is also vital for your health and happiness. Proper breathing will help you to relax and focus.

Let's look at the best breathing techniques from yoga.

Nodi Shodhana: Yoga Breathing Meditation

Nodi Sadhana (alternative nostril breathing) is one of the most popular yoga breathing meditations. It is used to produce calm, relaxation and balance. It does wonders for your health and research suggests it can even heighten longevity.

EXERCISE: Nadi Shodhana

1) Sit comfortably with good posture
2) Cover your right nostril with your right thumb
3) Breathe deeply through your left nostril
4) On the completion of the in-breath, uncover your right nostril and cover your left nostril (hence, "alternate nostril breathing")
5) Exhale through the right nostril
6) Continue in the same pattern, inhaling and exhaling.
7) Take 108 breaths in this fashion.

Use this breathing meditation before bed or for quick relaxation.

Kapabalhti Pranayama

This is a slightly more advanced type of breathing meditation from yoga.

Despite being more advanced, this technique is worth learning. It is said to clear out 80 per cent of the toxins in the body, massively increasing health.

The name Kapalbhati means "shining forehead".

EXERCISE: Kapalbhati pranayama

1) Sit comfortably with good posture
2) Place your hands on your knees with the palms facing upwards
3) Breathe in
4) Exhale

5) While exhaling, pull your navel in towards your spine. This should be done with force. Push your breath right out. Focus on the exhalation.
6) As you relax, let your breath flow inwards naturally, unforced. Focus on the inhalation. If you breathe out fully, your inhalation will be quite forceful.
7) Take 20 breaths. This is one round of kapalabhati pranayama.
8) Spend a few moments observing your body.
9) Repeat the above process for two more rounds, (to take 60 breaths in total)

Benefits of Kapalbhati meditation:

- Increases metabolic rate
- Helps to activate and balance the chakras
- Stimulates vital organs
- Improves blood pressure
- Makes the skin glow
- Reduces stress
- Tones the stomach
- Teaches us to breathe properly

Nine Round Breathing Meditation

The "Nine Round" method is a Buddhist breathing meditation technique beginners can use for calm and focus. Traditionally, it's used by Buddhists to remove the states of ignorance, confusion, anger, hate, desire and attachment. It originates from the most esoteric collection of meditations in tantra. It is a pre-tantric purification process that calms and centres the mind.

It is a truly powerful technique that you can use to clear up the energy centres in your body and to clear your mind of anger, hate, confusion, doubt, attachment, ignorance and desire, and the other negative states that Buddhism teaches us about.

When you try the method, you will probably notice how Nine Round Breathing is similar to Anapanasati meditation, which creates calmness and equanimity.

The tantra text teaches that there are "winds" in the body. Those winds are energies that serve the mind. But if the winds get blocked, the energy will not flow, and the mind will not function properly.

Because of these benefits, it is best to use Nine Round Breathing at specific times:

- When you're feeling angry or hateful
- When you have the same negative thought repeating over and over in your mind.
- When you're suffering from some sort of mental delusion, for instance, you are unable to accept your present reality.
- When you are feeling mentally foggy or confused.
- When you are unable to let go.

Tip: Use Nine Round Breathing for 5-10 minutes before your proper meditation session. This will calm and centre your mind ready for the next meditation.

In the tantric Nine Round Breathing exercise, you visualise the three energy channels in the body. This is very helpful for purifying the mind. It's often used at the start of a meditation session in order to calm and centre the mind, ready for the meditation ahead.

EXERCISE: Nine Round Breathing

1) Start by imagining your body as completely empty.
2) Now focus on the central channel, which starts in the same spot as the Eyebrow Chakra.
3) The Central Channel flows down the skull straight down to a spot that is precisely four fingers width under your naval. It is coloured a transparent blue about as thick as a thick piece of string. On either side of this Central Channel are two more channels. Both of these are transparent and are as thick as a piece of string. The left channel is white—the right one red.
4) To start, breathe in through your left nostril with the right nostril closed.
5) Feel the air passing into your nose and right to the start of the Central Channel.
6) Feel the airflow down the Central Channel to the left and right channel.
7) Close your left nostril. This will make you breathe out the right channel.
8) Breathe in again and image that your breath is like pure white light.
9) Let all attachments and desire leave you like a black smoke exiting your side channels.
10) Repeat the above three times.
11) **Time for the second round.**
12) Inhale white light through your right nostril.
13) Imagine all anger and hate exiting your left channel like smoke.

14) Repeat three times.
15) **Now for the third round.**
16) Imagine inhaling white light through your side channels.
17) Imagine those channels connecting to your central channel, which can get blocked by confusion and ignorance.
18) Breathe out all that confusion and ignorance as smoke until it comes pouring out from between your eyebrows.

Breath of Fire

Breath Of Fire is a Kundalini Yoga meditation technique that uses a particular style of pranayama (yogic breathing) to relax the body and mind.

There are many benefits of Breath Of Fire Yoga. You can use it to reduce chronic pain, improve mental health, and increase core strength. But a warning: As a meditation teacher, I frequently teach Breath Of Fire Yoga. And many of my students tell me that they sometimes feel light-headed doing this method (at which point I advise them to stop and go gently with it). This light-headedness is one of the side effects of the technique. So be mindful and keep an eye out for any adverse side effects, in which case, stop. That said, there are many benefits of Breath Of Fire Yoga too. Let's take a look.

Benefits

Breath Of Fire is one of the best ways of using yoga to build positive energy. It clears your mind and relaxes you. And it also gets a lot deeper than that.

One of the most amazing things about Kapalbhati pranayama is that it strengthens both your mind and your body at the same time.

The International Journal Of Medical & Pharmaceutical Sciences conducted a study in which they asked young and healthy participants to practice Kapalbhati pranayama for 12 weeks, starting with 30 times for one minute a day, then increasing to 5 minutes/day, twice daily, thrice/ week for 12 weeks. by one minute each day. The researchers concluded that "12 weeks of Kapalabhati pranayama training showed improvement in the cardio-respiratory parameters with significant decrease in [respiratory rate] may be attributed to a calm and stable mind-emotion complex in our subjects. Hence we conclude that pranayama training is useful in reducing [respiratory rate] through psycho-somatic mechanisms and that this enhances the health and well being of young subjects."

It also calms the mind. When you breathe properly you are naturally more relaxed, right? Well, by regularly practicing Breath Of Fire Yoga you will cleanse your lungs and diaphragm and this will make your breath easier and more relaxing. In turn, your mind will naturally calm.

It helps circulate blood around your body more efficiently, and this removes toxins, helping your body to detoxify.

By eliminating toxins and relaxing both the mind and body, Breath of Fire meditation also reduces pain and soothes your aching muscles. This can help with chronic pain, and it can also help you to relax after a workout if you have strains.

It's huge for your mind, too. Research shows that regular practice of Breath Of Fire helps reduce negative emotions, lower stress, and fight anxiety and depression. You can really feel the emotional release when you practice Kapalbhati pranayama. It will also strengthen your cognitive function in just a few weeks. The increased blood-flow to the brain helps your neurons to stay active, boosting cognitive functioning.

EXERCISE: Breath Of Fire

1. Sit tall and straight. You want to create good space between your navel and your heart.
2. Take a few relaxing breaths through your nose just to relax.
3. When you exhale, press your abdomen in. When you inhale, press your abdomen out.
4. When you inhale, imagine that your diaphragm is like a balloon filling with air. Then observe the air flowing out of you as you exhale, pressing your abdomen in.
5. Gradually increase your speed. Your breath will be loud and fast. You want to aim to make your inhales and exhales last the same amount of time, so you're establishing a rhythm.
6. Once you've finished, continue to meditate but relax and stop forcing your inhales and exhales. Let the breath come and go naturally (like you do when practising Anapanasati).

Tips

Now you know how to do Breath Of Fire yoga properly, here are a few helpful tips and pointers:

When you're taking breaths, aim to make inhales and exhales the same length and do not pause between them.

Make sure that you are always breathing through the nostrils rather than through the mouth.

Be careful if you ever practice this technique when you have sinus issues. If you have any kind of respiratory problem (like asthma), make sure you consult a healthcare professional before starting.

You can make kapalbhati pranamaya more effective by exhaling until the point where you can feel energy rising naturally in your stomach. Let this energy take over as you naturally take a big inhale. You will still feel energised, but it will be a more natural energy that is causing the inhalation.

If you notice that you are making funny facial expressions (such as squinting) or that there is tension in your body (such as clenched fists) you are not performing kalapabhati pranayama correctly. Stop. Relax. Now try again with more ease.

You will probably want to practice Breath Of Fire for more than 3 minutes. This is a mistake a lot of beginners make. As you probably know, most meditations last twenty minutes or longer, but this one is different. It is a short and intense practice and should not be done for long periods. Once you have practised the method a few times, you can go for a little bit longer, but don't exceed 10 minutes.

If you are not used to doing deep-breathing exercises, you may experience minor side-effects of kapalbhati. You might experience mild dizziness or light-headedness. This is normal. It is only because you are not used to taking in so much breath. If you do start to experience more severe side-effects, stop immediately and switch to a more relaxed, easier meditation technique.

WARNING: DO NOT USE THIS METHOD WHEN PREGNANT.

Lion's Breathing

You will definitely have heard your yoga instructor telling you to take a Lion's Breath. What does it mean?

Lion's breath is a simple yoga breathing exercise that is

really easy to do and is often used in kids' classes because it's fun. All you have to do is take a deep inhale through your nose, lean your head back and breathe out through the mouth with your tongue out. This stimulates the flow of breath through the body.

Skull Cleanser (Kapalbhati)

This is one of the best yoga breathing exercises for beginners because it promotes lymph circulation, which is beneficial to overall health and wellbeing. It is actually one of the Ayurveda techniques.

EXERCISE: Kapalbhati

To do this exercise, first, choose a mudra.

Now follow the instructions below:

1) Sit comfortably
2) Place your hands in the mudra of your choice.
3) Breathe into your belly and observe the sensation of your breath filling your body
4) Inhale through the nose
5) Contract your lower belly to force your breath out
6) Immediately release the contraction. Allow your body to automatically breathe in again
7) Continue the process above at a rate of approximately 70 contractions per minute, then gradually increasing. If you feel faint stop immediately.
8) After each minute of exercise take one deep breath to relax.

Ujjayi Breath

This is one of the most popular yoga breathing techniques, and you can do it while you're actually doing your yoga session. It has a very relaxing effect.

To do this technique, you breathe both in and out through your nostrils. Take a deep breath in and then imagine that you are sucking through a straw (you can actually hear your breath like an ocean wave when you do this). Gradually take deeper inhalations and slower inhalations. This will relax both body and mind.

Bellows Breath

This is a brilliant yoga breathing exercise for beginners who want to boost their energy levels, especially during Power yoga. You can also use it any time you're feeling bored or sluggish, to heighten your awareness.

To do it, place your hands in fists and raise them to the sky. Take an in-breath through your mouth. When you exhale, drop your elbow to the side of your body while vocalising a "Ha" sound. This sound should feel like it's arising from the very bottom of your lungs. Make it loud and proud!

Pranayama

Though not technically a "meditation", if you are a yoga practitioner you might like to know how to breathe properly during your yoga sessions. Here are some tips.

1: Exhale when bending forward

When we exhale, it is easier to extend the depth of a fold.

This is because when we exhale our lungs empty and the torso becomes smaller. Essentially this means that there is less of a mass between the upper and lower body. This makes it easier to bend forward. Also, exhaling has a calming effect and slow the heart rate down. That's why it is best to exhale during poses that are calmer.

2: Also exhale for twists

Following on from the rule above, when the body contracts there is less room for breathing. That's why we should exhale when we do a twist. By exhaling when we twist, we help the body to relax, which makes it easier to extend the pose.

3: Inhale during backbends

It is easier for the body to fill the lungs when there is space between the upper and lower body. When you do a backbend, you open up the space in the torso and the lungs, which makes it easier to fill the body with breath. At the same time, when we inhale the heart rate increases, which produces a feeling of alert awareness.

CANDLE GAZING MEDITATION (TRATAKA)

Candle Gazing Meditation (or "Trataka Meditation") is a meditation technique in which we focus our gaze on a candle.

There is a scientific link between the eyes and the brain. As you likely know, sight is the most powerful of our five primary senses. We perceive the world through sight firstly, and then touch, taste, smell, and hearing. Plus, unlike other senses, we can actually perceive the world indirectly through sight in the way of photographs and video. Because of this, an estimated 80% of our perception of the world comes via the sense of sight.

Not only do we create the majority of our perception of the world through sight, there is also a direct relationship between mental health and eye movement patterns. This is why highly perceptive people can actually determine how you are feeling simply by looking in your eyes. Numerous mental health conditions like ADHD and anxiety correlated to increases in erratic eye movement. The breath works similarly —most people are already aware of the fact that when they are stressed or anxious they begin to breathe shallowly.

Now, if mental health conditions cause erratic eye movements, what would happen if we deliberately held the eyes still? This is a question that yogis were interested in answering. And they discovered that by focusing the eyes and holding them still it is possible to relax the mind.

That's why when you feel stressed or anxious you might like to try Trataka meditation. Benefits of the technique include: relaxation, better mental health, and enhanced concentration.

Science is now beginning to realise the benefits of still-gazing. The therapy known as EMDR (Eye Movement Desensitization and Reprocessing) [1] has been used since 1987 to help cure problems such as trauma and PTSD—indeed, in one study by the National Institute of Mental Health, EMDR was found to treat PTSD more effectively than medication.

In summary, we know from science and from yoga that still gazing can improve our mental health, and this is where the benefits of Candle Gazing Meditation come from.

Candle Gazing Meditation / Trataka Benefits

As we saw when we looked at the science above, when we are anxious or stressed our eyes make more microsaccades, which are microscopic jerking movements. This happens because if we hold our gaze still for long enough objects tend to disappear from our vision. One of the benefits of Trataka meditation is that the gaze is still, stopping those microscopic motions and allowing the mind to become still too.

Put simply: Still eyes = still mind.

Little distractions in the mind cause the eyes to move. But when we deliberately hold the eyes still the mind settles. This is one reason why Zen and Tibetan Buddhism, yoga, and other spiritual sects have adopted meditations with the eyes open.

Plus, the side the eyes move to has an effect on the dominant half of the brain and on our emotions. By focusing the eyes on an object directly in front of us we create harmony between the two hemispheres of the brain

This is where the majority of Trataka Meditation benefits come from.

Although there is little research to substantiate the benefits of Candle Gazing Meditation, general agreement among experts is that it offers the following benefits:

There has been very little scientific research in this practice (example). So what we know in terms of its benefits is mostly all anecdotal evidence from practitioners that have devoted years to its practice. In this context, trataka is attributed to have the following benefits:

Trataka Meditation Benefits

- Enhances concentration, memory, and willpower
- Heightens visualization skills
- Clears accumulated mental/emotional complexes
- Allows suppressed thoughts to surface
- Can reduce insomnia
- Heightens cognitive function
- Increases nervous stability
- Makes eyes cleaner and stronger
- Helps with anxiety
- Balances brain hemispheres
- Can help with numerous diseases of the eyes
- Enhances self-confidence and patience

EXERCISE: Trataka Meditation

The principle behind Trataka meditation technique is focusing the eyes in a relaxed way on an object directly in front of you, and then closing the eyes and holding the image inwardly.

Here is an example of Trataka meditation with a candle.

1: Focus on the external image

You can choose any object to focus on. However, most people like to focus on a candle flame.

Place the object directly in front of you so that you are not looking to the left or right. Focus on the object while holding your eyes still. Part of the key to the technique is holding your eyes as still but also as relaxed as possible. After three minutes you will notice tears rising. Gently close your eyes for a brief period and then open them and continue to gaze at your object. When you finish this section, wash your eyes with cold water. Do not practice every say or you could potentially end up with a permanent image on your retina.

Make sure you do not strain your eyes at any time during the practice. And if you have cataracts, do not meditate on a candle.

You can also practise meditating on the tip od your nose.

2: Internalising the process

After you have gazed at your object internally, close your eyes. You will see an image of your meditation object behind your closed eyes. Meditate on this internal image for ten minutes.

Trataka, or "Candle Gazing Meditation" is a powerful method for calming your mind and developing your focus. It also make a wonderful alternative to the conventional eyes-closed meditations, which is why many people like to use this method as a complement to their primary practice.

Sadly there is less scientific research into Trataka than into certain other form of meditation (like Vipassana or Mindfulness) so it is hard to advise this as a primary discipline. However, I do recommend you try it and see what benefits you observe.

KUNDALINI

Kundalini meditation has earned something of a cult reputation amongst yogis. It is revered as a powerful meditation technique that can fully awaken your conscious awareness. It is said to do this by awakening *kundalini energy*, which is a life-force energy usually dormant in the base of the spine at the root chakra.

There are many different ways in which we can awaken kundalini energy in yoga, including:

Breathing techniques

Mudras (hand and body positions)

Spiritual mantras

Asanas (yoga poses)

However, perhaps the number one way to awaken kundalini energy is meditation.

Through a combination of exercises it is possible to shift the kundalini energy from the root chakra to the head, which will increase spiritual awakening and perhaps even lead to enlightenment.

As with meditation in general, the first mention of the Kundalini meditation technique is found in the Hindu religious text the Upanishads, which were written around 600 to 800 B.C.

Originally, the Kundalini meditation technique was only taught to yogis who had reached an advanced level of spiritual awakening, and even today it is not generally considered ideal for beginners. If you are relatively new to meditation I highly advise you to practise simpler techniques and only to practise Kundalini meditation techniques once you reach an advanced level.

In 1968 Yogi Bhajan started teaching Kundalini meditation technique in the West, stating that the method would offer numerous health benefits and help people to lead healthier, happier, more conscious lives. This, of course, was before Yogi Bhajan was accused of sexual, emotional, and physical abuse —which made many people question the legitimacy of Kundalini meditation technique. Despite those allegations, however, very many yogis are interested in learning the method, perhaps because of the promised benefits of Kundalini meditation.

Potential Benefits of Kundalini Meditation

There is precious little scientific research to substantiate the supposed benefits of kundalini meditation. However, those who have practised the method state that they have observed the following benefits:

- Clarity of mind
- Inspiration
- Enhanced communication
- Enhanced mindfulness
- Heightened compassion
- Awakening to their true self
- Heightened sense of purpose
- Clearer intentions

There have been a couple of scientific studies into the technique, and those studies do indicate some benefit, although the benefits that are scientifically backed are universal to most other meditations. For instance, a 2017 study showed that Kundalini meditation techniques offers stress relief and could potentially be beneficial for certain health conditions including cardiovascular disease and insomnia.

Another study in 2017 showed that Kundalini can enhance cognitive ability in older adult and improve memory.

A 2018 study showed that kundalini meditation can help with generalised anxiety.

However, the same benefits of seen in other meditations. Therefore, scientifically speaking, there is no evidence that the benefits Kundalini meditation are different to other methods.

Given the rising popularity of the technique, however, you might be intrigued to try it. So let's look at how to do it.

EXERCISE: Kundalini Meditation

1: Dress comfortably in light clothing. Traditionally, most kundalini yogis wear shawls over the heads to protect energy flow.

2: Spend five minutes performing a basic breathing meditation to relax your mind.

3: Sit up with good posture on a chair or on the floor. Place your hands in Anjali mudra (prayer position) and gently lower your chin as though praying. Close your eyes but leave a very slight opening.

4: Focus on the Ajna chakra (third eyes chakra located between the eyebrows). With your eyes closed, focus on this post.

5: Recite a mantra, preferably a kundalini mantra, which are written in the sacred Indian language of Gurmukhi. The exact mantra you choose doesn't matter too much. You can use "Om" if you like.

6: Breath mindfully, inhaling and exhaling through the nose while focusing on the sensation of breathing. Gradually slow your breathing such that inhales and exhales last for approximately four seconds (so one breath will take 8 seconds). Mindfully observe how your breath creates energy in your body.

7: Add a mudra (hand position). For beginners I recommend using Gyan mudra. This is the iconic meditation mudra in which the thumbs and second finger touch and the remaining fingers are held out straight. The hands are placed gently on the lap.

8: Breathe in parts. When breathing in, breathe in in 4 individuals inhales, and then out on another four individual exhales. As you inhale, drawn your naval towards your spine.

9: If your mind wanders, gently guide your focus back to your breath.

10: Continue for five minutes.

11: To conclude your kundalini meditation practise, take one deep inhale and exhale. Raise your arms out at full length and relax.

Potential risks of Kundalini meditation

There are some health risks of Kundalini meditation, especially for beginners. You may notice that you're feeling uncomfortable or slightly dizzy. If this occurs, stop.

SELF INQUIRY

Self inquiry meditation benefits you by helping you to see the nature of your true reality. The self inquiry meditation technique (instructions below) will help you to detach from Maya (the illusion of yourself and the world) and discover your innermost being.

If you've tried the breathing meditations and techniques like Vipassana, you might be looking for a way to take your meditation practice further. And while being mindful is great, there are so many more things you can get from meditation. Self inquiry is an example of another path that meditation can take.

Arguably the best benefit of self inquiry meditation is that it helps you to realise that you are not what you think you are.

When someone asks you, "Who are you?" what do you say? You probably describe yourself by telling them about your job, your family situation, and perhaps some of the core elements of your personality. But these *factual* things are not the real you.

Anyone who has ever felt a moment of true enlightenment, or what in Zen is called "Kensho" (which translates to "seeing the true nature"), will tell you that we are pure energy. But it can be hard to see ourselves that way because the mind is lured to matter-of-fact things, like your job and your family status.

In order to truly see our innermost selves, we need to silence our regular thoughts and perceptions. There are several ways to do this. One is through koans, which are riddle-like questions that Zen monks use to see the true nature of things. One such koan is, "Show me your original face before your mother and father were born." Questions like these make us challenge our usual mode of thinking.

Another such question is *"Who (or What) am I?"* These obscurations are called *Kleshas* by Buddhists and *Vasanas* or *samskaras* by Hindus and yogis.

The purpose of the koan *What am I?* is to guide us past our ego-induced delusion of ourselves and to perceive our true reality: that we are an empty and timeless energy.

And here we come to the principal benefit of self-inquiry meditation: seeing our true nature. However, this is just the tip of the iceberg, because once we see our true nature, we are set free of the pressures and strains that come from our delusional perception of ourselves.

Self Inquiry Meditation Benefits

The primary way in which self inquiry meditation benefits us is that it lets us see past our delusional view of ourselves and to realise the fact that we are pure energy.

However, this is just the beginning. Because once you realise that you are pure energy you are set free of many of the pressures and strains of life.

If you think about the stresses and pressures you face, you will realise that most of them are created by your perception of yourself. For instance, "I must work overtime this week because I'm a hard worker". Your idea that you're a hard worker forces you to overwork in order to substantiate your belief of yourself: that you're a hard worker. Many times, this belief will not aid you (how many people have succumbed to illness because they worked too hard and faced too much stress?). Then you have those people who believe they are victims, who thus always seek relationships with people who will make them victims (it is scientifically proven that people with victim mentality are more likely to enter relationships with abusive people).

What is happening is that your invalid beliefs about yourself are causing you to live a life *in accordance with the person you believe you are*. And you are unlikely to overcome this pattern of *belief-becoming-reality* until you change your perception of yourself.

Thankfully, self inquiry meditation let's us see the true pureness of ourselves, beyond our thoughts and misconceptions, such that we can then be freed from our ingrained delusions.

Ask yourself: How are negative beliefs about yourself effecting your reality? If you meditate on this question you might be surprised by the answer.

And so, the number one benefit of self-inquiry meditation is that it frees us from the trappings of our own delusions.

However, if you consider the impact that your delusional perception has on your life, you will see that the benefits of self inquiry meditation are potentially limitless. For instance, if you believe you are an overweight person, self inquiry will stop that belief from affecting you so that you can successfully lose weight. Or if you believe you are a lazy person (and thereby act lazily in order to substantiate that belief), self inquiry meditation will get you past that idea of being lazy so you can actually be productive.

In this way, it's impossible to give an exact list of self inquiry meditation benefits, because they depend entirely upon the individual and their perception of themselves.

In a nutshell: Self inquiry meditation benefits you by letting you see the true nature of yourself and letting you overcome your delusions about yourself (and the influence thereof).

So how do you do self inquiry meditation technique?

EXERCISE: Self Inquiry

Sit quietly somewhere peaceful. It is best if this place is a relaxing neutral ground devoid of anything that informs you about yourself. For instance, you don't want photos of yourself around, nor any personal property. For best results, perform self inquiry meditation in a forest.

As usual with meditation, spend a short time doing mindful breathing so you relax.

Once you feel calm, ask the question, "What am I?" (I prefer this question to *Who am I?* because *Who* immediately suggests that you are a person, which carries with it ideas of what a person should be, where *What am I?* is a much more open question that permits you to be anything).

Hold the question calmly in your mind. Do not grapple with the question or seek answers. Just let the question rest in your mind. Do not spoon-feed yourself answers either (yes you might want to be a spiritual enlightened person, but do not force that answer upon yourself).

Perceive the originator of the thought. Where is the question "What am I?" rising from? Seek the origin of the question by gazing inward.

Continuing to think, "What am I?" focus on the *I*. What is the *I*? Where does it arise from? Seek the very depth of that *I*.

Continue to tune inwards as the question permeates your mind.

Eventually you will realise that the centre of the *I*, the point from which the question arises, is complete emptiness. And this is you.

When you find the emptiness, meditate on it. It will liberate you from all pressures of the material world.

Self inquiry meditation is a powerful method. The reason it is so powerful is that it connects us with our innermost being, and helps us to realise that we are not subject to nor victim to this material world. We are pure energy that cannot be touched. Do not be surprised if you feel somewhat invincible after doing this method!

CRYSTALS

Crystals offer an additional method of meditating. Plus, they offer some benefits that other methods do not provide. Different gemstones have different benefits, such as purifying the emotions and calming the mind. That's why you might like to add some gems to your practice.

Before we look at exactly *how to meditate with crystals*, you need to ask yourself an important question: Which gemstone should you meditate with?

When meditating with crystals, you are allowing a powerful stone to influence your state of mind.

That's why you must choose the correct gemstone. So, let's start by looking at the different kinds of crystals.

What are the best crystals for meditation?

Just as different types of meditation are better for certain people, the best crystal for meditation is entirely dependent on who you are as an individual.

That said, everyone can benefit from meditating with crystals.

With the best meditation crystals, your practice will dramatically improve. The best meditation crystals can help you to take your training further for several reasons. For starters, meditation gemstones have unique properties that can help to boost your mind-state. Some gems help with anxiety, some help with depression, some help you focus, and so on. They provide unique energy that can alter your mental state.

They also help to ground your meditation.

When you meditate on an object, you bind your energy to that object. For instance, if you have a Buddhist prayer bead mala, that mala will be full of peaceful energy. So, when you wear your mala, you feel more relaxed.

Meditation crystals do a similar thing. They carry unique energy that helps return you to the state you were in when you meditated with the crystal. For instance, if you use meditation crystals for anxiety, the relaxed state of mind that you feel when you meditate with the crystal will stay with the crystal. Then, when you see or touch the gemstone, you feel that calming energy.

Finally, a third benefit is that they can help you focus. It can be easier to meditate on an object, and this is something Buddhists have been doing for millennia with a technique called *Samatha Meditation*.

If you want to know how to choose a meditation crystal, start by determining your own needs.

Ultimately, you are choosing a meditation crystal to create specific desired states. So, of course, the best crystals for meditation are the ones that have the properties that you want to see in yourself.

This will ultimately depend on who you are, your

strengths and weaknesses, and what you want to achieve in your life.

- So to choose a meditation crystal, ask yourself what you want to achieve
- Do you want to achieve inner peace? If so, buy a meditation crystal for inner peace.
- Want to ace your exams? Get a meditation crystal for focus and concentration.
- Want to cure anxiety? Get a meditation crystal for anxiety.
- Want love? Get a meditation crystal for love

You cannot choose your best meditation crystal until you determine what you want to get out of your practice.

So take a few minutes right now to answer this question: What would your best meditation crystal do do you?

For more specific uses, here are the properties of different meditation crystals.

Amethyst: This crystal is used to quiet the mind in order to allow insight and wisdom to arise to the conscious level. Amethyst also enhances visualisation and alters consciousness.

Aquamarine: This is a wonderful gemstone which you can use to improve self-awareness. It is very useful if you have lost touch with your centre.

Carnelian: This one focuses the mind and heightens concentration. Carnelian is very useful when studying. It also cures "monkey mind".

Charoite: This stone is used for creating tranquillity

and relaxation.

Crystal Cluster: This is a fantastic stone to use when meditating with someone else. It will heighten your connection to the other person.

Fluorite: This anchors you and grounds you, improving concentration.

Jade: Jade is a wonderful stone for calming the mind and for curing negative thinking.

Jasper Brown: If you are hoping to achieve a deep meditative state, this stone will help.

Labradorite: This helps to heighten your state of consciousness.

Lapis Lazuli: This enhances wisdom and insight.

Moonstone: Moonstone puts you in harmony with your unconscious mind, and promotes relaxation and peace of mind.

Obsidian: Used for spiritual protection.

Prehnite: Use this crystal to achieve clarity of mind.

Quartz: Quartz is a brilliant overall psychic enhancer, helping to heighten focus and concentration, to raise consciousness, and to improve mental clarity.

Sapphire: (Blue): This brings calmness to the mind and allows deeper intuition to come to light.

Cleansing your crystal

Just as we must cleanse mala bead stones before using them, we need to cleanse gemstones too.

When you first get your meditation crystal, it will have been around for many years and will likely have been handled by many people. That means that the energy of the crystal will not be pure.

So before we look at how to meditate with crystals, we need to cleanse our crystal so that it is pure for you and unaffected by external energies.

But first a friendly warning. Be careful with your meditation crystal. Some meditation crystals are fragile, and some may fade in sunlight. It's a good idea to wrap them in velvet or silk when you're not using them, which will help to protect them.c it.

One of the easiest options for cleansing crystals is to simply bury them in the ground, which will remove negative energy from the crystal.

Another option is to use sea salt. To do this, pour dried sea salt into a glass, delicately place the crystal in the salt facing downward, and leave overnight.

Another alternative is to use water. To do this, hold your crystal in a natural source of running water (or a tap if no natural sources are available)—make sure that your gemstone isn't soluble (some gemstones are more water-soluble than others).

The very best way to cleanse them, however, is with cleansing crystals. Crystals such as carnelian and quartz have cleansing properties. Put a cleansing crystal in a bag with other crystals to cleanse them.

Cleanse your crystal once when you first get it. That will purify it. And then cleanse it again every so often to keep it clear of negative energy.

Now that is has been properly washed, we can start meditating with the crystal.

Exercise: Meditating with Crystals

1) Choose your crystal [see above]. A good crystal may include lines and patterns that help you to get lost in it.

2) Find a quiet and peaceful area where you will not be disturbed [it's best to have a room of the house dedicated to practice]. Hold your crystal in front of you, making sure you can see it clearly. Breathe deeply and calmly, slowing the rate of your breathing gradually.

3) Look at your crystal and observe its every detail. Meditate on the crystal.

4) Close your eyes and take a deep breath in. Now imagine that you are inside your meditation crystal. Allow yourself to become absorbed in the gemstone. Let any thoughts you have subside. Quiet your mind. Move into the crystal, allowing yourself to explore it.

5) Continue meditating in this fashion for ten minutes. When ready, take ten deep breaths and gradually return to psychical reality.

6) Remember the way you feel after doing this crystal meditation.

7) Repeat again tomorrow.

TAOIST MEDITATION

There are eight major types of Taoist meditation techniques, including Zhan Zhuang, neiguan and "Emptiness". They're famous today mostly because they're the Bruce Lee meditation techniques that he spoke about in his movies and interviews.

Despite the fact that he was mostly Zen Buddhist, Bruce Lee did Taoist meditations, which are some of the most powerful methods ever. If you listen to Bruce Lee on meditation, you will hear him say such things as, "There is nothing to try to do, for whatever comes up moment by moment is accepted, including non-acceptance."

The idea, of accepting reality moment by moment, is the core philosophy of Daoism.

Bruce Lee trained himself to have complete acceptance of the present moment through the practice of Taoist meditation techniques like neiguan, Emptiness, and movement meditations like Tai Chi and Qigong. And you, too, can achieve the same thing.

Through Taoist meditation we cultivate acceptance of the present moment and we learn to live as our true selves.

Taoist meditations are a way to clear the mind so that we can have clear perception and acceptance of reality. They are also used to cultivate and control chi, the energy that is the life force behind all living things.

Taoism (or Daoism), is one of the three main religions in

China. Approximately 13 million Chinese people identify as Taoist, and there are approximately 20 million Taoists worldwide.

Taoism (Daoism) began in the 6th century BC with Chinese Philosopher Lao Tzu. Indeed, most meditations used in Daoism are Lao Tzu methods (we'll look at Lao Tzu's meditation techniques in just a moment).

Lao Tzu believed that it is important to live in harmony with nature—both our inward nature and the outward natural world. This is the core belief of Taoism. In order to achieve this, Lao Tzu created a philosophical and practical belief system called the "Tao". Through the Tao (the "way"), Lao Tzu taught people to purify the mind and to live with inner peace, in harmony with the natural world. And the main way he did this is with Taoist meditation techniques.

Ultimately, Taoists believe in harmony, self-acceptance, and following "The Way".

You'll probably notice how so many movies cover these themes, such as Star Wars, which even portrays Taoist techniques when Yoda meditates. There are lots of pop-culture reference to Daoism. However, not many people in the West know how to do Taoist meditation techniques properly. So let me show you how.

The principle of Taoist meditation revolve around the idea of chi.

Chi has a storied background in traditional Eastern healing, which speak of the nadis, meridians, or "energy channels". In the East, life is considered to be the result of vibrational energy, a life-force that flows through all living things. For this reason, much of Eastern healing science is based on techniques and exercises that get this energy flowing, such as through qigong and tai chi.

Chi is made of yin and yang and flows through the body via rivers. If you look at the medical science of countries like Thailand and India, you will find words like "Sen" and "Nadis" describing the energy channels in the body. When the energy channels in the body become blocked, we experience illness. And hence why Eastern healing focuses on curing the blockage to help energy flow. There is some scientific evidence to support this. MRIs and EKGs reveal that our bodies are electromagnetic. And many healing techniques such as meditation and "Shiatsu" (massage) have been scientifically shown to stimulate electromagnetic energy in the body.

Guide To The Taoist Meditations

Taoist meditation techniques are about living in the present moment, accepting the self, and purifying the mind.

One of my favourite quotes by Bruce Lee on meditation is: "The less effort you put in, the more powerful you will be." This expresses the core principle of Taoist Meditation. When we stop striving, we become our true selves.

This is the central philosophy of Taoist meditation techniques. Whichever Daoist meditations you do, you should strive for quiescence.

When describing meditation, Lao Tzu said: "Abide in stillness. The ten thousand beings rise and flourish, while the sage watches their return. Though all beings exist in profusion, they all end up returning to their source. Returning to their source is called tranquility."

This Lao Tzu quote reveals the basic philosophy behind Taoist meditation techniques.

Breath Technique

The best place for beginners to start is with some of the simple breath-based Taoist meditations.

These are perfect ways to develop quiescence. Like in Buddhist meditation, in Taoist, we use the breath to calm the mind and to cultivate inner stillness.

Speaking about meditation, Bruce Lee said, "Be like water,' by which he means that we should be free to flow with the moment in an accepting way. That is what you should aim for when you do Taoist meditations.

EXERCISE: Taoist Breathing Technique

1: Sit with good posture. Sitting in the lotus position is optional but certainly not necessary. What matters is that we sit in a way that supports good spinal health. Alternatively, it is perfectly acceptable to lie down or stand up.

2: Place your hands in your lap with the tips of the thumb touching, like the position used in Zazen, which is a mudra called the Cosmic Mudra, which we discussed in the section on Zen.

3: Imagine chi flowing straight up the spine and out the top of the head. The head and neck should be relaxed, and the chin should be tucked in a little. This helps chi to flow freely.

4: While you are in this posture, make sure you are relaxed. You should feel balanced and free of tension.

5: Bring your attention to your breath. In the Taoist method, we breathe deep in a relaxed way, and always through the nose. Your diaphragm should move, and your breath should flow freely into your lower abdomen. This is the same breathing style used in other meditations and in singing. The flow of the breath into the body will massage the organs, producing a deep sense of relaxation. Continue to focus on breathing for ten minutes.

6: While you are sitting and breathing, place the tip of your tongue on your lower palette. Why do we do this? One of the more interesting parts of Taoist philosophy regards the energy pathways in the body. Like your chakras, certain points serve as hubs for the energy that flows through the body. Two of the most important energy pathways in Taoism are the "du mai" and the "ren mai". Du mai is a pathway up the back of the body. Ren mai is a pathway down the front of the body. These two pathways converge at the hard and soft palate in the mouth. So, by placing the tongue over that spot, we complete the pathway, which helps chi to flow.

7: Notice how saliva is building in your mouth. This is important. Taoists have a very interesting belief about saliva. They believe it is a precious substance, so precious, in fact, that they call it "golden dew". Saliva contains hormones, proteins and other vital substances. That's why, when you notice a build-up of saliva on your tongue while meditating, you should swallow forcefully. This will help the saliva to move deeper into your body (though Western medicine may not agree with this, so you might like to ask a doctor before you try this).

Unlike Buddhists, Taoists do not advocate sitting still for very long periods. This, they say, will cause your energy to become stagnant).

EXERCISE: Advanced Breathing Method

Now that we've practiced just sitting still, let's advance our practice.

1: Sit comfortably on a chair or a cushion, or alternatively, you can lie on the floor provided you can do so while maintaining focus

2: Rest the tip of your tongue on the top palate and start deep breathing through your nose. As you breathe in, visualise chi entering your body as pure white light. The light fills you as water fills a jug. It fills your body and your mind. Notice how the light enters areas of your mind and body that are tight and tense. As it enters those parts, the areas relax, until you experience complete relaxation.

3: As you breathe out, impurities leave your body as black mist. Using your inner eye, watch as that black mist dissipates, being replaced by white light.

4: Breathing deeply and slowly, let the pure white light wash away your sorrow, worry, fears, physical tension and all other negatives. Continue this for twenty minutes.

5: This Taoist meditation technique ends with palming the eyes and face. Rub your hands together many times until they are warm. Now gently, soothingly, brush your palms down your face a few times.

8: Carrying the pure white light with you, come back to the present moment as you open your eyes.

EXERCISE: Chi Meditation

1) Begin breathing naturally while focusing your mind on your breath moving in and out of your lower abdomen. With your eyes open, focus on a point at eye level in front of you. This point should be approximately six feet away. Try not to move your eyes. Continue to focus on this point for 5 minutes.

2) Move your eyes to a position approximately 3 feet away and 45 degrees down in front of you. Focus here for 5 minutes.

3) Continuing to breathe in the same fashion, move your gaze to a point between your feet. Try not to move your head too much; only move your eyes. Focus here for 5 minutes.

4) Continuing the same pattern, focus on the tip of your nose for five minutes. Both your eyes should be fixed on the same point.

5) Close your eyes while still pointing them towards the tip of your nose. Feel your breath entering through your nasal passage and moving through to your abdomen. The air will feel quite cold as you breathe in and quite warm when you breathe out. Continue for five minutes.

6) Focus on the sound of your breathing for five minutes.

7) Now focus on your lower abdomen for five minutes.

8) Still sitting with your eyes closed, breathe in this fashion: breathe in for three counts, hold for three counts, then breathe out for six counts.

9) Imagine all impurities leaving your body as you breathe out. Rub your palms together counter-clockwise so that the palms warm, then hold them over your eyes, warming your eyes.

10) Place your hands down on your lower abdomen. Now open your eyes and sit still for a few moments.

More Taoist Meditation Techniques To Try

We have looked in-depth at one of the most important Taoist meditation techniques. However, there are many more Taoist meditation techniques that you might like to try.

> "When I let go of what I am, I become what I might be." ~ quote by Lao Tzu on meditation.

Emptiness Meditation

Taoist Emptiness meditation is precisely as it sounds. It is sitting quietly and emptying the mind of all thoughts and mental images, including feelings, imaginings and so on. When we do this, we experience a deep state of inner peace.

You may have heard of the Confucius technique "Heart Mind Fasting". Emptiness meditation technique is similar. This is one of the main Bruce Lee meditation techniques that he did often.

EXERCISE: Emptiness

1: To practice Taoist Emptiness Meditation technique, sit still and allow your mind to empty. This gives your mind an opportunity to let go and to move towards emptiness, which is a state in which the vital force and spirit is replenished.

2: Let your thoughts and feelings rise and fall unimpeded, so that your mind flows as freely as the tide upon the shore. The secret to successfully performing this method is to let go of your mind. Let your thoughts rise and fall as they will. Do not try to control them.

Even though this method sounds incredibly simple, it can be challenging. Many people become distracted. If this happens to you, you might prefer to use a more involving Taoist meditation, such as tai chi.

Zhan Zhuang (Pole Standing)

Zhan Zhuang (Taoist meditation when standing) is arguably the main meditation Bruce Lee did. Zhan Zhuang, or "Taoist Standing Meditation", is a method used in tai chi and martial arts to cultivate inner stillness and to create physical strength. It loosely means "pole standing". It is precisely how it sounds: standing still.

Zhan Zhuang is technically considered a "dynamic" method, although it is usually practised standing still in specific stances. For instance, martial artists will stand in one of the fighting stances and will maintain the position for many minutes.

So why would you want to stand still like a pole? Firstly, if you are into martial arts, Zhan Zhuang is one of the best ways of mastering stances. If you are into tai chi or Qigong, Taoist Standing Meditation (Zhan Zhuang) helps you to become aware of how the structure of the body works, as well as practising specific positions (such as Parting The Wild Horse's Main). It is also a great way of developing your concentration.

Zhuangzi

Zhuangzi is a Taoist breathing method. It's an exercise used to bring your mind into harmony with the flow of chi. It is very similar to other breathing exercises.

When he was explaining Zhuangzi meditation, Lao Tzu said we must, "focus vital breath until it is supremely soft." You can do this sitting (as you do in the Buddhist Anapanasati method).

A quote by Lao Tzu on meditation reads: "To circulate the Vital Breath: Breathe deeply, then it will collect. When it is collected, it will expand. When it expands, it will descend.

When it descends, it will become stable. When it is stable, it will be regular. When it is regular, it will sprout. When it sprouts, it will grow. When it grows, it will recede. When it recedes, it will become heavenly. The dynamism of Heaven is revealed in the ascending; The dynamism of Earth is revealed in the descending. Follow this and you will live; oppose it and you will die."

Otherwise referred to as Heart-mind fasting, Confucious described Zhuangzi this way: "Maintaining the unity of your will, listen not with your ears but with your mind. Listen not with your mind but with your primal breath. The ears are limited to listening, the mind is limited to tallying. The primal breath, however, awaits things emptily. It is only through the way that one can gather emptiness, and emptiness is the fasting of the mind.

Neiguan ("Inner Observation")

Neiguan is an advanced Taoist meditation technique that I would not recommend for beginners. In Neiguan we visualise the inner processes of body and mind. This gives us insight into the nature of our being. The proper procedure requires personal tuition because it is a highly advanced method.

Qigong

Qigong translates to "life energy cultivation", which perfectly describes what the practice is all about. It is a mind-body exercise that promotes health and wellbeing and while also providing a gentle workout. Bruce Lee was known to do this along with Tai Chi.

Whenever I practise Qigong, I feel like seaweed swaying under a tide. It is a soothing and relaxing style of movement.

The National Qigong Association tells us, "Qigong is an integration of physical postures, breathing techniques, and focused intentions. Qigong practices can be classified as martial, medical, or spiritual. All styles have three things in common: they all involve a posture, (whether moving or stationary), breathing techniques, and mental focus."

Qi Gong is 2500 years old and over that time, it has become a very detailed and in-depth system. There are very many different Qigong moves, and much like yoga, it also incorporates specific breathing exercises that are used to nourish mind and body.

Because Qigong is so in-depth, it is best to learn from a book or DVD. However, it certainly is one of the best Daoist meditation techniques.

Tai Chi

Tai Chi is very similar to Qigong, and for most intents and purposes, the two can be grouped together. This is another of the movement meditation Bruce Lee helped make famous in the West. Tai Chi and Qigong are both about cultivating chi, slowing down and being mindful of movement.

The best way to think of Tai Chi is as a gentle and soothing exercise that creates mental and physical wellbeing.

The Tai Chi For Health Institute tells us, "The flowing movements of tai chi contain much inner strength, like water flowing in a river, beneath the tranquil surface, there is a current with immense power—the power for healing and wellness."

Benefits of Taoist Meditation

There are significant benefits of Taoist meditation techniques and Taoism in general. Writing for UrantiaBook.com, Meredith Sprunger says, "Taoism is more a philosophy than a religion. It is concerned with the quality of life and has little interest in the heavens, gods, rituals, or life after death." The philosophy of Daoism is ultimately about health and well-being, and because of this, it offers substantial health benefits.

At a glance, Taoist meditation techniques are about creating, transforming and circulating inner energy, which Taoists call "chi". You've probably heard Bruce Lee's meditation quotes when he speaks about cultivating your inner energy. That inner energy is chi. Taoists believe that chi is the universal life energy that resides in all living beings. It is a soft, flowing energy, but a powerful one.

A famous Lao Tzu quotes says, "Water is fluid, soft, and yielding. But water will wear away rock, which is rigid and cannot yield. As a rule, whatever is fluid, soft, and yielding will overcome whatever is rigid and hard. This is another paradox: what is soft is strong."

You can understand the real purpose of Daoist meditations from this Lao Tzu quote. It is about liberating the energy in your body and mind so it can flow freely, unobstructed.

One of the real masters of Taoist meditation is Bruce Frantzis, author of the excellent Relaxing into Being. Frantzis tells us, Meditation can be defined as the process of releasing any blocked energy that is attached to any thought. Meditation is the ability to let go and change the structure inside of you.

Taoist meditation techniques are about removing blockages to improve the flow of chi. Think about Bruce Lee's meditation interview when he discusses being free like water. Water flows freely. And so should your chi.

"Blockages" of chi are detrimental to health. Simply think of how you feel when you are happy and healthy—free and flowing, correct? Now think about being ill; you feel blocked and obstructed. Hence, health can be thought of as a natural unobstructed flow of energy.

When I was 30, I went through depression. My mind was absolutely stuffed full of negative thoughts. My mind and chi were obstructed. It was the same when I was a pudgy-faced kid. I had asthma and was often in the hospital. To this day, when I think back, I can still feel the blockage in my chest. Funny how asthma and depression both gave me the same feeling of blocked energy.

When our energy flows freely, we are healthy and happy. When it is blocked, we are unhealthy and unhappy. Taoist meditation is about removing blockages and freeing energy in the body.

One of the leading causes of blocked chi is a lack of self-acceptance. It is hard to let go and be happy when you do not accept yourself. And so, just as Buddhists advocate self-love and self-acceptance, so too do Taoists. Writing for PersonalTao.com, Casey Kochmer says, "The path to understanding Taoism is simply accepting yourself. Live life and discover who you are. Your nature is ever-changing and is always the same. Don't try to resolve the various contradictions in life, instead learn acceptance of your nature."

Already, we can see that Taoism and Buddhism are similar. And you might be wondering about the difference between Taoism and Buddhism.

There are lots of similarities between Buddhist meditation and Taoist meditation. Bruce Lee did both. Both styles are about purifying the mind, letting go, and living in the present moment. However, Taoist meditations focus on energy (chi) more than Buddhist ones do. Because of this, many Daoist practices involve movement. Because of the similarities, it is a good idea for beginners to practice Buddhist and Taoist meditations. See which works best for you (I do both).

CHRISTIAN MEDITATION

There are many bible meditation methods Christians can use to get closer to God. And there are Christian meditation mantras too (I'll share them below).

If you have wanted to advance your practice of Christianity, or to feel closer to God and to understand The Bible better, meditation can help.

By meditating, we focus the mind, and when we focus the mind on The Bible, Jesus Christ or God, we bring ourselves closer to our faith. We remove any blocks that might be preventing us from fully experiencing Christianity.

In fact, most of the world's meditation techniques can be adapted to be suitable for Christians.

When we are meditating, we focus the mind absolutely on one thing. When we meditate as a Christian, we meditate on the Bible, Jesus Christ, or oneness with God. This could be done with Christian mantras, with contemplation techniques, or with other biblical meditation methods.

You might wonder whether the practice of meditating is different for you, as a Christian. In reality, most Biblical meditation techniques are similar to other meditative exercises.

Just like other methods, Christian meditation techniques are about focusing the mind on one thing, the only real difference is that Christian meditations focus on God.

Just as traditional methods of meditating are about purifying the mind, transcending the self, and achieving enlightenment and oneness, so too are Bible meditation methods. We still focus on purifying the mind and correcting thoughts, but we also strengthen our moral character because we are meditating on The Bible, Jesus Christ, and God. So, in some ways, Christian meditation methods are better than other techniques.

Are Bible Meditation Methods The Same As Prayers?

When I'm teaching Christian meditation techniques to beginners, I'm often asked how these meditative practices compare to prayer. Are the two the same? And if not, how exactly are they different?

As a mindfulness instructor, I find that meditative practices are about listening. Biblical meditation techniques for Christians are all about listening to God. So, when we look at biblical meditation vs prayer, the main difference is that in prayer, we talk to God, and when meditating, we listen to God.

Let's think about that for one moment. When we pray, we are consciously communicating with God. We select a prayer, or we talk to God, and so we are actively involved in that communication process. Meditating is all about listening.

That's why meditation and prayer work very well together. difference between prayer and meditation

Some people ask whether meditation is better than prayer. Seems like a fair enough question, right? Problem is it's unhelpful. It doesn't matter if meditating on the Bible is better than praying, or the other way around. Why not do both? All Christians pray. And one way to go further with prayer and also with our faith is to combine prayer with bible meditation methods. Do both. After all, both bring us closer to God.

Prayer is when you talk to God. Meditation is when God speaks to you.

Where Yogis and Buddhists use their practices as a way to train the mind, Christian meditation techniques are all about getting closer to God and listening to God, mostly through the words of the Bible.

EXERCISE: Christian Meditation

1: Pick up your Bible and mindfully observe how it feels to have that most sacred book in your hands.

3: Choose a passage of the Bible.

3: Read your chosen bible passage to yourself.

4: Now begin to meditate on it contemplatively.

5: You might like to slowly repeat the passage in your mind and focus on the words and their meaning. Be conscious of any thoughts or ideas that arise when you do this. Perhaps the passage is telling you something. Maybe the Bible is communicating with you, sending you a message from God. Be conscious of those messages.

6: Invite insights from God and Jesus into your mind. If you hear their wisdom, promise to take what they tell you and apply it to your life.

This exercise is similar to other meditative practice because we are focusing the mind on one thing. However, we are also interpreting the Bible. This helps us to absorb the teachings of the Bible into the soul.

Not only are we coming closer to God through meditation, but we are also getting the many health benefits of general meditation. So Christian meditation techniques are a win/win!

Benefits of Biblical Meditation:

Grounding

Focuses the mind

Makes us one with God

Helps us to listen to God

Helps us understand the meaning of the Bible and specific psalms

Eliminates negative thoughts

Brings us closer to Jesus

Purifies the mind

Helps us develop the positive characteristics of Jesus Christ.

What The Bible Says About Meditation

As a Christian, you might well wonder whether meditation is

in line with your Christian faith.

The Bible states that meditation is an essential tool for Christians. It tells us that Christians meditate as a way of contemplating the Bible and thinking on good Christian themes such as love and compassion.

"Psalm 143:5 I meditate on all your activity; I eagerly ponder over the work of your hands."

In other words, we meditate on God's word.

As you can see, Christian meditation techniques are about quieting the mind so that we can be conscious of the work of

God and Jesus Christ, and this strengthens our moral character. We do this by bringing to heart the values of the Bible, such as the compassion of Christ.

With biblical meditation, Christians become more like the perfect representation of man, Jesus Christ, by planting the fertile seeds of a moral character.

Psalm 1:3: "He will be like a tree planted by streams of water, a tree that produces fruit in its season, the foliage of which does not wither."

As you can see, what the Bible says about meditation is very positive.

That said, there are some rules that should be applied when you perform Christian meditation.

Rules For Christian Meditation

Scholars advocate that there are three essential rules of Christian Meditation techniques that must be followed:

- Christian meditation practices should be grounded in the Bible. The reason given is that the God of the Bible is a personal God who is sacred to Christians and whose words are holy. Mantras (see the Christian mantras below for examples) given by mystics and by gods outside the Christian faith are generally discouraged. Meditate on God's word. Meditate on God's love.

- Secondly, Christian Meditation techniques should focus on God's love.

- Christian Meditation practice must be done in the interest of heightening worship of God.

In his book The Catholic Catalgoue Catholic author Thomas Merton says, "The true end of Christian meditation is practically the same as the end of liturgical prayer and the reception of the sacraments: a deeper union by grace and charity with the Incarnate Word, who is the only Mediator between God and man, Jesus Christ."

"Reading the Bible without meditating on it is like trying to eat without swallowing."

Christian meditations techniques And Mantras:

Meditative Prayer

Meditative prayer is a type of contemplation. When we do a meditative prayer, we repeat the words of prayer similar to repeating a mantra (though, arguably, without the energy resonances that mantras produce). Below you can try some Christian mantras from the Bible.

Try using these psalms for your meditation

Second Peter 2:9 "the Lord knows how to rescue the godly from trials, and to keep unrighteous under punishment until the Day of Judgment."

Corinthians 13:1 "If I speak in the tongues of men and of angels, but have not love, I am a noisy gong or a clanging cymbal."

Romans 5:8 "But God shows his love for us in that while we were still sinners, Christ died for us."

Meditation on God's Love

Meditating on God's love is another popular meditation for Christians. In this exercise, the individual opens their heart to God and asks to be made one with God (which is identical to the Bhakti method we looked at earlier).

Christian Meditation for Kids

We are agreed that Christians can meditate, right?

Do you also think that it is right for Christian kids to meditate? I do. It's good for their health and their faith.

One of the best Christian meditations for kids is to meditate on God's love quietly with closed eyes. Ask your kids to feel God's love and to focus on it.

Another good Christian meditation for kids is to choose a simple bible verse for contemplation, and then have them contemplate the meaning of the verse. When they're done, discuss the verse with them and lead them to a good understanding of the underlying meaning of that verse.

My favourite biblical meditation

If you're looking to learn how to do Biblical meditation, the best place to start is with Psalm 119:15, which instructs us to "Meditate on God's precepts and ways."

But just how exactly do we do this biblical meditation technique?

If we are going to focus on the word of God, we first need to choose which specific words to focus on.

Choose a passage of the Bible you would like to use for this exercise. Take pride in picking the perfect passage (I have recommended some above). Make sure the passage you choose resonates with you on an individual level. It should feel special *to you* (not to your mother, father, priest or friend—but to *you*).

Once you have selected your passage, write it down.

Exercise: Biblical Meditation 2

1: Go somewhere quiet and peaceful, where you will not be disturbed. The church is an obvious choice.

2: Close your eyes and sit comfortably with good posture.

3: Focus your mind on your breathing for twenty breaths. Relax. Focus.

4: Once you feel focused and calm, read your chosen bible passage to yourself. Read it once and then hold the words in your mind.

5: Focus on God's words, meditating on them. You should hold the words in your mind lightly. Allow the words to be present in your mind.

6: At times you will lose focus. This is natural. Do not be angry about it and do not feel defeated if you lose concentration. Simply return to focusing on the words of the Bible.

7: Your mind will sometimes bring up thoughts, feelings and ideas that might be unhelpful. For instance, if you are meditating on the compassion of Jesus Christ, you may feel unworthy. Do not fight this feeling. Simply acknowledge that it is a feeling and nothing more. Say to yourself, "This is just a thought / idea / feeling".

8: Return to meditating on the bible passage.

9: Continue for 100 breaths. This will take approximately twenty minutes (if you are more relaxed it will take slightly longer). While meditating, consider how the words are relevant to your religious life, or to your life in general. You may also consider how you might make use of the words, how you might go about enacting the words of God. Permit yourself time to reflect on the words of God from a variety of angles.

10: Finish by expressing gratitude. Thank God for being with you during this time and for being there with you in your life. Promise yourself that you will meditate again soon.

4 Biblical Mantras

Try meditating on these 5 Christian mantras in the way we

discussed previously when we looked at mantras.

"**Jesus**": The most obvious Christian mantra is simply, Jesus. Meditate on this mantra to feel closer to Jesus.

"**Yahweh**" This is the first proper Christian meditation mantra. Inhale and say "Yah". Then say "Weh" on the exhale.

"**Lord have mercy**": This is one of the best Christian mantras. It reminds us of the mercy of God.

"**Thank you, Lord Jesus**": This Christian mantra teaches us to have appreciation and gratitude, which are good for mental health. It also teaches us to feel closer to Jesus.

Continual recitation of Christian mantras will help you to develop a higher understanding of God and of your own relationship to God.

DYNAMIC MEDITATION

"Life begins where fear ends." — Osho

One of the most wonderful but also most misunderstood of all meditation techniques is dynamic meditation.

Simply trying to trace the origins of dynamic meditation is the proverbial mystery wrapped in a riddle inside an enigma. So many different spiritualities and religions have used what could be called "dynamic meditations" or "movement meditations".

Take Hinduism, for instance.

Dance is an essential part of Hinduism. Hindus believe that the entire universe is the manifestation of the Supreme Dancer Nataraja. All Hindu gods have their own style of dance and there are 23 celestial Apsaras, beings who dance to please the gods and who express the *supreme truths* via their movements.

In temples throughout India, and particularly in East and South India, dance was traditionally a part of a sacred ritual in which devadasi's (girls dedicated to worship) worshipped the divine through a complex system of gestures and mimes. This sacred ritual evolved to become the South Indian Classical Dance, which is still practiced today. It is said that many of those who perform the South Indian Classical Dance are incarnations of apsaras.

Modern Christianity also uses a form of spiritual dance to bring a person closer to God. Beginning in the latter half of the 20th Century with the modernisation of Christianity, churches have used music and dance as a means of worship.

Judaism, too, involves a sacred dance: the messianic dance or Davidic dance (in reference to King David, who is said to have danced before the Ark of the Covenant).

Then there's the Buddhists, who dance to offer their body to Buddha. To do this they practice three main types of dance: the butterfly dance, the cymbal dance, and the T'aju (eight-fold path dance).

I could go on. Dancing is ubiquitous throughout spiritualities and religions, and also ubiquitous throughout cultures too.

If you like to travel you will probably have seen many different types of meditative movements that are not strictly religious or spiritual. In Japan, for instance, one very popular type of exercise is Katsugen Undo (Regenerating Exercise). It's a wonderful exercise in which you give up your conscious control of your body and allow your body to heal itself. In China, similar exercises called Zifagong, Re-do and Zi Ran Qigong are also popular.

Iran and Turkey likewise use similar unconscious movements and dance exercises. The Mevlevi Dervish is a spontaneous type of movement that, like Katsugen Undo, involves giving up control of the body. These Sufi movements are said to have been created when Rumi was walking through a marketplace one day. He heard the goldbeaters hammering rhythmically away and in a state of bliss he spontaneously broke into dance, spinning in a circle.

> **Rumi:** *a 13th-century Persian poet, jurist, Islamic scholar, theologian, and Sufi mystic. One of the most influential spiritualists in all of history.*

All the forms of dances and movement exercises that we've looked at so far could easily be considered "meditative dance" or "dynamic meditation". And there are many, many more exercises that could also be done in a meditative way.

Evidently, "dynamic meditation" is a very broad term, and could easily be made applicable to countless techniques from a whole spectrum of cultures and spiritualities. But today, when people discuss "Dynamic Meditation", they're referring to a very specific meditation technique that was created by 20th Century mystic, guru and teacher, Chandra Mohan Jain, "Osho".

Osho believed that it would be impossible for a person in the modern day to simply sit still and enter a meditative state. He said, "I never tell people to begin with just sitting. With a mad dance, you begin to be aware of a silent point within you; with sitting silently, you begin to be aware of madness."

Osho was also not focused on the idea of meditation being strictly spiritual or religious. He believed that meditation could be used for connecting to the divine, for self realisation, or as a way of healing and exercising the mind and body.

These principles of non-religious meditative movement are the backbone of the techniques that Osho created. So, bear these points in mind as we now continue onto the Osho Dynamic Meditation technique.

EXERCISE: Basic Osho Dynamic Meditation Technique

There are a few important starting notes that you need to bear in mind before attempting this technique. Firstly, dynamic meditation is entirely about moving when you're body feels like it. Unlike yoga, in which we move through specific poses (asanas), with dynamic meditation we are moving as the body dictates. It's important to allow your body to dictate the way you move, rather than controlling your body with the mind. It's also important to make sure that you are not inhibiting your body in any way. Move entirely as the body dictates, not more and not less.

It is also important to practice dynamic meditation in the right place. The right place for dynamic meditation is a large room where you have plenty of space to move without worrying about bumping into anything. Try to remove any distractions from the space so you will be able to focus.

With these steps in mind, follow these instructions.

1) Stand up and close your eyes. Focus on your breathing for five minutes to relax.

2) Now focus on your body. Meditate on the sensations in your body as you would when performing body scan meditation. Before long you will find an impulse to move. It will be as though your body is asking your mind to allow it to move. Go with it. Let the body control the mind. Let your body dictate its own movement. Be loose enough (mentally) to listen to your body and to let it move itself.

3) After ten minutes begin to get more and more into the dance until you are moving quite actively. Continue

to focus on your body while you dance. Dance for twenty minutes with or without music, whichever you prefer. You should feel no distinction between mind and body and no distinction between yourself and the dance. You're no longer the person dancing. You are the dance.

4) When you are ready to finish, shake out any tension and lie on the floor. Meditate on your surroundings for five minutes.

The above technique is the basic Osho Dynamic Meditation practice, but there are many more similar practices that have been created by Osho, his contemporaries, and other spiritual leaders throughout the years. Among the most popular of Osho's other techniques is *Nataraj.*

Osho's Nataraj meditation is named after Nataraja, the supreme god whom in Hindu mythology created the universe through his divine dancing.

Nataraj is considered a "total meditation", a meditation in which inner division vanishes and we are left with a completely relaxed state of awareness.

When you practice Nataraj meditation, aim to forget about being a "dancer". Aim instead to become the dance itself. Connect to the divine energy inside of yourself. Let go.

EXERCISE: Nataraj Dance Meditation.

1: Stage 1 is the longest stage and should last 40 minutes. In this stage you must dance with your eyes closed. Allow your unconscious mind to completely take control. Make sure that you are not controlling your movements and that you are not aware of the steps. Just dance. Become one with the dance.

2: 20 minutes

The next stage is done lying down and meditating on everything. Meditate on your body and on the environment. Be still and silent.

3: 5 minutes

This final stage is a celebration. Let go, dance, and have fun. Dance how you want to, listening to your body and moving how it dictates. Enjoy the movement. This should be a truly joyous activity.

Turning traditional exercise into meditation

As well as practicing these specific dynamic meditation techniques, you can also meditate while doing traditional exercise.

Whether you're into yoga, tai chi, dance, walking, running, or any other *safe* exercise, you can quickly convert that exercise into a meditation technique. There's just one caveat: You should only ever meditate when performing exercises that cannot possibly lead to serious injury. Obvious example: Running through a field? Check. Running next to a busy road? Scratch. When you meditate you often forget where you are and become what you're doing. That can potentially lead you to being unaware of your surroundings, which could cause an accident. So always be safe, and when in doubt check with a professional before continuing.

Once you've ensured that your exercise is entirely sae fto use for meditation, begin to consider the purpose of the exercise and the manner in which you exercise.

Purpose, or *intent,* is key. When you meditate on an exercise you are *not* burning calories. You're not losing weight. You're not getting in shape. You do not have an end destination. These things *will happen,* but they are not the *intent.* When you're meditating on an exercise the intent is to *become* the exercise. Your mind is one with your body and your body *is* the exercise.

When running *be* the running. Don't be the person trying to drag their body down the road to burn some calories so you can fit into skinny jeans. Make it more divine than that. Make your mind the running. Perform the exercise mindfully. Consciously lift your foot, move it forward, plant it carefully down on to the ground, transfer your weight onto the other foot, and repeat. That's the entire process of running. That's the process your mind should pass through with each and every step you take.

When dancing, don't try to look sexy. That's just inhibition (and inhibition is not sexy). Liberate yourself. Connect with the energy inside your body. Make your mind that energy. *Be* it. That's divine dancing. That's what the devadasi's in the sacred temples of India do. That's what's best for you when you dance.

When you meditate on exercise you're going to notice many wonderful things. For starters you're going to notice that exercise is not as painful as many people think it is. Too many people get bogged down with thoughts like "this is hard work" or "I'm exerting myself" or "I'm shedding the pounds". Those mental thoughts are like weights that your mind carries. It's easier to run when you're not carrying physical weights. It's also easier to run when you're not carrying *mental* weights.

You're also going to notice that exercise is a lot more fun than many people think. If you're too caught up in idea of becoming fit and healthy you lose the whole point: You lose sight of the fact that exercise makes you feel fantastic. When you let go and let your mind be consumed by the activity and the movement, you get to truly experience exercise in a way you may never have experienced it before.

When you meditate on exercise you will develop your appreciation for the miraculous biological architecture that is your own body. Too many people take their body for granted. They think it's a burden that has to be exercised and that stops them from eating all the chocolate and cakes they desire. They miss the beauty of it, the fact that their body is a temple, a sacred, complex, and beautiful thing. But when you let go of your thoughts and you allow your mind to be one with your body, when you finally notice all those million operations and movements that your 206 bones and 640 muscles do to enable you to move, suddenly you realise how amazing your body is.

More than anything, when you meditate on exercise you will enhance your mind body connection and you will feel much more aware and much more appreciative of your body and of your physical reality. That's a truly fantastic thing, because as soon as you're aware and appreciative of your own body you start to make better decisions. Instead of thinking "I want that McChicken Sandwich but I can't eat it because it's fattening" you think "My body is a divine and miraculous abode. I will honour it and love it by making healthy choices". It's a far more positive mental space to be in.

The human body is the best picture of the human soul. – Ludwig Wittgenstein

BODY SCAN MEDITATION: TUNING IN TO YOUR INTERNAL ANTENNA

"Your body is your antenna, always transmitting and receiving signals. Tune in. Listen."

When I finished my tour with The Canterbury Tales and The Marriage Of Figaro I happened to be idly chatting to people on MySpace when up popped a Canadian woman called Jeannie. She was beautiful, cultural, and intelligent—everything I looked for in a woman. But she also happened to be in Canada. Still, I couldn't help but chat to her. The hours past as we chatted on MySpace and then by phone and wouldn't you know it as time passed my heart grew fonder and I made the decision to move country, just for a couple of months, to see if that spark had what it took to become a burgeoning flame. I kissed goodbye to my Oxfordshire home and headed for Heathrow.

My stomach was knotted with nerves as British Airways flight 0097 hurtled through the sky towards Toronto's Pearson International Airport that autumn of 2007. Suddenly I was struck by the reality of what I was doing: moving home to meet and live with a romantic interest that I'd never actually met. What if she wasn't who she said she was? What if she was, in actual fact, some psychologically disturbed criminal who took unsuspecting romantics like me and locked them up in a dungeon? I mean, you never truly know what someone's like until you meet them (and often not even then).

All the time I'd been safely at home in England it never occurred to me just how big a risk I was taking. But at about hour four of the flight the nerves struck me. There was a definite quivering in my stomach. It wasn't the in-flight dinner—a surprisingly good stuffed roast pepper. It wasn't the turbulence. No, it was definitely either some sort of avidya or lack of mental hygiene that was afflicting my stomach.

Have you ever had those moments when you're aware of nerves you're just not entirely sure why? Your body starts sending you signals, like sweaty palms, cold feet, or the classic butterflies in the stomach, and you've no idea why.

The truth is, your body is an antenna. It is always transmitting and receiving signals. When your mind picks up on a source of stimulation (food, drink, raised voice, an attractive person, etc.) your body transmits signals to your brain. These signals are designed to inform you that you are changing mental state.

Imagine walking into a bakery. There're delicious buns oozing with gooey icing. The aroma of freshly baked breads hangs in the air. The cutest little pink cupcakes are fresh out the oven. Your mind picks up on the splendour of the food. Your body reacts. Your mouth waters and your pupils dilate (as they always do when you see something you like). You immediately feel a desire for the food.
Thoughtless, you grab yourself a few treats and gorge on them. Your body is now loaded with sugar. And suddenly you remember you're on a diet.

This is the case for many overeaters. They're not conscious of the sensations in their body, so their body is free to transmit all sorts of signals to their brain, toying with them like a puppet-master.

Those signals trigger them to pick up some food. They eat, mindlessly, and soon feel guilty about it.

Observe what happens when you visualise a delicious cake.

If you're mindful you'll notice subtle sensations in your body (the sensations would be amplified if the cake were real). You might notice that your mouth waters a little, your tongue moves slightly forward between your lips, and your eyes flash. When you're mindful you're able to notice all those little signs and, noticing them, you're able to consciously say to yourself "Those are simple physical sensations". But when you're not mindful, you don't notice those sensations. Going unnoticed the sensations amplify. Your mouth waters more, your stomach begins to prepare for the food, and before you know it you feel hungry.

If only we could have stopped for one minute to consciously say to ourselves "That rumbling in my belly is just a feeling. My watery mouth is just a sensation. I don't have to give in to those things". If we'd have done that we would have taken control of our cravings and not eaten that slice of cake.

The same is true for smokers. A physical sensation occurs in the body that transmits a signal to the brain saying it's time for a cigarette. And the person instinctively grabs a smoke. It's the same process for all addictions.

The same phenomenon happens to all of us. We received a signal from our body. If we're not mindful that sensation becomes thoughts, feelings, and cravings. We then act on that original sensation, as though we're slave to it.

Think of the last time you were angry. Someone suddenly cut you off on the road. Your heartbeat quickened. Your fists clenched. You felt flustered. Before you knew it you yelled at the other driver.

Those body sensations happen very quickly. It really is a case of "blink and you'll miss it". But if you're awake and aware of the sensations in your body, you're able to say to yourself "That's just a feeling. I don't have to act on it". You can then breathe deep and relax.

It's easy to take control of those physical sensations once you know what to do. And the best thing to do is to start practicing body scan meditations.

Body scan meditations are one of the types of meditation I teach most, because the technique is applicable to so many different issues. Drinkers, smokers, overeaters, people who are burdened with excessive emotions… No matter who you are, body scan meditation will most definitely make a difference in your life, helping you to gain more self mastery and particularly helping you to stop cravings. So, how do you practice body scan meditation?

EXERCISE: Body Scan

Before you begin the actual "body scan" you'll want to make sure you're relaxed and that your mind is focused. You might find it helpful to practice the <u>breathing meditations</u> we discussed earlier. Alternately simply lie down, close your eyes, and take five minutes to relax, unwind, and prepare your mind.

Once you've relaxed, take a moment to check your posture. Good posture is essential to the flow of energy in your body and to the balance and focus of your mind. Make sure you are comfortable and that your spine is in proper alignment.

With your eyes closed, focus on the sensations throughout your entire body. Simply observe the way your body feels. It has a vibration and an energy. Get in contact with that energy. Feel it. Investigate it. Is it soft or hard? Warm or cool? Is the vibration fast or slow? Focus the mind on those sensations.

Now direct your mind to the crown of your head. Notice the sensations there. Meditate on the way the crown of your head feels. Take a moment to connect the mind to that part of your body before continuing.

Now gradually begin to move your focus down your body, through your face, your neck, your shoulders, your arms, all the way to your fingers. Then proceed back up your arms to your shoulders, and then down to your feet and toes. Meditate on each part of the body before moving on.

Once you've reached your toes, reverse the procedure until you are once again focusing on the crown of your head.

Now take five minutes to meditate on the sensations throughout your entire body.

Once you have finished, take a few moments to relax before returning to normal.

When you get in contact with your body and the signals it transmits, you'll gain further power over your feelings and emotions.

The first thing you'll notice about body scan meditation is that there's a lot more going on in your body than you may have realised. There are a million vibrations taking place throughout your body. There are also varying degrees of tension and strain. Some areas will be more relaxed than others. Some areas may be quite painful. By being aware of the tension you can take steps to alleviate the problem. This can help to prevent injury and even illness, as you catch the warning signs early on and can then take steps to cure the problem.

You will also notice that different emotions create different kinds of sensations in the body. For instance, worry is almost always matched with a tightness in the chest. When you are aware of the early physical signs of oncoming emotions, you can begin to take control of those emotions. When you feel tightness in your fist, for example, you will have an early warning sign of approaching anger. You can then take countermeasures to address the situation (which in the case of anger would mean taking a deep breath or perhaps going for a walk).

Those same physical sensations are also early signs of cravings. If you struggle with any kind of addiction you will notice that cravings begin with a certain physical sensation. If you smoke you might find that your fingers itch because they want to be holding a cigarette. By being aware of your cravings in their early stages, you can take preventative measures before it's too late; you can do something different instead of submitting to your craving.

The best way to understand the benefits of body scan meditation is this: consider your body to be an antenna. It's receiving signals constantly. Those signals are valuable. They tell you that in a moment you'll be craving a smoke or feeling angry, or that you have tension in your body that could indicate an onset of some condition. Listen to those early signals. Then you can do what you need to do in order to prevent the situation from escalating.

MORE MEDITATIONS FOR THIS REVISED EDITION

CHANTING

There are many benefits of chanting meditation for beginners to look forward to. This meditative style is traditionally used in Buddhism as well as in Hinduism yoga, and Christianity.

In this guide, I'll share everything you need to know to get started with chanting meditation.

What is chanting meditation— A Beginner's Introduction

Chanting meditation is essentially the practice of meditating while reciting various chants, which are often in the form of various *mantras.*

You'll find this style of meditating very relaxing. The gentle humming sounds soothe you with their vibrational qualities and can help to promote the parasympathetic nervous system for a feeling of calm and inner peace.

What's best about chanting meditation for beginners is that it is an effortless and relaxing meditation. You do not require any advanced knowledge or any formal tuition to get started chanting mantras. If you have friends who like to meditate, you can get in a circle and practise chanting meditation with them too, for a fun group meditation.

Whether you're Buddhist, Christian, Hindu, another religion, or an atheist, you will find that there are different kinds of chants perfect for your individual beliefs.

Different spiritual groups use chanting meditation in different ways. The Tibetan Buddhist chanting meditations use a style of choral singing with different performers chanting different pitches. Hindu chanting and yoga chanting tends to focus on the Bhakti tradition, which is focused on loving devotion to god(s). Christians use choral chanting in the church to show devotion to God or Jesus Christ. Meanwhile, non-spiritual individuals use chanting meditation for relaxation and various health benefits.

Speaking of which; there are many different health benefits of chanting meditations.

The Staggering Health Benefits of chanting meditation

Scientific research has revealed that there are significant health benefits of chanting meditation. Naturally, meditation, in general, has significant advantages, but there are also some specific benefits of meditative chants.

For starters, research shows that chanting helps with illnesses. In his book "Human Sounds", Jonathan Goldman researched a group of French Benedictine monks who chanted daily. When these monks decided to stop chanting, they became sick, and during periods when they were chanting daily, they rarely if ever became sick. Does this mean chanting is good for healing?

According to Dr Alan Watkins [Imperial College, London], chanting does help us heal. One reporter even stated that he knew a Buddhist monk who healed his leukaemia by using Buddhist chants.

Are you feeling stressed?

One of the benefits of chanting meditation that you can feel for yourself is the way it reduces stress and anxiety. The gentle vibrations that chanting creates in the body help the muscles to relax and also stimulate the parasympathetic nervous system. Scientific research conducted by the University of Hong Kong revealed that chanting reduces the physiological impact of anxious moments in our lives.

Chanting is also possibly one of the best meditations to lower blood pressure. A study by *Telles, Nagendra, and Nagarathna* revealed that people who practise chanting meditation have better cardiac output and lower pressure.

Want to improve your mood? An fMRI study conducted by the *International Journal of Yoga* revealed that chanting stimulates regions of the brain including the parahippocampal gyrus, thalamus, amygdala, hippocampus, anterior cingulate gyrus, insula, and orbitofrontal cortex. These effects serve to improve our mood and can even help with Post Traumatic Stress Disorder.

Chanting can even help with addictions. In 1991, *Sethi, Golechha, Deshpande, & Rani's* research revealed that chanting for six weeks twice a day in the morning and nighttime led to a reduction in delta and alpha brainwaves, which enhances the sensation of inner peace.

You might also like to use chanting for sleep. Studies show that the gentle act of chanting helps stimulate the relaxation response to let us get a restful night's sleep.

Amazing, isn't it?

I'm sure you'll agree with me that the benefits of chanting meditation are significant. So how do you do it?

EXERCISE: Chanting

Let me teach you an effortless chanting meditation for beginners to use. It uses the sound "Om" (pronounced "Aum"), which is the universal sound in Buddhism.

Sit or stand comfortably with good posture. You should feel stability in your body. This is important because you want your lungs to open fully so that the chant comes from deep within, and the vibrations of the sound stimulate the entire body.

Take 27 mindful breaths. Feel your breath filling your lungs deeply, but do not force this. When you are relaxed, your breath will become deep by itself, effortlessly. While breathing, focus your mind on the sensation of your breath moving through your body.

Start to chant "Om"— you pronounce it "Aum". You should feel the sound resonating between your rounded lips. Relax your throat, so there is no tension. You should feel a connection between your abdomen (the lowest part your breath reaches) and your mouth (which is where the sound will resonate).

You are going to chant "Aum" 108 times. While you do

this, focus your mind on the sound between your lips. It should be a resonant and relaxing sound.

When you get to the 81st breath, meditate on the feeling of the sound resonating in your body. You should be able to feel gentle vibrations that are calming your body, almost like a massage.

Continue until you reach 108 breaths. Open your eyes. How are you feeling? Relaxed and happy? I thought so.

Traditional chanting meditation in Buddhism

It is traditional to use chanting meditations in Buddhism. When we do this, we usually perform chants in Pali. These Buddhist chants are performed for various reasons, including as a sign of devotion to Buddha, to repeat certain important Buddhist philosophies, and to help with training in dharma.

If you ever visit Buddhist temples, you might hear them chanting the popular Buddhist chants. These include:

Buddhabhivadana

Tiratana (The Three Refuges)

Pancasila (The Five Precepts)

Buddha Vandana (Salutation to the Buddha)

Dhamma Vandana (Salutation to his Teaching)

Sangha Vandana (Salutation to his Community of Noble Disciples)

Upajjhatthana (The Five Remembrances)

Metta Sutta f(Discourse on Loving Kindness)

Reflection on the body (recitation of the 32 parts of the body).

The traditional chanting in Khmer Buddhism is called Smot.

Don't you just love chanting meditation?

There are so many great things about chanting meditation for beginners to enjoy. You'll love how simple it is to get started, and you will quickly see impressive benefits, such as relaxation and reduction in the symptoms of stress and anxiety.

FALUN GONG

One form of meditation many people have never experienced is Falun Gong meditation.

Traditionally, Falun Gong was devised as a way of spiritual ascendance through a combination of exercises and meditation. It encompasses a moral rectitude that is centred on Truthfulness (Zhen), Compassion (Shan) and Forbearance (Ren). Developing these mental traits is a key part of Falun Gong.

Practicing Falun Gong involves two key parts Firstly, the refinement of character through the development of virtues, including giving up desires and attachments, similar to in Buddhism. Practitioners develop compassion, truth and tolerance and remove negative thoughts and behaviours, like fighting, greed, and ideas of personal profit. The second part is through physical exercise.

The 5 Falun Gong Meditations And Exercises

As well as the moral development that we looked at above, Falun Gong also includes four exercises that are done standing, and one seated meditation. These are seen as essential but not as important as the moral development aspect.

Exercise 1: Buddha Stretching a Thousand Arms: This

series of exercises is used to open the meridians and to let energy flow freely.

Exercise 2: Falun Standing Stance: This involves four static poses that resemble holding a wheel for an extended time. This is similar to the Taoist meditation Zhan Zhuang. This is said to enhance wisdom and increase strength.

Exercise 3: Penetrating the Cosmic Extremes: A series of three exercises to release negative energy and absorb positive energy.

Exercise 4: Falun Cosmic Orbit: This is done to circulate energy through the body.

Exercise 5: Falun Gong Meditation ("Reinforcing Supernatural Powers"): This is a meditation that is held for as long as possible.

Traditional Benefits of Falun Gong Meditation [and Those Proven by New Research]

Traditionally, it's said that Falun Gong will develop moral character and create a number of "shentong", which are supernatural abilities such as telepathy and divine insight. These are developed through the trinity of moral development, exercise and meditation. Many of these "supernatural abilities" are psychic.

Until recently, there had been very little scientific research into the benefits of Falun Gong and its meditation practices.

New research was published in 2020 by the journal *Brain and Cognition.* The research provides strong evidence there are indeed many benefits of Falun Gong and its meditation.

Ben Bendig, Ph.D., and a team of researchers were fascinated in the effects of Falun Gong meditation for a number of reasons. First of all, Falun Gong became very popular very quickly when it was first released to the public in China in 1992. By 1999, there were an estimated 70 million to 100 million practitioners across China. Then there is the fact that many people who practice Falun Gong claim to experience huge benefits, including clarity of thought and improved health. In '98, the Chinese government surveyed Falun Gong practitioners and found that 98% of the 31,000 people surveyed experienced significant health improvements quickly after practice. 90% of the people who were surveyed had an illness prior to beginning Falun Gong, and 70% claimed that the practice had cured their illness.

Many people believe, understandably so, that these claimed benefits were exaggerated. But there was no scientific research to prove it either way. Bendig wanted to change that. He himself had been successful in using Falun Gong to cure depression and chronic pain. But other than his own personal experience he couldn't scientifically validate these benefits.

"Obviously there was a personal interest," he said, "but primarily it was because it's such a popular qigong practice, and very little research has been done on it."

It would be impossible to research *all* the claimed benefits of Falun Gong. So Bendig decided to focus on the mental health aspects. In particular, they were interested in studying the long-term psychological effects of the practice. They took two groups, one group had at least two years experience with Falun Gong, the other group had no experience and so were taught the exercises. Both groups were given cognitive tests before the study. The groups were tested again, later, after a 90-minute Falun Gong session.

Bendig states, "Practitioners showed improved cognition, particularly for conditions that required coordination of both hemispheres of the brain [the left hemisphere is used for logic, the right hemisphere for creative tasks]. They had a huge improvement after meditating for dealing with this inter-hemispheric character that the novices did not improve."

One of the most observable benefits of Falun Gong, the researchers said, was a boost in emotional processing. Unlike most other forms of exercise, Falun Gong is gentle and slow. Some of the specific postures and held for long periods of time. And the eyes remain closed while Chinese meditation music is played in the background. It is a very relaxing experience. The meditation itself is about focusing on being clear minded, as opposed to focusing on a meditation object or on the breath (the more common form of meditation). This trains the mind to be able to enter a "quiet spot" to connect with inner peace.

Bendig's study adds to the growing amount of evidence that shows that meditation improves emotional control. If you have been struggling to get into meditation, or you're looking for a new way to meditate, Falun Gong seems to be a great option. Why not try this method in your next meditation session, and see what benefits you experience from it?

GONG BATH

There is nothing quite like a gong bath meditation. This ancient healing technique offers benefits for anxiety, sleep, stress and many other mental health problems. Not to mention, they are serenely relaxing. I personally find them utterly divine.

You may have noticed how popular they have been getting. If you visit a bigger city like London or Manchester in the UK, or Chicago in the U.S, you will definitely find yoga studios and sound therapy centres that offer gong baths.

So, what, exactly, is a gong bath?

A gong bath meditation is an old form of sound healing meditation that is rapidly becoming popular today in 2020.

Gongs are one of the oldest of all sound healing instruments. They have been used for almost 6,000 years.

One of the masters of these age-old healing instruments is Don Conreaux. Speaking about the benefits of gong bath meditation, Conreaux says they are "transformative. [They] release tone resonance and complex harmonics that are transferred to the recipient."

There are a variety of different instruments that are

used in gong baths. Of course, meditation gongs are the best. In my experience, when you meditate on these instruments you gain all sorts of benefits, from incredibly personal insights to serene relaxation.

What Happens in A Gong Bath Meditation? Zen, That's What

In a gong bath meditation, we lie down with our heads near the gongs. The conductor then plays these gongs while they are right next to us. This creates vibrations that "bathe" us in the sound. You can feel the resonance of the instruments from your tippy-toes to your crown. You simply close your eyes and meditate while those divine sounds wash over you.

It's something you really have to experience for yourself. It is a divine sense of relaxation and inner peace that you receive when you meditate in a gong bath. It heals both the mind and body.

The Principles Behind Gong Bath Healing

You might wonder just where exactly a gong bath's healing properties come from. Just like when you meditate on Tibetan Singing Bowls, the instruments create specific frequencies that heal the mind and body.

Everything in the universe vibrates at a certain frequency. This includes you and me, as well as all objects in the universe. There is always a vibration. If you meditate you will likely sense your own internal vibration. All of your organs are vibrating. The exact frequency of these vibrations effect both mind and body. Optimally, there will be a uniform frequency in your internal vibrations. This unity creates a sense of inner stillness and peace. However, periods of stress or anxiety can throw your internal vibrations out of whack, and at these times you might like to do a gong bath meditation to restore your optimal internal frequencies.

When you lie down in the yoga pose called *Shavasana*, and let the sounds of the gong bath wash over you, your body syncs to the frequencies of the sound bath, and this heals every part of you.

HEALING EFFECTS AND BENEFITS OF GONG BATH MEDITATION

There are many benefits of gong bath meditations—and not just the fact that they make you feel so utterly relaxed! Here are 5 of the best benefits of gong baths.

1: Healing Anxiety

Perhaps the number one benefit of gong baths is for their effect on anxiety. The frequencies of sounds created in gong baths activates alpha and theta brainwaves, which are associate with inner peace and relaxation—precisely what you want when you have anxiety.

Although specific scientific research on gong baths is limited, we know from research into binaural beats that we can heal the mind by producing two sound tones simultaneously. This produces a third tone, which is the tone the brain sync's two. When this tone is of a certain frequency is manifests in healing properties for both mind and body. This is how gong baths help with anxiety, stress and other mental health problems.

2: Better Sleep

Gong baths help you to sleep better. They do this by producing alpha and theta brainwaves.

We know from science that during the first stage of sleep there is increased activity in both alpha and theta brainwaves. The theta brainwaves continue to increase as we go deeper into the first stage of sleep.

So, part of entering sleep is the activation of alpha and theta brainwaves. These are precisely the types of brainwaves that gong baths produce. And this is why gong baths help you sleep.

3: Nervous system and blood pressure

It is a well established scientific fact that when we are relaxed the nervous system functions better and our blood pressure normalises. Many studies have shown how certain sound healing instruments can help our inner system to relax and therefore to function better. For instance, research conducted by Landry, J.M., revealed that singing bowls can lead to physiological and psychological benefits. The research suggests that instruments that create similar sounds to singing bowls will offer the same benefits. And one such instrument is a gong.

4: Helps you go deeper in meditation

Probably the most common problem people experience with meditation is that they can't relax enough to get into it. One solution is to use tools and instruments to help your mind to relax while you meditate. A gong bath is the perfect example of this.

Listening to a gong bath produces alpha and theta brainwaves that help you to relax. This, in turn, will help you to go deeper in meditation.

5: Therapy

Because of the benefits that we have looked at above, it is not unusual for gong baths to be used in therapy for anxiety, depression and other (mostly) mental health problems. Indeed, they are one of the longest standing therapies in traditional Eastern Medicine.

Basically, they're divine

There are so many benefits of gong bath meditations, as we've seen above. But to be honest with you, what I love most about gong baths is that they are simply divine. They're so relaxing. It really is a unique experience. That's why I recommend you try one.

F.A.Q

Are gong baths good for you?

There is limited empirical evidence to suggest whether gong baths are good for you. However, from research into other forms of sound healing it is likely that gong baths help with mental health conditions and overall have a therapeutic effect on the mind and body.

What should I bring to a sound bath?

The yoga studio or sound therapy studio will provide everything you need. Simply wear comfortable clothing.

What does a gong bath do?

In a gong bath you are submerged in the sounds of gongs. This produces alpha and theta brainwaves that are associated with inner peace and relaxation. Therefore they help with stress, anxiety and other problems.

Are Sound baths dangerous?

As of date of writing, there are no scientifically established dangers of sound baths. People with pre-existing mental health problems should consult a healthcare professional before doing gong bath meditation.

How do you feel after a gong bath?

Most people feel very relaxed after a gong bath. If you have ever experienced a deep and restorative night's sleep, gong baths have a similar effect.

CONTEMPLATIVE MEDITATION TECHNIQUES

There are many different kinds of contemplative meditations that are used in numerous spiritualities around the world techniques in use today, and these methods can help to awaken your mind to new perceptions about yourself and the world around you.

As a meditation teacher who has spent thousands of hours meditating, I've discovered some truly amazing things about my mind and life in general. For instance, I've learned that I have a potent sense of empathy that I used to take for granted.

Finding your spiritual strengths like that can open up a new chapter in your life.

The moment I learned I had heightened levels of empathy, I set about healing other people.

That's just one of the ways that the insight gained from contemplative meditation has helped me.

As a unique individual, you will have your spiritual strengths, and a few spiritual weaknesses too. Once you find those strengths and weaknesses, you will gain an all-new, enlightened perspective of yourself and the world around you.

Four contemplative meditation practices will unlock your insight and transform your perspective. Let's take a look at each of them.

4 Contemplative Meditation Techniques

Note that you'll get way more out of this if you meditate in a place that has contemplative architecture, such as a church or by the water.

1: Meditating on a spiritual text (like the Bible)

One of the oldest forms of contemplative meditation techniques is meditating on a spiritual text, for instance, meditating on the Bible.

Meditating on the Bible, the teachings of Buddha, the writings of Lao Tzu, or on any other spiritual text, is a powerful way of gaining a fresh perspective of spiritual life.

Books like the Bible and the Gita are perfect for contemplative meditation. Techniques like biblical mantras (reciting mantras from the Bible) are excellent for developing your faith.

Never meditated before? Then this meditation is perfect. It's one of the best contemplation meditation techniques for beginners. And it is immensely enjoyable and rewarding.

Simply choose your favourite spiritual text and find a

passage in it that truly resonates with you. Now sit somewhere peaceful and take five minutes to relax your mind (focusing on your breath helps).

Once you are focused and relaxed, read the spiritual text out loud and focus on the words. You can focus on the imagery of the words, the underlying meaning of the words, the sound of the words, or on the way the words make you feel. This turns *contemplation* into a contemplative *meditation technique*.

When you do this, you may begin to think of the text in new ways. Let this happen. Let the text reveal its true meaning to you, similar to how *magic eye* images reveal their picture once you are looking at them the right way.

This is one of the best contemplative meditation techniques. It will deliver valuable insight and transform your relationship with the text.

As an alternative to this, you might also like to try meditating on a sacred mantra.

2: Contemplating the divine

Most spiritualities that practice meditation have at least one contemplation meditation technique used to connect with the divine.

- In Hinduism, it is called Bhakti technique.
- In Christianity, it is biblical meditation.
- In Buddhism, it is the Dhyana method.

To be a spiritualist implies seeking the divine. And most spiritualists enjoy meditating and contemplating on the divine.

A way to go further in this contemplation technique is to find oneness with the divine. Focus on a representation of divinity (a statue, sacred passage, religious image, etc.) or your idea of divinity. This can become quite a deep contemplation technique.

Go further with this contemplation-meditation by bringing to mind your deity and observing how the mind conceives of that deity (whether it be by a mental image, a specific feeling or a mental sound). Finally, focus the mind on this conception, such that you are meditating on the way your mind conceives of divinity.

This is one of the most rewarding contemplative meditation techniques. It brings us into contact with the sacred in a way many people have never experienced.

3: Practising contemplation-meditating on an object

As well as using meditation to contemplate the divine, we can use it to contemplate physical objects.

There are very many physical objects on which to meditate. They range from the elements to meditation crystals to aspects of nature.

No matter which objects we focus on in contemplative meditation, we practice in the same way. We bring the object to mind (either by looking at the object or by visualising it) and we focus 100% on the object. When we do this, we do not judge the object. We simply allow the object to rest in mind, focusing on it 100%.

This practice helps us to perceive the reality of physical objects. These types of contemplative meditation techniques can be powerful sources of insight.

FOREST BATHING

I love forest bathing meditation. In Japan it's called "Shinrin Yoku" [1], which literally translates to "Forest Bathing". The meditation script, benefits, and tips in this guide will help you to start this rising form of meditation.

Nothing feels better than sitting by a willow tree, closing your eyes, taking some deep breaths, and meditating on nature in the forest. Even if you've never tried it, you can easily imagine how relaxing this activity is. It helps you to feel calm, centred, and connected with nature.

The tradition on Shinrin-Yoku started in Japan in the 1980s [1], making it one of the most modern types of meditation (although thousands of years ago Buddhist monks would sit in the forest to meditate, they did not refer to it as "Forest Bathing Meditation" or "Shinrin Yoku").

Nature bathing, the practice of letting yourself be one with nature, caught on quickly, largely thanks to its many health benefits and the fact that it is one of the most enjoyable meditations you can possibly do.

It's an incredibly refreshing practice in this day and age, and offers an escape from the busy city. According to the Environmental Protection Agency (EPA), the average American spends 93% of their life indoors. That's a whopping chunk of time. And it reveals how we are becoming disconnected from nature.

As we live busier lives in noisier environments, it is becoming imperative to take the time for ourselves to head out into nature and reconnect with the trees, the water, the birds, and the natural world.

And if you cannot get outside to do this technique in the ideal way, studies show that you can get many of the same benefits by meditating on natural sounds and natural virtual environments [2], such as by playing relaxing birdsongs on Youtube. Alternatively, you might like to create a meditation garden area to practice in.

Whether you practice inside or outside, there are many benefits of Forest Bathing meditation. Let's take a look at what this technique will do for you.

EXERCISE: Forest Bathing Meditation

1: Follow the basic rules

You can choose to do forest bathing meditation with a partner or by yourself.

Be mindful and do not overthink.

Don't go into forest bathing meditation with a goal. Have an open mind towards the experience.

Aim for a minimum of twenty minutes. 20 to 30 is ideal according to research. [3]

If you're walking instead of sitting, do not treat it like a workout. It's a meditation.

2: An ideal place

Despite being called "Forest bathing meditation", you do not need to do it in a forest. The name comes from "Shinrin-Yoku", which literally translates to "Forest Bathing". It's a Japanese word. In Japan, there are many forests. Maybe you, however, do not have a forest nearby. In that case, any natural environment will do. Although ideally, you will have the sounds of water and birds around you.

3: When you enter your forest or natural environment

When you enter, take a moment to connect with the forest or the natural environment. Notice the place you are in, the sights, the sounds, the feelings. Breathe in the forest.

Tune-in to your body. Notice how you are standing or sitting. Feel the sensations through your body. You might also like to touch parts of the forest, like stones and trees, to experience that connection.

4: The actual forest bathing meditation script

1. Sit with good posture. Take a few deep breaths to relax. Close your eyes.
2. Practice a "Five Senses Meditation". This is where you go through each of your senses, meditating on them one at a time.
3. Touch the ground mindfully. Feel the sensation of the forest on your hands.
4. Now sit with your legs crossed and eyes closed. Take 108 breaths as you practice *open meditation*

(Be aware of the entirety of your environment, meditating on each of the five senses).

5. When you finish your meditation, take a moment to express gratitude for nature. Think of all the ways nature benefits of you. Remember that you are always connected with nature.

Benefits of Forest Bathing Meditation

In my experience, you can immediately feel the benefits of forest bathing meditation the moment you start doing it. The relaxing breeze brushing past your face. The sweet calls of birdsong around you. The grass at your feet. It is immediately relaxing. And science shows it works. Not only does it give you the regular scientifically proven benefits of meditation, it does much more besides.

A 2010 study on Shinrin-Yoku found that forest bathing meditation helps reduce cholesterol, lower blood pressure, lower pulse rate, and increase parasympathetic nerve activity and lower sympathetic nerve activity for people who usually live in cities or other busy environments.

MaryCarol Hunter [an associate professor at the University of Michigan School for Environment and Sustainability] conducted a study last year (2019) that was published in the journal Frontier in Psychology. She discovered that spending twenties minutes in nature (meditating or doing other activities) lowers stress hormone levels. They described it as a "nature pill".

For the study, the researchers took 36 volunteers from

the Ann Arbor area and asked them to spend a minimum of ten minutes a day in nature, for at least three times a week. They could do this when and where they chose, provided they felt connected to nature.

The researchers took saliva samples before and after the nature-exposure period. The samples revealed that spending time in nature reduced the stress hormone cortisol by 21.3%. Researchers note that it is optimal to spend 20 to 30 minutes in nature. Anything less provides less benefits. Anything more does not provide additional benefits.

Exposure to nature also has many other benefits. It improves sleep quality, improves immune system functioning, improves mental health, reduces stress, reduces inflammation, and increases focus. Those benefits are the mental health aspects. There's also the fact that forest-bathing brings with it lots of fresh air and Vitamin D.

Given the fact that meditation has so many health benefits, and that walking in nature in one of the best hobbies for mental health, it is easy to see how forest bathing meditation benefits you.

APPLICATIONS

Now that we have looked at the most important meditation techniques, let's discuss some of the main ways in which you can use meditation in your life.

If you have pre-existing health conditions, consult a healthcare professional before using the techniques in this book.

ANXIETY

As a meditation teacher, one of the main reasons people ask me for help is for anxiety relief. The good news is that scientific research proves that meditation is effective for the relief of anxiety, and there are many different methods you can choose to use.

Here's the list.

10 Best Meditation Techniques For Anxiety

I recommend trying each of these exercises and finding the one that works best for you. When you find your best method, use it daily for continual relief

1. Mindful Breathing

The ideal place to start is with a simple breathing meditation. You would have heard many experts touting the benefits of this practice, including Jack Kornfield and Dr. Oz.

This type of meditation soothes the mind and generates inner peace. It is fundamentally like a breath of fresh air when you're feeling anxious.

A study published by the National Institute of Health in 2016 found that daily mindful breathing yielded large effects in the reduction of anxiety and increased positive thoughts.

2: Vipassana

One of the best Buddhist meditations for anxiety is Vipassana.

Vipassana is a meditation technique in which we label our emotions while meditating on the breath. For instance, if we are meditating on the breath when we suddenly feel worried, we tell ourselves "this is just a feeling."

So why is this one of the best meditations for anxiety and depression? When you practice vipassana, you learn to dissociate from feelings so that anxious thoughts don't affect you so much. In 2001, the Journal of Scientific Research found that a 10-day training program in vipassana meditation "may help mitigate psychological and psychosomatic distress."

3: Mindful Walking

I couldn't write this list of meditations for anxiety without mentioning mindful walking, a truly relaxing method that combines the relaxation of walking with the mental health benefits of mindfulness.

This is one of the best meditation techniques for anxiety if you prefer to be a little active, and especially if you happen to have a relaxing natural environment to spend time in, such as a beautiful park.

A trial published by the American Journal of Health found that ten minutes of meditation followed by a ten-minute walk reduced anxiety significantly better than a walk by itself.

4: Self – Guided Meditation For Anxiety

When you think sad thoughts, you become sad. When you think thoughts that make you anxious, you become anxious. Simple, right?

One of the best ways to take control of your symptoms is by controlling what's in your mind. And one of the best ways to do that is by using self-guided meditations for anxiety. "Self-guided" means you lead yourself through a visualisation that alleviates your symptoms. Essentially, we imagine specific things to produce specific changes in the mind.

CalmClinic states that "Visualisation… is a relaxation strategy that makes it much easier for you to cope with your anxiety symptoms during periods of high stress."

5 Guided Meditation For Anxiety

Research from the journal Behavioural Brain Research shows that guided meditations are helpful for anxiety. The research reveals that listening to a guided meditation for 13 minutes a day for eight weeks significantly reduces anxiety.

6: Body Scan

Another of the best daily meditations for anxiety is "Body Scan". This exercise reduces the physical symptoms of the condition. It does this by systematically relaxing the body. This system was devised by Jon Kabat Zinn and is a fundamental aspect of the Mindfulness-Based Stress Reduction program.

One of the critical reasons to use meditation techniques for anxiety is that when you meditate you become aware of bodily sensations, which are often the causes of the problem. When you feel your physical symptoms coming on, you might enter a panic attack. Controlling the initial symptoms of panic attacks is half the battle. With Body Scan, you learn to recognise the very early stages of an upcoming panic attack. You can then take steps to cut-off those symptoms before they get any worse.

A study published on the National Institue of Health showed that women with breast cancer who used MBSR [Mindfulness Based Stress Reduction, in which Body Scan is the primary technique] "experienced a significant improvement in 16 psychosocial variables compared with [a control group]. These included health-related, [breast cancer] specific quality of life and psychosocial coping, which were the primary outcomes, and secondary measures, including meaningfulness, helplessness, cognitive avoidance, depression, paranoid ideation, hostility, anxiety, global severity, anxious preoccupation, and emotional control."

6. Mindfulness

Scientific research has proven that arguably the very best meditation technique for anxiety is mindfulness. Like Lao Tzu says: "If you are depressed, you are living in the past. If you are anxious, you are living in the future. If you are at peace, you are living in the present moment." Scientific research has proven that this is an excellent technique for social anxiety, depression, and for stimulating the relaxation response, so you experience less "fight-or-flight".

Anxiety.org tells us, "Research has shown that mindfulness helps to reduce anxiety and depression. Mindfulness teaches us how to respond to stress with an awareness of what is happening in the present moment, rather than simply acting instinctively, unaware of what emotions or motives may be driving that decision."

7. Emptiness

This form of meditation originates from the teachings of Lao Tzu, the father of philosophical Daoism. Emptiness meditation refers to the act of emptying the mind by focusing on nothing. This creates a sense of space in the mind, which is very relaxing. Definitely one of the best meditations for anxiety because it gives your mind a break.

Pranayama

Pranayama refers to the way we breathe when we do yoga. It is a deep style of breathing that is coordinated with movements of the body. By meditating on the breath in pranayama while doing yoga, we relax both the mind and the body, which is one of the best ways of handling anxiety.

A study published in the International Journal of Yoga in 2013 revealed that students who practised pranayama for one semester significantly reduced their anxiety and improved their test results.

9: Mindful CBT (Cognitive Behavioral Therapy)

An alternative type of meditation for anxiety is Mindfulness-Based Cognitive Behavioral Therapy (MBCBT). MBCBT is an extension of cognitive-behavioural therapy. It is a method of using specific strategies of thinking to change negative thoughts.

10: Loving Kindness

Loving kindness is the best meditation for anxiety that involves other people. For instance, social anxiety and relationship-anxiety. The reason why this is better than other methods is that it involves creating positive feelings about other people. It trains us to receive love from others and to give love too. This creates a sense of emotional support that helps relieve symptoms.

A 2015 study by Evidence-Based Complementary And Alternative Medicine found that loving-kindness led to significant reductions in depression and anxiety, with less rumination of negative thoughts and increase in positive emotions.

What Are The Best Meditations For Social Anxiety?

The best meditations for social anxiety are ones that change the way we feel about other people. And, importantly, ones that change the way we *think* they feel about us. For instance, the two Buddhist methods Loving Kindness [Metta] and Karuna [Compassion] are all about developing feelings of love, kindness, and compassion towards other people. While doing these techniques, we visualise giving and receiving love and compassion for and from other people.

These are the two best meditations for social anxiety because they help us to develop compassionate relationships with others.

Stefan. G. Hoffman [Department of Psychological and Brain Sciences, Boston Universit] conducted research into the effect of Loving Kindness Meditation on social anxiety. In his conclusion he wrote, "Adding an LKM component to traditional psychotherapy (such as CBT) that primarily targets negative emotions, might significantly enhance the efficacy of treating mood dysregulation, possibly by enhancing adaptive emotion regulation. We also predict that such a strategy might be beneficial for treating anxiety disorders, such as PTSD, generalised anxiety disorder, and social anxiety disorder.

You can also use general mindfulness meditation technique for social anxiety. This is a technique where you simply observe how you are feeling in the present moment. This helps you to recognise that your feelings are just feelings and that they are unimportant.

It's also worth using daily mindfulness meditations for social anxiety. You can do this by practising mindful breathing during panic attacks or using apps like Headspace and Calm, which have quick exercises you can do. The main benefit of using mindfulness meditations for social anxiety is that they quickly return your focus to the present moment, and this helps you to relax.

Best Meditations For Relationship Anxiety

Similar to social anxiety, meditation techniques can help us build better relationships by making us more compassionate towards other people. Buddhist Metta and Karuna [which are basically about visualising yourself giving and receiving love and compassion from other people] will help you with your relationship. They are the best types of meditations for anxiety in a relationship because they cultivate more compassion and understanding.

In his book Altered Traits, internationally renowned psychologist Dan Coleman explains that with Loving Kindness Meditation "You handle stress better, you're calmer, you're less triggered, and you recover more quickly." He goes on to explain that LKM leads to heightened compassion and empathy, which makes us more understanding of our significant others, which in turn reduces the symptoms and effects of relationship anxiety.

Best Meditation Techniques For Anxiety Attacks / Panic Attacks

The best types of meditation techniques for anxiety attacks (or "panic attacks") are a little different. Panic attacks are different to other forms of anxiety. They are about very heated feelings that come on out of nowhere.

In my experience, as someone who has personally used meditation for anxiety attacks, the best option is mindfulness and Mindful CBT [cognitive behavioural therapy]. Any technique that immediately brings you back into the present moment (such as mindfully holding an ice cube, or taking a cold shower and meditating on the sensation of water on your body) are also good options. Techniques like these can cut through the panic attack and snap you back into the present moment.

Best Meditation Techniques For Anxiety In School / Exams

We all know what it can be like to be stressed about your school or university work. Thankfully we can use meditation for exam anxiety. One of the best ways to do this is to take mindful breaks.

One of the primary reasons for anxiety when studying is because we cram the mind with too much information. This is equivalent to lifting too many weights at the gym. Studying hard makes your mind ache. And just like your body, your brain needs a break.

For this reason, the best meditations for anxiety in school are easy methods that let you relax and take a break, such as basic mindfulness. When you feel stressed about exams, meditate on your breath. Simply close your eyes and take 108 mindful breaths. Do not listen to a guided meditation, which is just more noise. Your breath should be your guide.

Best Meditation Techniques For Anxiety At Work

It's best to use some relaxing and easy meditation techniques for anxiety at work. If you are feeling the pressure or you're stressed, your mind is telling you that you need a break. And when the brain needs a break, it wants silence and stillness. For that reason, the best meditation techniques for anxiety at work are easy mindfulness exercises. Take some mindful breaths, or do simple mindful exercises such as tai chi or yoga, which will also help to relax your body if you have been sitting for too long.

DEPRESSION

There are many meditations that can help with depression. They start from the very basic breathwork to guided meditations and traditional methods. These methods can significantly reduce your symptoms as well helping with grief and other complicated emotions.

The easiest is breathwork. When you focus the mind on the breath, you silence your thoughts, which helps you to escape from depression and anxiety.

Like a cup, if the mind is full, nothing more can be put in it. No new information can enter a full mind. A problem. Because just as the body needs water, the mind needs new information. Meditating empties the mind. Then, new, healthy, positive information can enter. Meditation helps us let go of what is there, and put something happier and more pleasant in its place.

Meditation can also help with many of the root causes of depression, of which there are many. Causes of depression include everything from family history to childhood trauma and certain events in life. These circumstances can lead to mental health problems, including low self-esteem, self-criticism, sadness, and feeling depressed.

According to research by Princeton, depression is caused when fewer new brain cells are produced. The link between daily meditation and depression is that meditation increases the production of new brain cells and balances certain chemicals involved with depression.

Specifically, meditation helps depression by effecting the following brain chemicals:

Serotonin: Serotonin is the "feel good" chemical and often plays a pivotal role in depression. Low levels of serotonin are linked with depression. Most brain cells are affected by serotonin. The chemical aids in communication between parts of the brain, and has a significant influence on mood. Research by the University of Montreal shows that mindfulness and meditation help by bathing neurons in feel-good chemicals that reduce stress, which is one of the leading causes of low serotonin levels.

Norepinephrine: Norepinephrine is a neurotransmitter in the central nervous system that increases arousal and alertness levels. Too much secretion of norepinephrine can cause anxiety. Too little norepinephrine can lead to depression. Meditation does not have an acute effect on the production of norepinephrine. However, it *does* block the hormone's effect. Because of this, hormone levels are not decreased, but we still get the calming effect

Cortisol: Cortisol is produced during stress. Too much cortisol destroys healthy tissues and prevents "good hormones" from being built, including serotonin. Meditation balances cortisol to prevent this from happening.

One of the most authoritative studies on depression and meditation was produced by The Lancet medical journal, which conducted a study of 424 British adults. The group was divided in two. Half the test group were allotted pills and the other half were given lessons in mindfulness. The latter group stopped taking their medication entirely after a winding-down period.

The results were impressive.

"The relapse rates in the two groups were similar, with 44% in the mindfulness group and 47% for those on the drugs," reports British newspaper The Guardian.

Lead author Willem Kuyken, professor of psychology at the University of Oxford said, "Our hypothesis was that [therapy would be more effective than pills]."

The results showed that meditation is equally as good as medication and does offer an alternative therapy. It also revealed that one of the best types of meditation for depression is mindfulness.

Nigel Reed, who has been suffering from depression and who took part in the study, says, "Mindfulness gives me a set of skills which I use to keep well in the long term."

The study also determined that mindfulness might work better than pills for people who are at high risk of relapse.

The best meditations for depression help us to stop negative thoughts.

It doesn't matter whether you're using a simple method like mindful breathing, an advanced method like VIpassana or a guided meditation for depression, one of the main reasons why meditation helps with depression is because it helps us control negative thoughts.

EocInstitute rell us, "Scientists estimate the number of human thoughts at around 50,000 per day — meaning a negative, depressed mind can literally generate dozens of pessimistic thoughts per minute!

You need to stop negative thoughts so that you can find peace and calm. You need to find a new, positive way of thinking. One way to change your negative thoughts is to use mindfulness-based cognitive behavioural therapy (MBCBT). This is a powerful way of boosting positive thoughts in your mind while reducing negative thoughts. To do this technique, essentially what you will want to do is meditate, listen to your thoughts and challenge any negative thought that comes along. This will help stop depressive thoughts.

As well as MBCBT, the following techniques can be particularly helpful:

Anapanasati

As we looked at previously in the book, Anapanasati is a mindful breathing exercise that cultivates relaxation and inner peace. It gives the mind a break away from depressive thoughts so you can begin to heal.

Zen Walking

I'm sure you'll agree with me when I say that when you're feeling down, a pleasant long walk helps a lot. A walk gives you the chance to escape and allows you to clear your mind. Especially if you go for a walk in a beautiful natural environment such as a park or a hike through the forest. The only thing better than a walk is Zen walking. Daily practise will cultivate inner peace and relaxation, especially if you walk outside. Being inside for too long can cause mental atrophy and general sadness. Getting outside and doing mindful walking will help to relieve the symptoms of depression.

Loving Kindness (Metta)

Scientific research reveals that Loving Kindness is one of the best daily meditations for depression because it helps to cultivate feelings of happiness, interconnectedness, and love.

Mindfulness

When you practise mindfulness, you train yourself to let go

of thoughts and to focus on the moment. This is very potent for sadness because it helps you to escape the perpetual cycle of painful ideas that can make you feel depressed. I especially recommend mindfulness if you are suffering from negative-thought depression.

The NHS tells us: "When we become more aware of the present moment, we begin to experience afresh things that we have been taking for granted."

Self-Guided Meditation

An alternative solution is to use guided imagery for depression. Guided imagery or "visualization" is essentially a method in which we lead the mind through different imaginings, such as imagining you are on a relaxing beach in the sunshine.

Try the following self -- guided meditation for depression:

1) Imagine standing on the beach beside the ocean
2) Sea the waves lapping to and fro at your feet
3) Hear the swoosh of the waves
4) See the horizon
5) Feel the warm sand at your feet
6) Taste the crisp air
7) Say to yourself, "I am relaxed and calm. It is a good day".

I'm sure you can see the benefits of using this self-guided meditation for depression, anxiety and other conditions. It trains the mind to think about positive, relaxing things and this cultivates peacefulness.

Body Scan

When you are depressed, you lose touch with the present moment. The condition causes the mind to become consumed by ruminating negative thoughts.

Comparatively, when we are happy, we live in the moment. Living in the moment essentially means focusing on reality instead of psychological phenomena. Body Scan technique gets you in touch with your body and puts you back in the present moment.

STRESS

Stress is one of the main reasons people start meditating in the first place. We are living in a world where stress is an epidemic. And it is easy to see why. With the pressure at work, the amount of financial stress we all face, health anxiety, relationship worries… there are simply so many things to be stressed about.

However, it is quite simple to start reducing the symptoms of all this worry and anxiety. And the best way to do it is to use some simple meditations for stress relief.

Meditative exercises reduce the inflammatory response to worry and to negative thoughts, which reduces the health impact of tension. Mindfulness also reduces activity in the amygdala and increases connections between the prefrontal cortex and the amygdala, which lessens reactivity and improves our ability to manage stress naturally. It also stimulates activity in the parasympathetic nervous system, which creates relaxation.

Here are some of the best meditations for stress-relief.

Try this simple exercise

Close your eyes for a few minutes. Breathe in through your nose and out through your mouth. Count to 27 breaths. Now recite the following words to yourself several times in your mind. "I am feeling tense at the moment, but it is just a feeling. This feeling will pass. I am safe. All is well. I am becoming calm". Now, continue to focus on your breath. On each inhale say the word "Relaxing". And on each exhale say the word

"Calming". Continue to count your breaths as you recite the words. Aim for 108 breaths.

Mindfulness

Arguably the very best meditation for stress relief is mindfulness. When we use mindfulness meditation for stress, we simply observe stress for what it is: an emotion with physical sensations. Often when we are stressed, we sink inside the mind. Do you find that you have lots of negative thoughts when you feel anxious? Do you get caught up in those thoughts? If so, mindfulness will help. It gives you the ability to get away from your worries and to step outside your negative thoughts so that you are not controlled by your emotions.

Buddhist Methods

There are many excellent Buddhist meditation techniques for stress relief. Methods range from focusing on the breath to going for a mindful walk.

The core philosophy behind Buddhist methods is that they help us to understand the processes of the mind, including the feelings of pressure and anxiety. When you practise Buddhist methods, you gain an understanding of how the mind works, and you gain greater control of your mind. So if you have felt like you don't understand how your mind works, and you feel like you don't have control over your worries and concerns, you will find Buddhist methods excellent, especially Vipassana.

Vipassana is all about observing your various mental states and processing them more healthily. When we practice Vipassana, we meditate on the breath, and we label our emotions and thoughts. For instance, if you experience a thought while meditating, you will simply say to yourself, "This is a thought" or "This is an emotion". It's simple but powerful. It trains your mind to process thoughts and feelings more rationally, so you are less reactive to negative states of mind.

Anapanasati is also beneficial. Anapanasati teaches us that it is natural to go through different states of mind and that invariably if we get caught up in one frame of mind, it will soon dissipate. This teaches us that mental states are impermanent, so we need not be too worried when we momentarily experience anxiety.

Taoist Techniques

Taoist techniques are all about living as our true selves and connecting with pure energy (chi) inside of us. Taoist techniques cultivate purity of mind and body and eliminate negatives, such as toxins in the body and anxiety in the mind. The reason these are some of the best meditation techniques for stress relief is that they cultivate inner stillness and tranquillity. We learn to let go of anything we don't need, and we live more naturally, in harmony with our true selves.

SLEEP

Science shows that one of the best ways to get to sleep is by using self-healing meditations. Meditation helps to quieten the mind and promote inner-calm so we can get a restful night's sleep.

Not only this, but meditation helps improve the quality of sleep too. It even reduces our need for sleep. Neuroimaging studies show that meditation helps sleep issues because it makes us need to sleep less. That means that even if you still cannot get to sleep after, you will reduce your symptoms of insomnia by meditating. Some studies show that for people who meditate, sleep requirements drop by about 4 hours per night.

So, how do you use meditation to get to sleep?

Mindfulness

Arguably the very best meditation technique for sleep is mindfulness, which is the simple act of focusing the mind on the breath and labelling any distractions. This trains the mind to stop reacting to stimuli, which ultimately helps us to switch off and get to sleep.

A clinical trial published by Harvard recently proved this. In the trial, a group of 49 middle-aged and older adults who had insomnia were divided in two. Half the group were taught to use mindfulness to get to sleep, as well as learning about other meditations. These meditations focused on present-moment mindfulness and the labelling of thoughts and emotions. The other half of the group were given a sleep education class. The groups met six times, once a week for two hours.

After those six weeks, the group that had learned mindfulness had significantly better sleep than the other group. Dr Herbet Benson, director emeritus of the Harvard-affiliated Benson-Henry Institute for Mind-Body Medicine, said, "Mindfulness meditation...evoked the relaxation response, which is a psychological shift that can help us to get to sleep by undoing the symptoms of stress, anxiety and depression.

Abdominal Breathing

Another excellent meditation technique for sleep is Abdominal Breathing. This is simply the practice of breathing deep and meditating on the movement of the breath through the body. To do this, focus your attention on your breath and imagine air entering deep into your lungs and filling your entire body. Breathe in for five counts. Pause. Then breathe out. Count breaths in cycles of tens, and aim for 100 breaths.

The National Library Of Medicine states that "[abdominal breathing] reduces negative subjective and physiological consequences of stress in healthy adults."

Deep breathing activates the relaxation response, which helps reduce the symptoms of stress and anxiety, two of the leading causes of insomnia.

Kriya Yoga

According to research that was published in 2009, one of the best meditation techniques for sleep is Kriya Yoga. This is an advanced form of meditation that requires a meditation teacher for proper instruction.

The study gathered data from 11 healthy subjects aged between 25 and 45 with chronic insomnia. The group was divided in two. Half the group were given two months of Kriya Yoga instruction. The other half were given a health education program. Both groups were given a sleep education program.

Ramadevi Gourineni, MD, director of the insomnia program at Northwestern Memorial Hospital in Evanston, said, "Results of the study show that teaching deep relaxation techniques during the daytime can help improve sleep at night."

Practising Kriya yoga and other deep meditation techniques helps us to get to sleep by training the mind to unwind. Therefore, some of the best meditation techniques for sleep are ones in which we enter a deep meditative state.

Tibetan Singing Bowls

Tibetan Singing Bowls are sound healing instruments that have been used for meditation for thousands of years. Research shows that when we listen to singing bowls, we activate theta and alpha brainwaves, which are the same brainwaves activated during the first stage of sleep.

A study published in the journal Evidence-Based Integrative Medicine found that meditating on the sound of a singing bowl for one hour helped relieve tension, anger, anxiety, depression, and stress, which are some of the leading causes of insomnia.

Another theory on Tibetan Singing Bowls is that the vibrations the instruments create helps to heal the whole body and stimulate the relaxation response. One study showed that practising singing bow meditations twice a week for five weeks led to improves sleep.

Rules For Meditating Before Bed Time

If you want to use meditation before bed, make sure you follow these simple guidelines.

1: Do It At Least One Hour Before Sleep

If you meditate while trying to sleep, you could inadvertently prevent yourself from sleeping. The reason is that meditation heightens your awareness and raises your consciousness, which is counterproductive to dozing off and catching those Zzzzzz's.

Leave at least one hour between meditation and sleep. One hour before bed, meditate so you relax and unwind. Then stop meditating, go and do something else, like reading or something else that is relaxing, and then hit the sack. This will stop your racing thoughts, relax your mind and body, and then let you drift off into sleep.

2: Stick To Relaxing Techniques

Some meditations are designed to release your emotions. Those are not the best types of meditation to do before bed. Instead, focus on some relaxing meditation techniques. You're spoilt for choice here. You could go for a Zen Walk or do some gentle movement meditations. But the best bet is just to do some simple breathing meditations.

3: Be Mindful When Lying Down

A lot of people like to meditate in bed lying down. Hey, I get that. It's been a long day. Your legs are tired. You want to relax. And besides, those pillows just look too darned comfy. No sweat. Meditate in bed. Just do it the right way. Lie down with good posture and make sure your mind is in a state of restful awareness.

4: Afterwards, Do Something Different

After meditating, before bed, do something to relax but also distract your mind. You don't want to stay in the heightened state of awareness you created when you meditated. You want your mind to start to drift off gradually. That's why it's best to do something that is relaxing but also distracting. My favourite thing to do between meditation and bed is to read a book.

Meditating before bed will help you to get to sleep at night. Just remember to leave an hour between meditating and going to bed.

THE PATH TO ENLIGHTENMENT

Meditation has become such a wide-ranging subject that it extends across religions, spiritualities, and cultures, reaching across all continents and all people. It is quickly becoming one of the most practiced health techniques in the world.

From the Samatha, Vipassana, and Dhyana techniques of Buddhism to the modern Binaural beats and guided meditations, meditation has spread across all branches of society. It is now such an expansive and wide reaching subject that it's almost intimidating to attempt to put it all together into one structured and digestible whole.

If you've attempted the various types of meditation that we've discussed, you may very well be wondering how you put them all together.

Thankfully there is a clear strategy, a way in which you can use the full spectrum of meditative techniques to achieve complete self mastery. I've called that strategy *The Path*.

Just as with any path, The Path will take you from wherever you are to where you want to go. But before you take the first step, you need to ask yourself *Where am I now?*

We're all at different stages in our journey. We're all at different levels of enlightenment. To get a good idea of where you are exactly, answer the following questions.

Where is your mind at? A quiz

To complete his questionnaire, enter an "X" in either Always, Rarely, or Never for each question.

Group "A" Questions

Question	Always	Rarely	Never
You find it easy to focus on one thing			
You are able to quieten your thoughts			
You feel like you have control of your mind			
You're rarely scatterbrained			
You finish one task before beginning another			
You are rarely irritated			
You live in the moment			
You are good at listening to people			
You rarely forget what you're doing			
You feel grounded and stable			

Group "B" Questions

QUESTION	Always	Rarely	Never
You accept other people as they are			
You are calm even when people act negatively			
You are happy around most people			
You understand that no one is perfect			
You are tolerant of others			
You enjoy the company of animals			
You appreciate nature			
You feel sad when others are sad and happy when they are happy			
You like to help other people			
You find it easy to forgive			

Group C" Questions

QUESTION	Always	Rarely	Never
You are able to forgive yourself			

You accept it when you underperform			
You think positive things about yourself			
You accept your own weaknesses			
You think other people like you			
You have a realistic view of yourself			
You feel proud of your accomplishments			
You give yourself time and space when you need it			

Group "D" Questions

QUESTION	Always	Rarely	Never
You are in control of your emotions			
You find it easy to be inwardly silent			
You rarely argue with yourself			

You rarely make life unnecessarily hard for yourself			
You rarely experience thoughts that surprise or alarm you			
You understand your own feelings and emotions			
You are aware of and listen to your intuition			
You understand your own actions			
You feel you have a good relationship with yourself			
You are willing to put yourself first when you need to			
You are aware of negative emotions before they become problematic			
You listen to yourself and accommodate your own needs			

Group "E" Questions

QUESTION	Always	Rarely	Never
You allow yourself to fully embrace the moment			

You allow yourself to fully enjoy good times			
You feel engrossed in meaningful conversation			
When you have a good conversation, it's as though there's nothing but you and the other person			
You are able to fully focus your mind on what you're doing			
You are able to perceive the beauty in the small things			
If you want to, you can get full engrossed in a good book or film			
At special times you feel one with another person, place, or thing			
You appreciate beauty			
You are able to focus on one thing with absolutely no distractions or thoughts at all			

Read through each of the questions in the five groups A to E. Give yourself 0 points for every time you answer "Never", 1 point for every time you answer "Sometimes" and 2 points for every time you answer "Always". Then add your score up.

The total score is out of 100. What did you score?

If you scored 0 – 30: This is the lower range and indicates that you need to spend more time meditating and also to make sure you allow yourself to relax. If you score in this range, try some of the easier meditation techniques. You might like to use guided meditations and binaural beats, along with simple breathing meditations, in order to calm and centre your mind.

If you score 30 – 60: This is the average range. This range indicates that you are able to focus fairly well but that you also get distracted by thoughts and feelings. If you scored in this range you will find it very helpful to practice some of the intermediate meditation techniques, like breathing meditations, Zen walking, and body scan meditation. This will help to improve your focus and to relax and purify your mind.

If you score 60 – 90: Congratulations. This is a fantastic range to be in. This range indicates that you have a high degree of self control and your mind is relaxed and focused. If you are in this range you already enjoy living in the moment and you are usually in control of your thoughts and feelings, which is why you often experience serenity and happiness. Try some of the advanced meditation techniques like Dhyana and dynamic meditation to improve your score even more.

If you scored 90 – 100: Amazing! You are top of the class. You have an extremely high degree of focus. You are completely accepting of yourself and of other people. Plus, you live in the moment almost all the time and are able to fully embrace and appreciate the fullness of life. If you scored in this range you really don't need to improve very much. Why not use your skills to help others? Try volunteering, or simply help your friends and family out so they can relax and focus and enjoy the serenity and equanimity that you already enjoy.

For everyone who scored under 90 on the test, you should consider where your strengths and weaknesses are as this will help you to decide what to do next.

The test is broken down into different sections, A to E. These sections are designed to test different mental traits. Let's take a closer look.

Each individual section (A to E) is marked out of 20.

If you scored less than 10 on group A: Group A is all about your calmness and inner stillness. A high score in this category means that you are in control of your thoughts and feelings and are able to silence your mind in order to focus. A low score indicates that your mind is full of noise, which prevents you from focussing.

If you score lowly on group A, consider taking steps to become calmer and to focus your mind. You will find it very helpful to practice Samatha meditation, breathing meditation, body scan, Zen walking, and other simple techniques, as well as using Binaural Beats and guided meditations to help you to relax.

If you scored lowly on group A you will likely score lowly on other groups too. Don't worry about those other groups yet. Focus your attention on creating inner calmness. Once you are relaxed you will be able to focus more, allowing you to move on to more advanced meditation techniques.

If you scored less than 10 on group B: Group B is all about your relationships to other people as well as to animals and nature. If you scored highly on group B you find it easy to accept other people and to forgive them of their shortcomings. If this is the case, you most likely enjoy a healthy social life and appreciate other people. If you scored less than 10 on this group of questions, try practicing Loving Kindness Meditation and Karuna Meditation, both of which will boost your levels of compassion and help you to accept and forgive others.

If you scored less than 10 on group c: Group C is all about your relationship to yourself. If you scored highly on group C it means that you are accepting of yourself, that you recognise both your strengths and weaknesses, and that you have a healthy relationship with yourself. If you scored lowly on group C you may find that you are often judging yourself and have negative thoughts about yourself. If you scored lowly on group C, practice both Loving Kindness Meditation and Karuna meditation *with a specific focus on boosting your compassion for yourself*. This will heighten your selflove and make you feel more positively about yourself.

If you scored less than 10 on group D: Group D is all about insight. If you scored highly on group D it means that you fully understand yourself and that you are aware of the workings of your own mind. You are also in touch with intuition and have good self mastery. If you scored lowly on group D you may often surprise yourself and find that you don't always understand your thoughts, feelings, and emotions. If you scored lowly on group D, practice Vipassana meditation. This will put you in touch with the inner workings of your mind and heighten your self mastery.

If you scored lowly on group E: Group E questions are all about your ability to be absorbed in the moment. If you scored highly on group E you will find that you are able to focus your mind 100% on any task you perform. You are also able to enjoy the moments of your life with absolutely zero distractions. Few people score highly on group E so if you're one of them, you should be proud! If you scored lowly on group E you will find that thoughts and feelings hold you back from being completely engrossed in the present moment. If you scored lowly on group E, practice mindfulness, Dhyana and Bhakti meditation, all of which will help you to live fully in the moment and to engross yourself in the richness of life.

If you scored lowly in more than one group (as most people do) focus on the first group you struggled with. For instance, if you scored lowly on groups A, C and E, focus on group A first before moving on to C and finally E.

These groups are ordered as they are for a specific reason. The first group of questions is all about your level of calmness and focus. If your mind is not calm and focused you will experience all manner of thoughts and feelings which will interfere with your day to day life. These distractions will prevent you from living in the moment and from enjoying life fully.

So the first group of questions regards calmness and serenity, which Buddhists call *Samatha*.

Samatha is the essential foundation on which all else is built, and it should be your first priority.

Beginner meditators can use breathing meditations, mindfulness, guided meditations, Binaural Beats and other entry-level techniques to quieten their mind and to find calmness and focus.

Once you have achieved Samatha you can then move on to groups B, C, and D.

Groups B and C can essentially be lumped together. Group B pertains to your feelings about other people. Group C pertains to your feelings about yourself. But both groups are essentially about compassion: Compassion for others and compassion for yourself. You can achieve both by practicing two meditation techniques: Loving Kindness Meditation and Karuna meditation.

Having focused and calmed the mind and then cultivated compassion for yourself and others, you will then be in the right mental space to begin to look deeper and to develop insights. Insight gives you mastery over self and also certain extra-sensory perceptions like intuition and clairvoyance. The path to developing insight is through Vipassana.

Once you have achieved calmness, focus, compassion, and insight, you begin to truly enter the deeper stages of meditation, the stages at which you can achieve oneness, the state of existing as one with an object, person, or thing. This is what group E is all about. Oneness can be achieved through the practice of Dhyana meditation and Bhakti meditation.

In the end, once you have scored highly in all the groups, A to E, you will have achieved a state of complete calmness and equanimity, you will have compassion for all, you will be able to access the deeper parts of your mind through insight, and you will be able to focus your mind to such a degree that you achieve complete oneness.

"The first step on a new path"

The journey we have been on has taken us through history, across culture, and within ourselves. And I hope that throughout our journey you have enjoyed every step and have perhaps picked up some gems and jewels along the way that you can take with you.

It is my great hope that the techniques that you have discovered in this book will help you now that you put this book down. The skills and knowledge that you've discovered in this book will be immensely valuable in everyday life. With mindfulness, loving kindness, insight, awareness, and an enlightened mind you can live every moment of your life with pure happiness and joy.

If you have enjoyed the book and found it useful, then I would like to ask if could please write a positive review of it on Amazon. This will help others to discover the book and to take the same journey that we have been on.

But the journey definitely does not end here. The end of one journey is but the beginning of another. If you would like to continue our journey, join me on TheDailyMeditation.com

The techniques we have discussed in this book, and the journey we have gone through, will lead to complete happiness and inner peace. That's why I would like to ask you to share this book with your friends and family. Let them enjoy the journey too and learn the same techniques that you have.

MORE JOURNEYS OF DISCOVERY LIE AHEAD IN THIS SPIRITUAL MUST-READ

THE 30 SECRETS TO SPIRITUAL LOVE

What is "Spiritual Love"? How can spiritual techniques help you to find true love and to create a perfect relationship? In The 30 Secrets To Spiritual Love, I reveal 30 ways in which you can find true love, make it work, and make it last. This is the perfect book for singles and for those looking to connect on a deeper level.

About The Author

Paul Harrison is a meditation teacher, journalist and author. As CEO and Editor In Chief of

TheDailyMeditation.com, Paul's writings and teachings have been read and enjoyed by hundreds of thousands of people around the world and continue to inspire people to live happy, peaceful, joyful lives.

Paul is deeply passionate about inspiring people to dream big and to live consciously.

Thanks for reading my book. I look forward to the next time. – Paul.

Printed in Great Britain
by Amazon